A BACKPACK, A BEAR,

AND EIGHT CRATES OF VODKA

Lev Golinkin

A BACKPACK, A BEAR,

AND EIGHT CRATES OF VODKA

a memoir

DOUBLEDA

New York   London   Toronto   Sydney   Auckland

All rights reserved. Published in the United States by
Doubleday, a division of Random House LLC, New York,
and in Canada by Random House of Canada Limited,
Toronto, Penguin Random House companies.

www.doubleday.com

DOUBLEDAY and the portrayal of an anchor with a dolphin
are registered trademarks of Random House LLC.

Grateful acknowledgment is made to Alfred Music for
permission to reprint an excerpt from "Won't Get Fooled
Again," words and music by Pete Townshend, copyright
© 1971, copyright renewed by Fabulous Music Ltd.
Administered in the United States and Canada by Spirit One
Music (BMI) o/b/o Spirit Services Holdings, S.a.r.l., Suolubaf
Music and ABKCO Music, Inc., 85 Fifth Avenue, New York,
N.Y. 10003. International copyright secured. All rights
reserved. Used by permission of Alfred Music.

Book design by Michael Collica
Jacket design and illustrations by Michael J. Windsor

Library of Congress Cataloging-in-Publication Data
Golinkin, Lev, author.
A backpack, a bear, and eight crates of vodka : a memoir /
Lev Golinkin.
pages ;   cm
ISBN 978-0-385-53777-3 (hardcover)—
ISBN 978-0-385-53778-0 (eBook) 1. Golinkin, Lev.
2. Jews, Russian—Ukraine—Kharkov—Biography.
3. Jewish refugees—United States—Biography. 4. Jews,
Russian—United States—Biography. I. Title.
E184.37.G655A3 2014
947'.004924092—dc23
[B]
2014005408

MANUFACTURED IN THE UNITED STATES OF AMERICA

10 9 8 7 6 5 4 3 2

First Edition

To Jeff, Bettie, Amanda, and Dr. V

CONTENTS

This book was born from a need to understand my past, and as such, everything recounted here is as accurate as memory, research, and reflection can allow. But this is not only my story: the narrative takes place in the context of a massive refugee movement and includes accounts of numerous individuals, some of whom weren't eager to publicly embrace a turbulent past. In light of this, and in the spirit of not being a jackass, I have changed the names of those who asked to remain anonymous or weren't available to provide consent.

A BACKPACK, A BEAR,

AND EIGHT CRATES OF VODKA

PROLOGUE

Chestnut Hill, Mass., May 2003

It was a hot day and the metal bleachers of Alumni Stadium channeled the sunshine directly into the center, where the graduates and I melted in our black gowns. The commencement speaker, a blind man who had climbed Mt. Everest, spoke about the journey of life, and ways to overcome obstacles, and the many lessons of college. He said other stuff, too, but I don't remember what it was. I couldn't listen. I needed to move. I needed a cigarette. I needed a pack of cigarettes, I needed coffee, extra-large coffee with cream and no sugar, and most of all, I needed to walk.

People and places I hadn't thought about for years—that I'd refused to think about—flashed through my head, drowning out the mountain climber. I had to find Linda, and Peter, and Eva, and the bald hotel owner, and the Bosnians. I had to find the pudgy man who pulled us off the Vienna train station and the blond girl from the house with the red door who gave me a jacket on a cold February evening when the wind howled down the Danube. There were others I had to find. Unfortunately, I didn't know their names, or where they were, or what they looked like, which was going to make looking for them a bit problematic.

The speech ended, everyone clapped, and we broke up by schools and shuffled off to various parts of the campus for the second half of commencement. On the way, friends swapped congratulations and contact info, and I made a mental note to clear my phone book and disable my e-mail account. Boston College was kind enough to let me participate in the graduation ceremony, so I crossed the stage and was handed a giant envelope with a little printout explaining why there was no diploma inside and I would therefore not be going to med school. I smiled and shook the dean's hand, Dad took a picture, and I scampered back to my seat without further thought on the matter. The only thing preventing me from graduating was a one-credit physics lab. I could earn my diploma in a month, and then apply to med school . . . or not apply to med school. At this point it wasn't important.

Commencement ended and the countdown began: we had to empty our dorms by 5:00 p.m. I hadn't packed and by the time Dad and two family friends scraped me out of my room and into a van, we were right at the deadline. Dad, a meticulous packer, was rechecking straps and calculating optimal suitcase alignment when I excused myself, ran back to the dorm, shut the bathroom door, and turned on the faucet. The water helped, for some odd reason. Even though there was no one else in the dorm, the rushing sound made me feel more alone. I've always needed that moment before the plunge, to stand and gather, and I've always preferred being alone by myself to being alone in a crowd.

The Soviet Union was waiting. The largest country in the world, a country the size of North America. The land that worshipped the embalmed body of a bald monster, the land that banned God, the land of black cars, illegal radios, crooked mirrors, and underground bakeries, where missiles and tanks rolled under the red flag. The guards were waiting, and the gas masks and the refugee camps. From the moment I stepped on American soil I had dedicated myself to forgetting, ignoring, and burying them, and still they waited. I felt my hands clenching the porcelain sides of the sink, felt the familiar panic radiate from my chest, crawl up my neck, choking me, urging me to run, get a new address, new goals, new friends, move, disappear, be somewhere else, but for the first time in my life, being terrified didn't matter. I had to go back, to Indiana, to the refugee camps in Austria, to talk to people, walk around, and reconstruct something resembling a past. College has many lessons; I stood with the blind man on that one. Some I'd forget, some I'd already forgotten, but the one thing that finally sank into my head is that you can't have a future if you don't have a past.

A thin film of vapor coated the mirror by the time I turned off the water and walked back to the van, where Dad was pacing. It was past 5:00 and the campus was nearly abandoned. The faculty had driven off to embrace the summer, and the grounds crew was stacking chairs and folding pavilions in a rush to move on. Maroon pennants with the BC logo flapped from lampposts making me think of other red banners flapping in other winds, in a country that no longer existed. Lanky shadows of campus towers chased the van down Commonwealth Avenue, like giant Gothic windshield wipers clearing away the school year, and then I passed out, and when I woke up we were getting gas at a rest stop in Jersey.

I spent the next two years walking.

Part One

We'll be fighting in the streets
With our children at our feet
And the morals that they worship will be gone
And the men who spurred us on
Sit in judgment of all wrong
They decide and the shotgun sings the song

—"Won't Get Fooled Again" by The Who

THE BEST PARADES IN THE
WHOLE DAMN WORLD

Kharkov, Ukraine, USSR, September 1987

Parades were the gold standard of the Soviet Union. Workers' parades, women's parades, Revolution parades, the Great Patriotic War parades, we had them all. We had perfected parades; we had the best parades in the whole damn world. St. Patrick's Day? Thanksgiving? *Please.* Macy's has balloons. We had intercontinental ballistic missiles rolling through Red Square. Parades were of paramount importance and attendance was mandatory, rain or otherwise. On April 26, 1986, the year before I entered first grade, the Chernobyl nuclear power plant (located less than three hundred miles from Kharkov) exploded, spewing a radioactive cloud over the Ukraine. Other, weaker countries would've had their citizens hunkering indoors and popping iodine tablets. But May 1 was International Workers' Day, canceling the parade was unthinkable, and so on we marched, blissfully unaware, soaking in the sunshine and the radiation. The reviewing stand was mostly vacant, of course, since local Party leaders had been alerted beforehand and had long evacuated the area, but the parade went off without a hitch. *That's* commitment.

The year after the radioisotope-enriched May Day festivities, Mom grabbed my hand and we walked to the September parade for the start of first grade. Aside from the occasional tram rattling by, Moskovskyi Prospekt was quiet: there were no lines outside the Kharkov Department Store, which hadn't received shipments in two weeks; the morning shift was already in the factories; and the *babushki* were staying indoors, cooking supper and complaining about the weather. Even the discarded newspapers that usually spun and danced in the wake of traffic clung to the pavement and slowly dissolved in the puddles. Mom and I passed by the Plaza of the Uprising, lined with maple and chestnut trees, turned left after the Hammer and Sickle stadium, and arrived at Kharkov School Number Three, where the parade was already under way.

This procession didn't have placards announcing how many tons of wheat had been harvested by the city's collective farms, or proclamations of the Malyshev Factory's churning out thirty tanks ahead of schedule for the millionth year in a row, or lists of proud citizens nominated for the Order of Labor Glory, Second Class, award. It was a quieter, smaller affair held outside the brick school building where Mom and I watched the teachers, followed by the fifth-graders through second-graders. Encouraging production statistics and Orders of Labor Glory aside, everything was immaculate: the sky was pure, dark steel; frigid rain poured down, but no one felt a drop. It was as if they were marching hundreds of miles away, in a sunny Cuba full of warmth and light. Unfazed, undazed, and firm strode the students, girls smiling with shy optimism, boys practicing to be the soldiers they would become. I clung to Mom's leg, covered partly by the umbrella, partly by her long white shawl.

The last soggy red pennant streamed by, and I straightened my uniform and went to check in with Anna Konstantinovna, my first-grade teacher, a tall woman with gray hair and a gray face that matched her gray blouse. First she taught us how to sit, because without proper posture, learning was impossible. We sat at our desks, backs stiff, eyes on the chalkboard, arms folded, right over left, fingers straight. (In the event of a question, the right arm was to pivot ninety degrees until perpendicular to the desk, but at no point were the fingers to separate.) Anna Konstantinovna paced down the aisles. She didn't so much teach as remind, as if I, the two brothers in front of me, and the rest of my classmates already knew everything we needed to know, and her job was merely to jog our memories. A photographer trailed her. His duty was to document and report that the new generation of Communists was ready to enter society. Anna Konstantinovna paced, the photographer clicked, and I sat, issuing silent orders to my squirming fingers.

The lesson on posture was followed by a two-hour briefing, which reaffirmed that as the children, we were indeed the future and would soon shoulder the burden of improving our glorious society and fighting the belligerent Capitalists. Our perfect Union wasn't always perfect, after all. It had been achieved only through the relentless work and genius of Lenin, but Lenin was dead now and it was up to us to pick up the torch. Everything from Pushkin to multiplication made up the arsenal we would utilize to spread happiness to workers and peasants around the globe. The responsibility dangled over our desks like the sword of Damocles.

To aid us in the upcoming struggle, we were taken to the cafeteria and fed milk and sandwiches. Hating milk is probably the first lasting decision I made, but, Anna Konstantinovna was quick to remind me, without its life-giving power, how was I going to stand up to the Capitalists? "Milk is strength. Milk is strength, Lev," she said, and I quickly gulped down the curdled mass in my cup. Everyone had to sacrifice for the common good.

Following lunch we were returned to the classroom, where Anna Konstantinovna sat at her desk, back straight, eyes fixed ahead, and making it look easy. I watched her arm drop down to her desk drawer, then reemerge with a small metal box. She tilted her wrist, scattering the box's contents, and I squinted. Our teacher's desk was covered with stars. Tiny metal stars.

Like all good dictatorships, the Communist Party of the Soviet Union recognized the importance of early-childhood indoctrination. The moment a child entered first grade he was fed into a finely oiled propaganda machine, the first tier of which was the Little Octobrist group. October was the month of the Revolution, and it held special significance for the Party (October saw parades galore; October parades made the other parades look weak, like St. Patrick's Day). It made sense to have first-graders begin at the beginning, at the origin of the Revolution. We became Little Octobrists by donning the official star pin. Symbols are crucial to both elementary education and totalitarian propaganda (the two have much in common), and a tried-and-true emblem of the USSR was the five-pointed red star. Every star on Anna Konstantinovna's desk had a cherubic Baby Lenin embossed in the center, and the golden, curly-haired child looked like a perverted version of the Baby Jesus pins that people in America put on their car visors to keep them safe. Anna Konstantinovna fastened our pins, and we walked to the Grand Assembly to watch the third-graders become Pioneers.

Pioneer was the next level after Little Octobrist, and it was a big deal. Being a Little Octobrist didn't entail much beyond wearing the pin: the Pioneers got to step forward and start serving the Motherland in earnest. Enrollment began in third grade, and it was optional. They didn't want to pressure us. They wanted it to come from the heart, and if the occasional child was too stupid or immature to join, they would eventually be forced to do so by the fifth grade.

To reflect the sobriety of Pioneer enrollment, the day's ceremony took place in a Grand Assembly, mini parade-like procession and all. Red kerchiefs, the symbol of the Pioneers, were everywhere, and banners emblazoned with slogans like ALWAYS BE READY TO FIGHT FOR THE WAY OF THE COMMUNIST PARTY OF THE USSR! and A PIONEER IS EVER VIGILANT! swung from the rafters. One by one, the third-grade inductees rose and recited the Solemn Pledge of the Pioneers:

"I, [last name, first name], joining the ranks of the Vladimir Ilyich Lenin All-Union Pioneer Organization, in the presence of my comrades solemnly promise: to love and protect my Motherland passionately, to live as the great Lenin bade us, as the Communist Party teaches us, to always carry out the laws of the Pioneers of the Soviet Union."

After tying on a red kerchief, each newly knotted Pioneer was paired up with a first-grader. My Pioneer was a pretty girl with very tight ponytails who gave me a book about some jackass named Don't Know Anything who found a flying car and decided to travel to the sun, where, after numerous misadventures (I vaguely recall an incident with an elephant at the Sun City Zoo), he finally learned that he really belonged back home, working hard with his fellow citizens to build a better society. The girl told me how Pioneers had these organizations called Squads and Watchgroups, and you got to be part of Committees, and be Friends with other Pioneers, and learn important Communist Skills and Pioneer Songs, and other great stuff. She asked if I knew the alphabet, and I said yes. "That's good," she recited. "The alphabet is the beginning of all beginnings; even Lenin began with it." (It sounds better in Russian; it's a rhyming couplet.) I just stared at her ponytails and at the canary-yellow book jacket, which showed Don't Know Anything revving up his flying car, ready to wreak havoc on Sun

City. Then the older Pioneers embraced their new comrades and lined up in Squads and Watchgroups and marched away, and that was my first day of school.

*   *   *

The olive-green gas mask over my face is a remnant from World War II—the Great Patriotic War, as people on the radio call it, or simply the War to everyone else. The mask is too big and is made of old, tough rubber, and Anna Konstantinovna had to really tug on the straps to make it stay on my head. The round eyepieces are also too big and encompass not just my eyes but also my cheeks and eyebrows. We're all wearing the masks, and our left hands grasp long, flexible hoses that end in some sort of tin filters. I'm in uniform: a starched blue suit, the dark red Baby Lenin pin twinkling from my lapel. Everyone has their Lenin pin. All the boys wear navy suits, and the girls wear brown French maid outfits and have large white bows in their hair, but today you can't see the bows because they're squashed under the gas masks.

Everyone in first grade is lined up in a hallway with brown walls painted with murals of Pioneers, boys and girls helping the elderly and planting trees. There are posters of bald Adult Lenin, too, with slogans like "Be Ready! Always Be Ready!!" and other quotes centered on readiness and the importance of education. Suddenly the boy at the front of the line is told to run and he runs and we follow, up the stairs and down the stairs, outside to the pavement and inside to the hallways, and the gas mask lenses are fogged up and dirty and all I see are gray cement blurs when we run outside, and red-and-brown mural blurs when we run inside.

It's October, so most of us have learned our way around the building, and the run goes smoothly. We loop through the school several times, corridor by corridor, classroom by classroom, and then we take off the masks and split up by class, and then I'm lying on the floor, my arms pinned by the tall brother, the older one, and someone's at my legs, the fat kid with the big head, I think, and my forehead's bleeding, and I'm trying to lift my head up, and it makes the blood flow into my eyes and down my nose. The blood obscures my vision but I can still make him out, the little kid, the younger brother, straddling my chest and shoving a shit-stained wad of toilet paper in front of my eyes. "This is what you are, this is what you all are," he hisses, and the shit is brown, and his face is tan, almost dark brown, and his eyes are receded and black, and his uniform is dark blue, and the Lenin pin is dark red, and what stands out from the whole dull palette are his bright white teeth that spread over half his face.

His face is frozen. I can hear *"zhid"* and "shit," and feel the spit as it shoots out his mouth, but his face is trapped in that gargoyle smile. They're all frozen—I see hands, pressing down on my arms and legs, I see faces in the periphery, still, immobile, bored—they're doing this all in a perfunctory way, as if they have to, and they're just frozen in the middle of their task. A Squad of Pioneers flutters by, or maybe it's a Watchgroup, I can't tell the difference, and their red kerchiefs look like a flock of colorful birds. The younger brother's grin is not happy, it's more of a scowl, a baring that cuts through the smell of the shit and the blurry red fog of the blood, and I see the teeth, and the brown of the hallway, and blue blurs of uniforms and the gray-and-white blur of Anna Konstantinovna as she opens the door and calmly reminds us that it's time for class. The late bell rings, a few more punches, another shit smear on my face, and my classmates and I head in to learn.

I'm still not clear as to why we had to run in the gas masks. Anna Konstantinovna briefly alluded to the Capitalists and said that it was vital to be prepared in case they attacked, and it must've been a satisfactory explanation, because I didn't push her for further clarification, and neither did any of my classmates. But that's the only regular school day I can vividly recall. The rest of it, Soviet poetry and Ukrainian grammar, blood and shit, Revolutionary history and gym class, it all blends together and I remember little. I probably wouldn't have remembered that day, either, except for the masks—the masks were kind of neat, and they made the day stand out.

*   *   *

To my memory's credit, I missed about half of my first two years of school. Mom drew on her contacts among city doctors to get me extended-absence notes whenever I fell ill, which was frequent, and so I stayed home as much as possible. Overall, I didn't mind being sick: there were always books to read, Grandma allowed me to hang out with her when she was cooking dinner, and at night my parents and sister came home and then I could tell Mom about what I'd read or hammer out plots to annoy my sister, Lina.

If the weather was nice, I'd tag along with Dad for a walk in a little lilac park behind the apartment complex. He was an engineer who traveled all over the Union to fix turbines, and he never failed to return with trinkets and stories. Dad told me of frost-shackled mining towns in the tundra, where temperatures plunged to minus forty and birds froze to the ground like little feathered ice lumps. Some of the workers would chip away the ice and tuck the birds under their armpits, and by the time they reached the refineries the birds would thaw out and fly away. My favorite were his stories from the 'stans in the south, where minarets stuck out into the skies and one madrassa built in the days of Timur the Lame had a niche inlaid with red stones, and when you stood just right the stones aligned to form an image of a Muslim saint. Dad, ever the engineer, spoke with delight of the Uzbeki and the Turkmeny, whose tribal ancestors had built huts in the deserts, drilling holes in the walls to create air currents that made the interiors feel cool and breezy. Often, Dad's thoughts would wander back to his turbines and he'd start muttering about blades, rotors, and diaphragms. Newspapers and other trash lined the paths, and homeless men bunked beneath the trees at night, and the park smelled like piss and lilacs. Long branches swollen with purple blossoms drooped overhead and I'd walk alongside Dad and dream of the day when I would be tall enough to have to bend under branches, too, and then I could help him with his turbine problems and maybe leave Kharkov and go see the minarets for myself.

When Dad was on the road, I spent the afternoons with my best friend, Oleg, who lived in the apartment across the landing from us. Our usual game was playing the German invasion of Russia in our housing block's common yard. Sometimes we'd be the Red Army, creeping back before the German advance, holding fortifications, making desperate stands, making sure the Nazi bastards paid a dear price for our city. Sometimes we did the opposite, trekking out to the far end of the yard, by the landfill and the army barracks, then turning around and taking the land bench by bench, foyer by foyer until we secured our apartment building by the bakery. Going that route meant being the Germans, of course, so Oleg and I just called it "starting at the far end" to make ourselves feel less unpatriotic. Attacking was more fun than defending, though, and more often than not we started at the far end.

Imagination wasn't required for the game. Kharkov *had* been destroyed by the Germans—four major Battles of Kharkov between 1941 and 1943 had made their way into the history books—and, forty years later, the scars remained. Our balcony wall was pockmarked with mortar holes. Memorial plaques and captured Panzer war trophies littered the city. Mom, Dad, and Grandma all remembered the frantic evacuation in the fall of 1941, when they were packed on trains and sent far to the east, Dad to the Urals, Mom and my grandparents to Central Asia. Back when Dad had returned to the city, there were more than just pockmarks. Dad and his school friends, many of them fatherless, would burrow into collapsed buildings and dig through the rubble for machine guns, grenades, and bones. They carried weapons to school, just because they were so readily available, and for a while Dad armed himself with a wicked SS dagger with German writing on the blade. When his father, Grandpa Lev, saw the knife, he brought Dad to the fields by the tractor factory.

"Somewhere around here are the pits where five years ago, the man who owned this knife, and other men like him, shot thousands of Jews in a single day," Grandpa Lev told Dad.*

He didn't order Dad to get rid of the dagger, but Dad carried a regular Soviet knife from then on.

For Oleg and me this wasn't like playing in a backyard; it was more like stepping onto an old movie set and reenacting the movie. We crept past the army barracks, hid behind the lilacs, crawled on recon missions over the hill by the apartments, dodged, seized, and raided until we reached our home building, grimy and victorious. Day after day, it was me and Oleg kicking ass against the yard: the older boys who congregated by the doorways and traded pins and coins, the girls, including Oleg's sister, Tanya, who

---

* Much later, the details emerged: the Nazi killing field was a ravine called Drobytsky Yar, on the outskirts of Kharkov, where 15,000 Jews were killed on December 15, 1941. The city refused to create a memorial for the Jews on the site until 1991, after the USSR fell apart.

plucked flowers and squealed whenever we nicked their dolls (or, as Oleg and I thought of them, "enemy combatants"), Mitya the yard keeper who mostly paid attention to his pipe, the *babushki* parked on benches who never missed anything, and the ghosts of the German and Soviet dead.

THE BLACK WITCH COMES
TO KHARKOV

Kharkov, Ukraine, USSR, 1980s

My mother was a psychiatrist who worked at one of the several large clinics in the city. The majority of her patients suffered from the standard psychiatric ailments: depression, mania, anxiety, an occasional psychosis. Mom and her coworkers made house calls or held office hours for the functional patients, and attended to the more serious, hospitalized cases in the clinic. It was a similar routine to that of her Capitalist counterparts, save for a little-known group of patients who were unique to the Soviet Union. These patients were rarely spoken of, because prior to being institutionalized they had been mentally healthy.

Political dissidents posed a tricky dilemma to the regime. These weren't your run-of-the-mill murderers or petty thugs (most were highly educated intellectuals). No, these individuals knowingly, willingly, and conspicuously rejected the Soviet Union, the Soviet way of life. They penned letters, attempted to organize rallies, spoke out against the system, and otherwise engaged in bizarre actions that had only one explanation. "No sane individual would oppose the USSR" was the official stance of the dictatorship. In other words, since: a) Communism was the ultimate form of human society; and b) it was natural for any normal person to aspire to the best; then c) anyone who shunned the best was clearly deranged. Deranged people belonged in asylums, which is exactly where the dissidents were incarcerated.

But locking them away wasn't enough; to erase all doubt, the protestors had to be officially classified as insane. To achieve that, the regime first required an appropriate illness, and in 1969 one was supplied by Dr. Andrei Snezhnevsky, a leading Soviet academic. "Sluggishly progressing schizophrenia," a disorder recognized nowhere outside of the Communist Bloc, was characterized by a sole key symptom: an irrational desire to fight perceived social injustice. Sluggishly progressing schizophrenia was considered an intractable disease that demanded the most aggressive treatment, and, once diagnosed, patients were subjected to electroshock, insulin-induced comas, sensory deprivation, tranquilizers, and potent psychotropics. Eventually, the diagnosis became reality.

Mom's workload always swelled around the holidays, when a KGB agent would present her boss with a list of names. "Surely you realize how certain individuals tend to get overly agitated this time of year. They go out in the streets, shout nonsense, pass out leaflets, and disturb the working men and women of our city. Please sign these orders so we can institutionalize them for a while. That way the public won't get harassed and everyone will have a safe and pleasant holiday."

It wasn't a request; the head doctor would sign and the black Volga sedans used by the secret police would hit the streets, off to ensure that everyone had a safe and pleasant holiday.

There was an area of Kharkov called Nemyshlya. It was a place rife with crime, a neighborhood the city had given up on; even ambulances stopped at the outskirts, and police entered strictly en masse. Mom was one of the few psychiatrists who made house calls to Nemyshlya. The taxis would drop her off and wait on the periphery, and Mom would enter on foot, unescorted, and hardened criminals would smile and part way for her, because they knew she was the only doctor who would take care of their friends and families. Her care wasn't limited to just the city. Kharkov, like other Ukrainian cities, was surrounded by villages and communal farms—many of which weren't readily accessible—and Mom's work took her on countryside excursions, via trucks, motorcycles, and, on one occasion, a horse and buggy.

Mom refused constant attempts to bribe her, but at some point long before I was born, word spread that she loved flowers. Our apartment was a garden, with fresh bouquets arriving daily. Tables and stools held vases of lilies and peonies, and bluebells poked through the laundry lines on the little balcony. One ex-patient, a farmer, would drive his truck into the city and fill our bathtub with tomatoes and cucumbers. Mom kept insisting that we couldn't possibly go through a tub of the plump vegetables, but the farmer, like all farmers, was a man of routine and the deliveries continued, year after year, with the cyclical surety of the harvest.

*   *   *

My sister, Lina, was twelve years older than me, and I devoted much of my time in the apartment to cooking up novel ways to annoy her. Lina's studies left her with limited private time for boys—it was a fact I leveraged to my benefit. The first time a romantic interest stepped into the apartment, he was bombarded with an onslaught of unpleasantries. Lina's shutting her door wouldn't help, since I'd make sure to disable the latch beforehand. Some of the more intrepid boyfriends managed to extricate me from the room, which was fine; I had backup plans. There were hidden alarm clocks set to buzz every few minutes, booby traps rigged above the bed, and, failing that, I could sing, loudly and badly. I never went to school and spent entire days in the apartment: this was my home court, and one had to do a little better than locking the door.

Soon, usually by the second date, the boyfriend would quit worrying about impressing our parents and grandmother and focus on me.

"There you are, Lev!" He would find me, waiting in the foyer. "I brought you candy!"

"Thank you."

"Now that we're friends, would you mind not gluing my shoelaces together? Deal?"

"I read about it in a book, you know.* There was this man, and he was in South America, in the pampas, and they were hunting these big ostriches, except in South America they're called rheas, and they would throw this rope around their legs when they hunted, and that's where I got the shoelace idea."

"How about this: I'll bring you more chocolate and you stop doing that."

"How about pirates: they're these sailors who attack other sailors, and they have bandanas, and peg legs, and parrots, and they bury treasure. Do you have any pirates?"

"I'll find you some pirate toys, promise."

"And chocolate. And be careful when you walk into Lina's room—I stretched some fishing line across the door. I read about that in a book, too."†

---

* *The Drunken Forest* by Gerald Durrell, which covers the author's wildlife collection expedition to Paraguay and Argentina. Many of Durrell's techniques for trapping large game can be easily modified for snaring sisters and their boyfriends.
† *Karlsson-on-the-Roof* by Astrid Lindgren. This tale of a boy and his magical friend is replete with ideas for using common household objects to inflict misery on loved ones. A must-read.

The boyfriend would tear the city apart, but by the next date I'd have my pirates.

Lina got back at me by telling stories. I'll never forget the evening she flew into my room to ask if I'd heard about the Black Witch, who made toys come alive and strangle kids at night. No one could determine which toys were possessed. The Black Witch was patient: some toys remained perfectly harmless for years, then pounced without warning. Lina's bulletin was timely; she wasn't a hundred percent sure, but she had it from a reliable source deep in the Witch's retinue that the Witch was heading to Kharkov. I hollered for Mom, but Lina shrugged it off.

"He asked me for a story, so I told him one."

"Is that true?" Mom asked.

"Yes, Mom," I said, frantically compiling an inventory of which of my soldiers were likely sleeper cell candidates.

"Stop asking her. You always ask and you always get scared."

"I know, but—"

"See!" Lina jumped in, beaming. "I told you he likes my stories."

She was right. I spent a week barricading myself in the bedroom, then lowered the threat level and came back for more. I couldn't resist. Sometimes she sketched pictures of her monsters to help me visualize the horrors that waited for the lights to go out. Sometimes she didn't even have to make anything up.

"Before you were born, when I was your age, the KGB detained Dad and started asking him about what books he owned [true]. They sat him down and detained him, and then, they raided our apartment and searched it! *Bang!* went the door, and in they burst! Thank God, one of Dad's coworkers warned Mom and Grandma beforehand, as soon as Dad was taken, so they burned all the illegal books we had [true]. By the time the KGB agents came in their black cars, dressed in their big black coats [the KGB and the Black Witch shared a penchant for the color], everything bad was already gone. So they let Dad go and didn't put him in prison. But who knows? The KGB's unpredictable. Maybe tomorrow they're not going to like the books you read—you know, like your fairy tales [poetic license: all children's lit had long been scrubbed free of undesirable religious and Western allusions]—and they're going to come for you, and *you* don't have any coworkers to warn you, do you? They'll come in their black cars and take you away."

She paused, waiting for the desired effect to set in.

"Go ahead and read your books while you still can . . . Watch out for the black cars."

She grabbed her schoolbag and rushed out, a trail of satisfied giggles lingering in the hallway.

Lina was *good*.

When Lina was in high school, she was working hard to go to med school. She was on track to earn her gold medal, an award given to high school seniors with straight A's that qualified them to pursue certain professions, such as medicine. Lina had the grades, and then in the fall of her senior year her high school director called Dad in for a conference. The director, an accomplished educator, looked concerned.

"Comrade Golinkin, your daughter is a fine student and a very nice girl. I asked you here because I admire her, and I don't want this to take her by surprise. She will get a B, only one B, which will preclude her from getting the medal; it's the best I can do for her. I have my orders, just like everyone else."

Dad was confused. Un-affirmative action policies of the Soviet Union shifted and varied depending on the year, the republic, and the whim of the dictatorship. Some years, certain ethnicities would be tolerated in certain professions and institutions; then, a nameless bastard in the nameless echelons of the bureaucracy would decide that too many *zhidi* were getting straight A's, and a memo would be generated and sent out. Dad knew all that; what confused him was why the director bothered to bring him in to discuss it.

"Of course, we *do* live in an open society, and you *do* have the option of filing a complaint with the administration. I know that Lina can be . . . tenacious, and may urge you to follow this course of action. But I must strongly advise you against it." The director leaned forward. "The teachers will then have to justify your daughter's not qualifying for the medal, and instead of a single B she will have to start receiving Cs and Ds. I don't want that to happen; I don't want her to be any more upset than necessary. I'm trying to help you. Do you understand?"

"I understand," Dad said. "Thank you for your time and for looking out for Lina."

On the walk home, Dad thought how lucky Lina was to have a school director who cared.

Lina *was* tenacious. She dedicated the next two years to mastering the medical academy entrance exam in the hope of overcoming the taint on her transcript. Her passion won Dad over, and he hired some of the best tutors in the city to prepare her. Lina took the exam twice. After the second attempt, an administrator from the academy phoned Dad and told him to stop torturing his daughter and send her somewhere she could get accepted. Lina became an engineering student.

From that moment on, medicine was no longer discussed. "Tomorrow afternoon you're getting your books, Sunday you're off, and Monday we're registering you at Kharkov Polytechnic— get to work," said Dad, and went out for a walk, ending the deliberations for good. I was three at the time, but even afterward and all through my teenage years I can't remember having or hearing a single conversation about this event in my sister's life; the same went for my beatings in school and in the yard. Adapt and endure was how generations of Russian Jews had managed to hang around under the Bolsheviks, and the tsars, and whatever the hell was there before the tsars. My grandfather Lev (my father's father and my namesake, who died shortly before I was born) was an orphan raised by a yeshiva, a Jewish religious school in a Byelorussian shtetl. Grandpa Lev showed promise in Torah studies, but when the Torah was outlawed and the rabbis killed, he became a factory worker, eventually rising to foreman. Years later, when Dad was sixteen and wanted to become a history professor, Grandpa Lev reminded him that a Jew would never be permitted to join a history faculty, so Dad took a walk and became an engineer.

Dad excelled in his field: back when Lina was a toddler, he had spearheaded a paper on turbines that was selected for presentation at an international Communist expo in Bulgaria. A week before the trip, a low-ranking KGB sergeant showed up at Dad's work with a letter *from Dad* to the expo committee. The letter explained that due to a recently broken leg, Dad would be unable to attend the exhibit and requested that the following [non-Jewish] coworkers represent the project instead of him. The only thing missing was Dad's signature.

"But my leg isn't broken!" Dad blurted out in a moment of idiocy (my father hated lying).

"Would it help if it were?"

Dad hastily scribbled his name, went for a walk, and returned the next day, ready to work. Adapt and endure, and those who had allowed themselves to be paralyzed by lamenting over pogroms, anti-Semitism in school, anti-Semitism at work, beatings in the yard, complacent teachers, friction, tides, gravity, and other unalterable factors were ground underfoot.

Lina was about to enter Kharkov Polytechnic, where nobody cared about her distressed state, where she would need her brain to function in order to have a career and have children. Dad was trying to help her, as were the school director and the administrator from the medical academy. Any way you look at it, *Be yourself* wasn't an option—being yourself was the problem.

OLEG AND THE MIRROR

Kharkov, Ukraine, USSR, November 1987

In November of the year I entered first grade, about a month after the gas mask drill, a period of unseasonable warmth settled over the city. Early American colonists called this late-fall phenomenon "Indian summer," because it gave the Indians time for one final raid before suspending their war campaigns until spring. The Russian name is *"babye leto"* ("old women's summer"), for it's the *babushki's* last chance to warm their bones in the sun before winter descends for good. Oleg and I didn't step out of our apartment building: the abnormal weather carried with it an element of risk, and not just for American settlers. An entire platoon of *babushki* was camped in the yard, any one of whom might start wondering why a pair of first-graders was slinking around outside when there was plenty of homework to be done. Telling the *babushki* to take a hike was ill-advised (I had attempted it once, with disastrous consequences), which meant that Oleg and I were best off indoors.

Everyone in my family had gone out to work, to school, or on errands, leaving just us and the empty apartment. We were bored, and amused ourselves by browsing through the various trinkets that Dad had brought home from his trips throughout the USSR. For a while we stayed in the master bedroom, then made our way into the hallway. Nothing special was there, just a couple of bookshelves, a coat rack, and a mirror, placed in the hallway as a courtesy for disheveled guests walking in from the elements. As we passed by the mirror, Oleg looked at me.

"Are you a *zhid*?"

"Zhid" was an ugly word with an ugly meaning. In English the best translation is "kike," but that doesn't do it justice, for "kike" is rarely used nowadays in America, whereas *"zhid"* was heard all around Russia. It meant more than a nasty Jew; it was the term of an epidemic, a sinister cancer many Russians felt was ravaging their country. *"Bei Zhidov, Spassay Rossiyu"* ("Crush the Jews, Save Russia") was a common slogan scribbled in the alleyways of Kharkov.

I was a Jew. I knew that. I didn't know what that meant.

"I don't know," I said, after a while.

Oleg was thinking.

"Let me look at you."

I said nothing. Somehow I found myself facing the mirror, straining to see the image through the dirty surface. Behind me, I saw Oleg circling, scanning, searching, trying to pinpoint something.

"You *are* a *zhid*. I know you are. You have the ass of a *zhid*, the face of a *zhid* . . . We learned how to look for them in school."

Despite the fact that we lived next door to each other, Oleg and I went to different schools. My parents had lobbied hard to get me enrolled in School Number Three, which was known for being tolerant toward Jews. Of course, I still received my share of beatings, but I suppose it was the school with the gentlest, most understanding beatings that a Jew could get. I thought the other kids didn't like me. But Oleg was different. He was my friend, my best friend, the veteran of a thousand Battles of Kharkov. Until I stood there with him, I did not make the connection between the beatings and being a *zhid*.

Oleg finished his inspection and stood to my left, looking at me in the mirror, his face showing a curious mixture of sympathy and disgust. I wanted to get out of there and away from the mirror, but I couldn't. I saw a protruding nose attached to a skinny face with thin lips above a long neck. Below was a stooping body with small hips and a flat ass. My familiar image was still there, but overshadowed now by those grotesque features. I wanted the thing in the mirror to be gone.

"I'll have to ask my mom about this." Finally I turned to Oleg. "I'm going to read a bit. I'll see you later?"

"Yeah, sure."

I let him out and watched as he walked across the stairwell to his apartment, just a few feet from mine. I wasn't angry at him: How can you get angry at someone for speaking the truth? I just turned the lock and leaned against the black leather upholstery stapled to the door.

A few months earlier, I'd snuck out to the bakery around the corner for some cheese-stuffed *vatrushki,* and a man with a long mustache started following me. "We're sick of you," he hissed, and he grabbed my arm. "Why don't you all just leave?" I yanked my arm free and spun away, and I felt him chasing me as I sprinted home. I managed to hold on to the *vatrushki* but I didn't want them anymore, and the whole time I couldn't understand why he was holding me if he wanted me to leave, and who "you all" were, and why he was sick.

Anna Konstantinovna's face floated up to replace the man's. She was a tall woman to start with, but the times I stared up at her from the floor, she appeared gigantic. I saw my gym teacher, whose name I wasn't sure of, winking at the fat kid and the brothers and shutting the locker room door for a long ten minutes. Then I was back in the apartment, overhearing Mom and Dad late in the evenings, when friends came over and they whispered of synagogues and "us" and other bad things. What had been disparate moments of fear and pain swirled around my mind until the answer came to me, resolved itself in the mirror.

I peeled myself off the leather door and went to bed. It wasn't even dinnertime, but I felt tired.

The last two things I said to Oleg were lies. Other than passing encounters on the stairwell, I never talked to him again. And I didn't even consider asking Mom anything. I remembered her dragging me along to meet with Anna Konstantinovna after the first few beatings, and the way her hand crushed mine on the walk home afterward, and her anger made me feel worse. In a country where parents didn't trust their kids and people got arrested for "holding subversive Jewish gatherings" in their houses, what could she have told me? What did she know about being a Jew besides the persecution? I don't know if I understood all of that at the time. What I did know was, this was something Mom couldn't help me with.

I tried hard to forget about the whole thing. I didn't want to be pitied. I hated myself and I wanted others to hate me. I wanted to surround myself with an aura of hatred. Mirrors became enemies, and anything good in them was transparent, like a vampire's reflection. I stayed in the apartment and read fairy tales and stories from faraway lands. The reminders of being a *zhid* still came, at school and in the yard, but over time something else began to creep up on me, in addition to the fear. I considered the bullies lucky: they only had to see me once in a while; I had to live with myself every day. I envied them.

DISARMING THE ADVERSARIES

Kharkov, Ukraine, USSR, Spring of 1988

Ideas are more powerful than guns. We would not let our enemies have guns; why should we let them have ideas? —Joseph Stalin

Tat-tat-tat-tat rattled the rotary dial, Dad's fist clenched and pale as he gripped the black receiver. "I'll take two bags . . . that's fine. Same as last year? Good, I'm leaving now." He replaced the receiver, grabbed a bag stuffed with rubles and flour, and hurried out into the rain.

Purchasing *matzah* in Kharkov required money, flour, and discretion. The money went to the underground bakers who operated out of apartments throughout the city. But even with the reforms that had begun to creep into Soviet society, it was still dangerous for the bakers to purchase large quantities of flour in the springtime. To avoid drawing attention, the suppliers asked customers to contribute flour along with rubles; that way, today's buyer provided ingredients for tomorrow's client. Discretion was necessary, because possession got you anything from a heavy fine to the loss of your job, depending on the political climate. For Dad, discovery likely meant being unable to work as an engineer. The bakers could face imprisonment.

Dad hopped on the trolley, mixing in with the rush-hour bustle, then ducked down a predetermined alleyway and exchanged
bags. He returned, visibly relieved to lock the door, and instructed
me to follow him into the kitchen.

"We are going to eat *matzah*," he said.

"Why?" I asked.

He wasn't sure, but he thought Passover was sometime around
now.

For a man who risked losing his beloved career, Dad didn't
know much about Passover. There were no holiday traditions, no
family gatherings, no Seder services (definitely illegal), and if you
were crazy enough to try hosting one, good luck finding someone
who spoke Hebrew or knew the prayers. Many lost track of when
the holiday fell, since Passover, like Easter, is a day that shifts
from year to year. *Matzah* was all that was left, that and rain.
"It's *Zhid* Easter," the ordinary Russians would grumble when
the first nice day of spring was ruined by a downpour. "Weather
always turns shitty on *Zhid* Easter." It was as good a way as any
to remember a forgotten holiday.

Incidentally, Christmas didn't fare much better. Christmas was
effectively destroyed by a series of anti-religious campaigns starting in 1928, shortly after the Revolution. But the people still
needed a winter holiday to tide them through the dark nights,
and that's when one of Stalin's propaganda geniuses suggested
it would be much easier to co-opt an existing tradition rather
than contrive a new one. Stalin agreed, and as a result, Christmas
trees, presents, songs, and decorations were uprooted, cleansed
of religion, and transplanted over to the New Year. Under this
system, families were ordered to celebrate the New Year with
New Year's songs around a New Year's tree adorned with New

Year's ornaments. Santa moved, too: every New Year's Eve, jolly, white-bearded Grandfather Frost, who looked *exactly* like Santa, would drop by in his sleigh with goodies for the children. This revamped holiday celebration debuted in 1935, seven years after the old, religious Christmas was outlawed. People are good at adapting, especially at gunpoint, and after a few winters the new tradition took hold nicely and no one but the old folks thought of or remembered what had been done before.

How could thousands of years of tradition—Jewish, Christian, Muslim—vanish overnight? What had become of them, the believers, the martyrs, defenders of the faith? The answer is chillingly simple: the martyrs, they were martyred. They were martyred by the millions. The first thing the Communists did upon attaining power was to exterminate the intelligentsia. They killed the priests, they killed the rabbis, they killed the teachers, they killed the judges, they killed anyone and everyone who was a source of knowledge and inspiration. Artists and writers were taken because they distracted the workers; engineers because there were power outages. Farming elders were killed because of food shortages, which led to more food shortages, which led to more dead farmers. They killed with diligence, they killed with pride, they killed and they killed until there wasn't a man left who could recite so much as a damned nursery rhyme, and with the leaders dead, their memories banned, the books burned, the relics confiscated (and sold to the West to purchase more bullets), the sanctuaries torn down and refurbished into gyms and Pioneer youth centers, the souls of the people left bare and trembling, the Communists' goal had been accomplished. The Bolsheviks knew: eradicate the culture, and the rest will wither accordingly.

*   *   *

My grandparents' generation was the last to know what things had been like before 1917, before the Revolution. By the time Grandpa Lev was a man, he spoke Yiddish, had become Bar Mitzvah, and was intimately connected to his history and customs. Many of his contemporaries lived in rural enclaves, governed by their own rules, their hours anchored by yarmulke and tallisim, prayers and feasts, daily reminders of who they were. Everything, from birth to death, was suffused with ritual and meaning. And, as my mother and every rendition of *Fiddler on the Roof* point out, Jews in that time were a bit snobbish, and viewed themselves with a certain measure of underdog pride. "The goyim [non-Jews] hate us because they envy us," the Jews of old averred, "because we have something—we *are* something—that they will never be."

It was far from an idyllic existence; anti-Semitism in my grandparents' time manifested itself in pogroms, violent raids often sparked by times of strife and unrest. Pogroms shattered and burned, raped and looted; pogroms flared up and pogroms died down, spreading through vast regions or smoldering in local provinces, sometimes petering out for decades at a time. Long centuries taught Jews to view them as seasonal calamities, unavoidable evils like famine or drought. The Cossacks and peasants who participated in these medieval riots were goaded by their own, medieval beliefs: Jews were witches; Jews concocted outbreaks of plagues; Jews crucified Jesus; Jews plotted to assassinate the tsars. The difference was, Jews before the Revolution knew what it was like to be Jewish. They possessed a language and rituals that were still connected to the meanings behind them. And as they rose, time and again, from burned villages and charred ghettos, they rose as a people. They rose as Jews.

"*Mayn zun, mayn zun,*" Grandpa Lev would say to my teenage father as he scrubbed the grease from his hands after returning

34

home from the tank factory. Dad watched my grandfather illegally rinse the bitter herbs, bless the Passover wine, break the *matzah,* reestablish the covenant of long ago. Dad soaked in the ancient words, grateful for a glimpse into an already-waning world. My father's generation had an immediate link to the pre-Revolution era. Dad couldn't learn Yiddish, or study the Torah, or become Bar Mitzvah, but what he did inherit was a yearning for something his father had once had. It was a blurry vision, but it was enough to draw him down the alleyway with a sack of money and flour, risking himself for an obscure holiday that he didn't comprehend.

But the afterglow was rapidly fading. The end of World War II was a watershed moment, for the war had destroyed personal records, and Jews began bribing clerks to falsify their passports, altering names and ethnicities to rid themselves of their Hebrew stigma. The yeshivas were gone, the shtetls destroyed. Many Jews had been herded into urban environments where paranoia and the secret police thrived. City life offered plenty of opportunities for informants to root out unwelcome cultural practices. Being a Jew was no longer a seasonal concern.

The anti-Semites also had changed, and the witch hunts of old were gone. With each year, both Jews and anti-Semites regressed into more basic survival mind-sets. The everyday Russian was just as affected by the secret police as the *zhidi,* for in the land of no trials, no one was safe. Such was the case with my father's boss who had spent ten years in the gulag. One afternoon, the supervisor, a Ukrainian without a drop of Jewish blood in him, was walking through the factory floor when he overhead a group of welders quietly snickering in the far corner. The supervisor paid them no mind until he was apprehended the next morning. It turned out one of the workers had told an anti-Soviet, Jewish anecdote, and since the incident took place in a factory, the supervisor was charged with fomenting Zionist propaganda with intent to undermine Soviet industry. The man pled that he was across the shop floor when the joke was made, he didn't even *hear* the quip, especially considering he was clinically deaf in one ear. Applying typical Soviet logic, the Party took the deafness into account, and instead of the standard twenty years in the labor camps, the man got ten.

"You nevertheless have one good ear to answer for, Comrade," the KGB officer admonished the supervisor as he was hauled from the sentencing chamber.

"Mayn zun, mayn zun," Dad said as he dragged me over to the sink.

"Why?" I asked when he thrust my fists under the faucet and told me to hold one fist on top of the other.

Dad always knew everything. He'd traveled all over the USSR. He could put turbines together and he knew all about power plants, and history, and books. But now he wasn't sure.

I craned my head to spy the sack of *matzah* squatting on an old chair in the parlor. I despised that pallid, tasteless substance, that ashen thing already crumbling into powder, as I despised this fists-washing thing. They were stupid, sad secrets, things to be beaten over. An idea crept into my mind, and I started laughing and slamming my fists against each other. Water splashed on the floor and hissed against the rusty radiator. Anger flashed across Dad's face, followed by disappointment. "Not yet," he whispered, and I knew it was finished, and I felt the blessed relief that comes when you try to outsmart an adult and hope desperately that they'll fall for it, and it works.

"He's immature," Dad said to Mom, who appeared as thankful as I was that the sham was over. "He doesn't understand."

Dad was right. I had no idea what it meant to be a Jew. I was repulsed by it, and was about as interested in Judaism as I was in cannibalism. But he didn't know either—scurrying down alleys and mimicking his father didn't yield meaning, and without meaning, symbols are useless and an ancient token of freedom and redemption crumbles into a bland, tasteless cracker. The anti-Semites didn't know—they hated because they had been programmed to hate, and they obeyed because they had to obey in order to survive. No one knew, no one understood, and, as the old saying goes, one will always fear what one doesn't understand.

A MARKED MIKHAIL WILL
DESTROY RUSSIA

Kharkov, Ukraine, USSR, Spring of 1988

It's an early weekday afternoon and the yard is quiet. Mom's at the clinic, Dad's fixing a turbine, Lina's in school, and Grandma's at the stove working on borsch, which I'm excited about, and potato pancakes, which I will find a reason to avoid eating. I'm supposed to be in school, but my last blood tests showed I was still low on iron and that was enough for Mom to score me another extended sick note. A couple of weeks ago I successfully wormed out of the Passover hand-washing, and now I won't have to worry about the end of first grade for a while. I have a good streak going.

Kolya rolls through the yard, lazily scanning benches packed with *babushki* greeting the spring, and lilac bushes where a few scrawny birds are trying to surprise the early crickets. The *babushki* position themselves three or four to a bench, where they discuss everything from Union politics to the far more interesting rumors of the apartment complex. Some of the more intrepid women have already exchanged their dark winter scarves for the brighter red and yellow spring varieties.* Mitya, the yard keeper,

---

* In Russian, *babushka* refers to the woman and not to the actual scarf, as it does in English. The difference is negligible, however, for one is seldom seen without the other.

is slowly stirring piles of runny snow, pausing here and again to relight his pipe. I wave my arms but Kolya ignores me. He saw me when I scrambled down to meet him from the balcony, but Kolya is never in a rush.

Everything about the kid is angular, from his lanky wrists sticking out of the sleeves of his older brother's coat to the bent spokes jutting from the wheels of his bike. The wheels are slightly flattened, which makes the bike lurch a little, but Kolya pedals standing up and that doesn't slow him down. The most peculiar part of the bike is the oversized seat, shaped like an upside-down helmet, which originally belonged to an old moped.

"You buying or gawking?" Kolya slings himself off the bike, hand hovering near the seat's lock.

"I'm buying, Kolyukha," I assure him.

"You better be," he says, but I know he's grumbling out of habit, and the seat snaps open. Coiled inside, wrapped in on itself, is an old stocking, several old stockings in fact, layered over one another and reinforced with electrical tape. Kolya unties the knot at the end and the coins spill out into his hand. Eastern European coins are the easiest to get and are always in Kolya's vanguard. There are Hungarian forints with plain wheat sheaves (wheat being the prevalent symbol used to demonstrate your country's commitment to Communism), boring East German pfennigs, each denomination bearing the same hammer, compass, and wheat mark, solid dinars from Yugoslavia with wheat wreaths and flames, intricate Czechoslovak korunas and Bulgarian stotinki (wheat wreaths and lions on both), bani and lei with cogwheels and factories surrounded by halos of wheat from Romania, and more. Kolya's long fingers pick through the wheatocracy with the surety of a seasoned dealer. He skips past the pfennigs—I already have those—and digs out a few stotinki, since I wanted to buy some the last time but didn't have the money. The coiled stocking gives birth to several little socks containing more exotic coins from Cuba, Angola, Vietnam, North Korea, South Yemen: our fellow wheat enthusiasts from around the globe. I buy some Cuban pesos, think about the Vietnamese coins with five-pointed stars on the back, haggle with Kolya over a few beat-up rubles from early Soviet Russia, but my eyes can't help being drawn to the far end of the stocking.

"I want to see the others," I say, carefully storing my purchases inside my jacket.

"I showed you the others, remember?" Kolya replies, but I'm not letting him play dumb today. I don't know how he managed to get out of school early—I'm sure he has an explanation, otherwise the *babushki* wouldn't have allowed him into the yard—but there's no other buyer around and I'm not letting the chance pass by.

"The *others*. The birds. The ones you showed Deniska and Fedya. I saw the eagles, over their shoulders."

Kolya squints, trying to make up his mind, then slowly reaches deep into the mouth of the stocking until the layers of nylon swallow his forearm. He positions himself so his back is between us and the nearest bench of *babushki* and works out the knot on the sock in his hand, glancing down at me from time to time.

I see them and I want them, the tsarist coins, illegal ones, dark, rusty kopeks and dull silver rubles. The two-headed eagles scream from the metal, wings spread out, talons clutching orbs and scepters, the ancient symbol of the House of Romanov proclaiming the might of a dead empire. *Kopiyki,* it says in the archaic spelling of the word, and something about it fascinates me, because no one spells "kopeks" like that anymore.

"There he is," Kolya whispers, "Nikolai the Bloody, the one they shot with all his family." A calm, bearded man appears in profile on the higher denominations, hair combed to one side.

"Ten rubles if you want two kopeks, but you better keep them hidden. I don't need you bragging to anyone about it."

I was ready to wrangle a better price out of Kolya, but nothing irritates me more than being treated like a child—I'm already eight years old—and I angrily shove a pink ten-ruble Lenin note into his hand. I'll show Kolyukha who can keep secrets. I already have a secure location prepared for the coins, a little baggie I can hide behind my teddy bear that no one will see.

"I get to pick which ones I get," I say as nonchalantly as possible, but Kolya doesn't budge. He's intently staring at a spot on a balcony directly across from the far entrance to the yard. Nikolai and the eagles have vanished into the sock and the sock into the stocking. Suddenly I see them. Five men in dark coats with red armbands walk into the yard.

Everything slows down. Kolya holds on to the ten rubles, but in exchange he's sorting through common Hungarian forints, counting them out into my hand. "This one, it's in great shape," he says, and I want to remind him that I already have them, I know I'm not getting the two-headed eagles but I want some Angolan coins or Vietnamese ones, but my mouth isn't working well and I just nod my head instead.

The yard is quiet. Laundry creaks on taut ropes, drying pins protesting the strain from the wind, the yard keeper's shovel clinks brisk and regular, but otherwise I can hear everything. The five men in red armbands stroll through the apartment block. They have the businesslike gait of wolves near caribou, purposeful but not hurried; there's always someone weak, injured, unlucky, and the pack will have its dinner. Wherever the men are headed, there's no need for improper haste. They're not KGB; you don't see those until they come for you in the middle of the night, and nobody hears about it until the next morning. They're not even policemen, the KGB's little brothers who handle official nuisances like filling out an arrest warrant long after the prisoner has vanished from the world. They're *druzhinniki,* neighborhood watchmen assigned to patrol for drunks and loiterers, but on their arms is the plain red band, the crimson banner of the USSR, and with it comes all the malice and paranoia and fear that the color has ingrained into my head.

Silence falls ahead of the *druzhinniki.* Kolya and I can hear them from all the way down the yard. They're chatting about the upcoming Sokol Kiev–Dinamo Moskva match. This is Sokol's year. Communism's goal is total equality, of course, brotherhood of workers and unity of nations—save for the hockey rink. In the arena, Sokol Kiev is going to feast on the marrow of their sorry Muscovite comrades and usher in a new era of Ukrainian dominance.

I don't know why I am afraid of the men. I don't remember learning to be afraid of them, the police, anyone in the government. No one taught me that Nikolai coins are dangerous or that certain words like "synagogue" are not to be uttered except in the apartment, but I know it, as surely as I know a hot stove will burn my hand and scissors are not to be played with. *Whisk whisk, whisk whisk,* the armbands rustle against the men's coats as their arms swing on the walk. *Keep walking, don't stop, not here, don't stop* pounds through my head. Mitya the yard keeper has developed a keen interest in corralling every dirty snow patch onto the sidewalk around him, and he concentrates on the slush, his pipe forgotten. *They're just* druzhinniki, assures the rational part of my brain, but my ears hear the *whisk whisk* of the armbands. *Don't stop here, keep walking,* my head echoes back. *Whisk whisk, don't stop / whisk whisk, don't stop,* goes the cadence. Kolya stares at a balcony and I stare at the coins, but the *babushki* stare at the *druzhinniki.* No *babushka*—Russian or Jewish—ever looks away. Something happens to a woman once she gets old enough to be called a *babushka*. Lina told me something about their surviving the evacuation and the war and the things before the war that no one talks about, times when people disappeared on a regular basis and the black cars were an everyday thing. "They stare because they're alive," said Lina, but I'm not quite sure what she meant. *Whisk whisk, whisk whisk* through the yard, and stolid scarf-wrapped heads swivel on benches to keep the men in sight.

Kolya presses the forints into my hand and tosses in some Polish groszy for good measure. We exchange meaningless words about not storing the coins near a radiator or anywhere else they can oxidize and develop a sickly blue-gray crust. Lina's tales of the KGB detaining Dad at his work flash through my head. I know that they took Grandpa, too, in this very yard, in our own apartment, back when Mom was a little older than me and the cars came for him. This was after Stalin died, as I would learn much later, and they thought dentists were hoarding gold, so they imprisoned and tortured every dentist they could get their hands on for a supposed plot to drive up gold prices. *Not here, keep walking,* the primordial prayer of survival screams inside my skull, and I hear its silent echo resonate through Kolya, and Mitya, even the *babushki,* through the birds, bricks, snow piles, and laundry lines of the yard.

Kolyukha carefully returns the jingling socks back to the stocking, cinches the end, and clicks the seat shut. The red armbands *whisk* by us and out the front of the yard, leaving behind tracks in the mush and predictions of Dinamo Moskva's upcoming demise. Gone are the eagles, as well, and I'll have to wait for another chance. I can still make out their faded wings on the brown copper when I close my eyes, but for some reason when I see the coins in my mind they're gigantic, like big copper tea saucers. Kolya was generous, because the fat bulge of Eastern European wheatage in my jacket is worth more than ten rubles, and I wave goodbye to his lanky silhouette as it half rolls, half lurches out of the yard.

* * *

"A marked Mikhail will destroy Russia," augured the old women sweeping the landing of my apartment complex. It was a few weeks after my unsuccessful attempt to get the tsarist *kopiyki* and I was running upstairs when I scurried past the two *babushki* in long coats and wool headscarves, their gnarled hands wrapped around old wooden broom handles. I paused outside my apartment, just out of sight. Mikhail Gorbachev, the new Soviet premier, had a conspicuous port-wine birthmark on his forehead. "That spot is an omen," the hushed whispers carried up the landing, "and so is his name. He's a marked Mikhail, and a marked Mikhail will destroy Russia." That's what the *babushki* foretold.

The old women knew their history, or at least the parts they considered important. The Roman Empire was founded by a Romulus and collapsed under a Romulus. Its descendant, the Byzantine Empire, was founded by Constantine the Great and collapsed under Constantine XI. And the "Third Rome," the Russian Empire of the Romanovs, which styled itself as the successor to the Byzantines, was founded by Tsar Mikhail I. These events didn't just transpire by coincidence, and logic dictated that should Russia collapse, it would do so under a Mikhail. In 1988, change and reform convulsed the land. The Soviet Union was mired in what was rapidly transforming into a humiliating and bloody defeat: the invasion (or, as it was referred to by the state media, the "liberation") of Afghanistan. And Mikhail Gorbachev, the man presiding over the chaos, was marked.

The *babushki*'s warnings were echoed by scarf-wrapped counterparts in apartments and farms throughout the land. Russia was rife with superstition, which permeated across class and ethnicity. Everyone took precautions against the evil eye, especially during weddings, births, and pregnancies. Peasants continued to eschew the word "bear," referring to the animal as simply "the boss." Using the boss's true name was unwise, lest the wind carry it and the beast come running to see who called for it.* Words in general were dangerous, and certain ones were not to be uttered for fear their innate power be unleashed, as I was to learn during one unforgettable evening. It started when *someone* placed hard, dried breadcrumbs under Lina's bedsheets, which had resulted in her tossing in bed the entire previous night.† Upon discovering the crumbs, Lina called me an obnoxious, underdeveloped fool.

"May you grow blisters on your tongue!" I fired back with an archaic curse normally reserved for witches and blasphemers (I read about it in a book).

The impact was devastating. Lina ran for Grandma, who, after a protracted chase, cornered me by the china closet and demanded I take back the curse. I held out for a good five minutes, intoxicated by my newfound abilities, but then Mom arrived to reinforce Grandma and I could only stare at the dessert on the dinner table until I hollered, with utmost sincerity, that I no longer wished for any afflictions, lingual or otherwise, to befall my sister.

Pagan custom had survived, and the deities of old still clung to the soil, thinly veiled as Eastern Orthodox saints. The Slavic thunder god, Perun, continued to be revered in the countryside, only now he was worshipped as Elijah, the ominous prophet who rolled through the skies in his fiery chariot. In Russian Ortho-

---

* Even the actual word for bear, *"medved,"* is a euphemism meaning "honey eater," which adds another layer of protection.
† This was directly inspired by Kipling's *Just So Stories,* in which a mischievous islander terrorizes a rhinoceros by putting crumbs under the rhino's coat. I didn't have a rhino but I did have Lina.

doxy, as in other syncretic religions, old deities don't die; they just get makeovers. Many people consulted *baby*, witch doctors, sort of like super-*babushki* who read fortunes and offered herbs, tinctures, and amulets, mysterious remedies for various diseases. These coexisted with modern pharmaceuticals: if a doctor didn't help, people went to a *baba*, or vice versa. Lives were beyond our control, affected by the stars, by goodwill and malice, names and spells, saints and talismans. The question was not whether Gorbachev was marked; he was. The birthmark was an omen; it meant something, required interpretation. The old women's warnings were issued in all seriousness and accepted as such.

Uncertainty surrounded the premier. He had risen rapidly and undetected. He spoke of change, *glasnost* and *perestroika* (openness and restructuring). The rhetoric alone was alarming. It naturally vexed the ruling class, who had no need for reform—they had nowhere to go but down. But it was also distressing to the population at large. "Change" is a tricky word for Russians. Russians fear change, and for good reason. "Life has improved, comrades; life became more enjoyable," quipped Joseph Stalin as he unleashed his Five-Year Plans, cheerfully massacring millions of his own people in the name of progress. Often, when restrictions were loosened, paranoia *increased*, because everyone realized that sooner or later some fool was going to poke his head out a little too far.

Change was the harbinger of the black cars.

Gorbachev came to office with dangerous ideas, such as private enterprise (limited, of course) and freedom of the press (extremely limited, of course), but his initial forays into reform were rather innocuous. To be honest, they were rather idiotic. The marked Mikhail kicked off his premiership by venturing to Siberia to assess the working conditions of coal miners and lumberjacks.

Raisa, his wife, accompanied him, which was a first, since previous administrations had a decidedly stag-party flavor, to the point where people wondered if their leaders even had spouses. In 1985, his first year in office, Gorbachev rolled out his anti-alcoholism crusade. "Fight the Green Serpent!" posters sprang up all over the Soviet Union. I remember seeing them at bus stops and on magazine covers, cartoons of sad men and women trapped in the coils of a sinister boa constrictor with puffy red eyes, as unpaid bills and unattended children huddled in the background. To the dictatorship—the Politburo, the KGB, the Red Army—Gorbachev was benign, a silly man who wasted his time on silly causes, and the hardliners were relieved. "Let him shit in the woods with his lumberjacks," they smirked. "Let him fight the Green Serpent." The population also relaxed, and all across the Union, from the halls of the Kremlin to smoky kolkhoz bars, Gorbachev's reforms were met with quiet derision as people raised glasses to toast to his health. The regime felt secure, the jokes circulated in droves, but the dull purple spot still remained on Gorbachev's forehead, and the old women muttered their warnings.

SOMETHING WAS DIFFERENT;
SOMETHING WAS IN THE AIR

Bucharest, Romania, Summer of 1988

Two *babushki* in a Ukrainian apartment complex weren't
the only ones reading the omens that summer. Six hundred miles
away from Kharkov, on the western fringe of the Evil Empire,
a man stepped out onto a Bucharest tarmac, drawn by the
same winds of change that troubled the old women. Unlike the
babushki, Amir Shaviv wasn't concerned with the influence of
birthmarks on the fate of nations; his interest in Gorbachev was
of a professional nature. The previous twenty years had seen an
erratic trickle of Soviet Jews fleeing the USSR to seek shelter in
the West. The biggest factor behind this flow of Jews was the
state of the Soviet government. During repressive times, emigration dwindled to a handful of families per year; when the regime
eased up, it spiked to a couple of thousand families. But whether
five or five thousand, any Jews crossing into the West became
the responsibility of Shaviv's employer, the American Jewish Joint
Distribution Committee (JDC or Joint), and *that* made Shaviv as
curious about the marked Mikhail as any *babushka.*

The journalist–turned–human rights worker was in Romania
trying to get a feel for the situation in Eastern Europe, since the
news filtering in from beyond the Iron Curtain was of change and
unrest. This had happened before, of course: the Prague Spring,

Khrushchev's Thaw, etcetera, etcetera—Soviet Cold War policies habitually cycled through periods of relative freedom followed by renewed cruelty. Nevertheless, the reports of 1988 were worth investigating. The triumph of the Catholic Solidarity movement in Poland, Gorbachev's decision to cede political independence to Eastern Europe and withdraw Soviet troops from Afghanistan; all these were intriguing, to say the least. In light of this, Shaviv and the delegation he was part of were dispatched by Joint, an overseas arm of the American Jewish community, to visit and assess key areas under the pale of Communism.

Bucharest was a good place to start. Its Jewish community was honoring Moshe Rosen, who had just celebrated his fortieth anniversary as chief rabbi of Romania. For four decades, Rabbi Rosen had kept the faith alive in the face of the Stalinist dictatorship of Nicolae Ceauşescu. Representatives from all over Europe were there to laud his efforts; their words would be a good indication of the degree of freedom in the Soviet Bloc.

It was a hot day, and the International Hotel, where the gathering was held, was not air-conditioned. People melted in their suits. The sluggish heat, however, didn't stifle the enthusiastic applause that erupted every time Ceauşescu's name was mentioned. Rosen's celebration, like all events held under the shadow of Communism, was infiltrated by government agents, and the speakers acknowledged their presence by invoking the Genius of the Carpathians on a regular basis. The mandatory thank-yous echoed by mandatory applause reminded the Joint delegation they were not in Manhattan anymore.

The unfortunately named Adolf Shayevich, chief rabbi of Moscow, was one of the orators. After the customary tributes to Rabbi Rosen's service, Shayevich's speech took a sharp turn.

"I stand here, and I address you not just as myself but as a representative of all Soviet Jews. And as I stand here, I think of what

49

we, as Soviet Jews, do. I think of how we gather over the holidays and sit around our tables and say 'Next year in Jerusalem.' "

The last sentence was a reference to an old Jewish custom from Passover, the world's earliest celebration of freedom. The Jews had spent the better part of the past 2,500 years scattered throughout the globe; over the centuries, they had developed the idea that each year, Jews in the Diaspora should strive to spend their next year in Jerusalem. This embodied the desire to have an autonomous Jewish nation unified around a single historic and religious epicenter. And for the past 2,500 years, this proclamation had remained as vague as "Next year, let's have world peace." But in 1948, the birth of the State of Israel transformed the saying from ephemeral nostalgia to concrete opportunity. Ben Gurion Airport was now open for business, and the Promised Land was a plane flight away, ready to accept its people—along with their money, education, and expertise. "Next year in Jerusalem" had become a dangerous idea. "Next year in Jerusalem" got the crowd's attention.

Shayevich continued. "And when we say 'Next year in Jerusalem,' are we just mindlessly reciting old maxims with nothing but superficial intentions behind them? Well, I am here to tell you that we, Soviet Jews, are saying 'Next year in Jerusalem,' and yes! we are serious, and yes! we mean it!"

Shaviv was shocked. Shayevich wasn't just the chief rabbi of Moscow—he was the *only* rabbi of Moscow; actually he was the only rabbi in the entire USSR. Adolf Shayevich was *allowed* to exist because the Soviet Union grew tired of dealing with gripes from groups like Amnesty International and the UN. The chief rabbi of Moscow was displayed in the capital so that visiting dignitaries could be told: "We certainly tolerate religion. Look! We even have a rabbi!" Seeing Shayevich take charge at that podium was a bit like watching Mr. Peanut come to life, strut into Kraft

Foods headquarters with his finest top hat and cane, and demand to be made CEO. Yet there he was, this nothing, this concession, promising the crowd, Ceauşescu agents and all, that he fully intended to get out of Dodge and take his people with him.

The way Shaviv saw it, there were only two explanations: either Shayevich was insane, or he knew what he could say and get away with. Shaviv's journalistic nature took over, forcing him to seek clarification, and he jostled his way through the crowd.

"Amir Shaviv, representative from Joint; a moment of your time, if you would. That was a powerful speech, Rabbi."

"Thank you. I'm glad you enjoyed it."

Excuse me, Rabbi, are you completely meshugah?

"Excuse me, Rabbi, are you . . . aware of the implications of that speech?"

A calm, measured response: "Yes, of course I am."

"And?"

"And what, young man?"

"And did you mean it?"

Now came Shayevich's turn to be surprised. "And I meant every word of it, young man." The short, bearded rabbi frowned. "Why else would I say it?"

Amir Shaviv was no therapist, but by the end of the conversation he felt comfortable enough to rule out any messianic complexes or delusions of grandeur. As strange as it was, Adolf Shayevich was both sane and serious.

*   *   *

On their way back to New York, the Joint team visited their Rome bureau. Residing nearby, in a Joint-run refugee shelter, were several families who had been fortunate enough to get out of Russia and were currently waiting to be accepted into the United States.

Shaviv began asking questions, the most important one being "How long did it take you to get your exit visa?" The responses he heard time and again surprised him. Every single family living in Rome had received their exit visas within six months. Not years—*months*. Shaviv was accustomed to hearing accounts of individuals languishing interminably in the Soviet system, getting fired, jailed, harassed. Compared with those stories, a six-month wait was practically no wait at all.

The team returned to Joint's New York headquarters with more questions than answers. As Shaviv told me years later: "Here was a Russian rabbi who either was looking for a one-way ticket to Siberia, or knew that he could say what he said and not be punished. Then there are these Russians living in Rome, none of whom waited longer than half a year to be allowed to leave. We felt something was different; something was in the air. We decided to watch and be prepared."

Amir Shaviv's instincts would serve him well and sooner than he thought. What neither Joint nor the Jews of Russia realized was that *glasnost* and *perestroika* were gaining a soon-to-be-unstoppable momentum of their own. A little over a year after Shaviv's trip to Europe, that momentum would trigger a series of frantic phone calls all over the Soviet Union, including my family's Moskovskyi Prospekt 90, Apt. 5. Those phone calls, in turn, would result in a massive flood of refugees bursting forth to become the last great Jewish exodus from the Soviet Union.

LAND OF ENDLESS TWILIGHT

Pärnu, Estonia, USSR, July 1989

Pärnu, the summer capital of the Soviet republic of Estonia, was a resort town renowned for healing: ancient mud baths and seawater spas, the calm, warm water of Pärnu Bay, tiny cottages and pleasant boardwalks, had for years drawn vacationers from all over the Union. Pärnu's beaches lacked the usual garbage and dead fish deposited courtesy of Soviet environmental policies, and many vacationing Soviets preferred its rugged Estonian shoreline to the filthy, manicured sand of the sanatoriums. Concerts and festivals filled the evenings. Old women sat on street corners, perched over sacks of ripe blueberries, and for a few kopeks, you got a rolled-up newspaper cone of berries with a liberal sprinkling of sugar. And then there were the White Nights, a high-latitude phenomenon that enveloped the land in perpetual twilight. This wasn't twilight as it is in most of the world; this was an ethereal glimmer that began at sunset, lasted for hours, and stirred something primordial in the soul.

But clean beaches and White Nights weren't the reason Mom and Dad brought me to Estonia in the summer of 1989. This tiny land, tucked away between Russia and Finland, had for centuries been ravaged by territorial conflicts. Unending cycles of occupation and counter-occupation had instilled its stern northern people with a deep passion for freedom. In 1940, Estonia became the last Republic to be "united" to the Soviet Union; it was a unification accomplished under the treads of tanks, but even those couldn't quash the resistance. Estonian patriots (molded by their harsh climate into consummate hunters) melted into the forests, and long into the occupation, many a careless Russian trooper stumbling home late at night never made it back to the barracks. Estonians *hated* the Communist Party, they despised the very idea of its existence, and offered safe harbor to Georgians, Jews, Armenians, anyone persecuted by the regime. That's what made it such an attractive getaway. Estonia meant movie screens playing films from the West and restaurants with European fare. It meant Jews speaking Yiddish in public. It was nice beaches and peace of mind, or the closest thing to it in the USSR.

And what a thrill it was to be in the Republic in the summer of 1989. One beautiful Friday afternoon, my parents and I hopped on a bus to Tallinn to wander around the crooked alleyways and medieval bastions that still gird the Old Town. It was the heart of the Singing Revolution, as the historians would come to call it, when crowds of Estonian patriots flocked to the capital to hold vigils, sing old folk songs long banned by the Soviet dictatorship, and demand independence. The cobblestone plaza around Tallinn's Town Hall was full of young musicians plucking guitars, poets reciting the *Kalevipoeg*, Estonia's national epic, and people clustered around radios playing illegal broadcasts from Voice of America and the BBC. Soviet censors tried hard to prevent citizens from straying into forbidden airwaves; all transistors were programmed to block radio signals beyond official frequencies, but intrepid Estonian mechanics learned how to bypass the system, and the crackle of makeshift radios mixed with singing all over Tallinn.

A procession snaked its way through the plaza, men and women holding hands and carrying placards. Mom got goose bumps. This wasn't an official parade; this was a *demonstration*, against, not by, the regime. The line drew closer—candles, and signs, and singing. Clapping and cheers broke out. Mesmerized, Mom took a step forward.

"Please, no families! . . . Please back up! . . . If you have a family, do not approach!" the demonstrators shouted as soon as Mom ventured too close. It was 1989 and yet, just three months earlier, a similar demonstration in the Republic of Georgia (another hotbed of anti-Soviet resistance) had ended in tragedy. Young Georgian women donned traditional Georgian bridal costumes and marched on Rustaveli Avenue in the capital city of Tbilisi. Georgia's governor, alarmed by the display of national identity, ordered the people to disband, but the protestors, perhaps buoyed by the spirit of Gorbachev's reforms, refused. The governor responded by calling in the Spetsnaz, the special forces unit of the Red Army. After the mêlée cleared and the tear gas drifted away, the bodies of nineteen young women in bridal costumes, faces bludgeoned beyond recognition by razor-sharp military spades, the trademark weapon of the Spetsnaz, lay sprawled on the avenue for the Union to see. Thus died assurances of freedom in the age of *glasnost,* and memories of the mutilated faces of those nineteen beautiful Georgian girls haunted the plaza in Tallinn. "Single individuals only; if you have a family, do not approach!" rang out the warning as hope and danger floated on the Baltic breeze.

*　*　*

One August evening back in Pärnu, Mom, Dad, and I came across about twenty-five people, some vacationers, some locals, gathered in one of the many small parks that dot the town. A slender

55

man with auburn hair, a thick mustache, and round glasses stood in the center of the group. Next to him was a pregnant woman with gray-blue eyes and jet-black hair. The man read aloud from a book, and often he'd pause to explain something in the text. His Russian was broken and strange because it was the first time I heard a foreigner use our language—in person, on TV, or anywhere. But the man displayed no discomfort. On the contrary, he spoke as if the essence of his words would overpower incorrect tenses and misplaced articles. Of Jesus he spoke, of Isaiah and God and Mary, of faith and endurance, and swords and plowshares.

The woman, black hair framing her pale face, struck up a melody, simple and moving, on her guitar. Everyone held hands as her music filled the park and the summer breeze tossed her hair. I don't know how long it lasted—maybe a minute, maybe five, maybe more. It was August, the White Nights were almost at an end, but it seemed that as long as this woman kept singing, the twilight would endure and hold the night at bay. At last, she reached the end of the chorus, chanting the final line over and over as the strumming faded into the night air. Her song ended and with it the dangerous thrill lifted, and the circle disappeared, reverting once more into a few strangers enjoying a summer night in a park, just as other strangers enjoy summer nights in other parks all over the world.

The pregnant woman shut her guitar case and approached us. "Shalom. My name is Rita."

Rita was an American. Her Russian was better than the man's, her husband, Ben. They were Baptist missionaries, holding sermons, donating clothes, speaking with people, listening and praying.

The Soviet Union persecuted all religions, but it hounded the Baptists without mercy. Other denominations had the decency to conduct their affairs underground, but the Baptists just didn't get it. Suffering was a part of their faith, and they walked serenely to the gulags, knowing the earthly torments of the Soviet Union meant nothing compared with what awaited those who abandoned their god. This stoic temperament unnerved the USSR, who hated the Baptists and feared them.

Rita offered us a Bible.

"It's a gift from Christians from all over the world," she said. "This is the thousandth anniversary of Russia's conversion to Christianity."

Dad nodded. "Yes, I've heard rumors of that on Voice of America. But didn't the Soviet Union reject your gift?"

"Of course it did." She shrugged. "So we figured we'd just distribute them ourselves."

"But how were you able to come here?"

"With God's help"—she smiled at her partner—"we managed to bypass the system."

The book she held out was lightweight, printed on wafer-thin paper, portable and concealable. Dad, ever a lover of books—especially forbidden ones—accepted the gift, tucking it deep into his tote bag.

"Aren't you concerned about your public . . . activities?" he asked.

"We've been doing this for a long time. And besides, Estonia's lightened up a lot in the past year, thanks to Gorbachev. We've been to worse places." Something about Rita's tone gave her credibility, and Dad loosened up. He told her about our family, specifically about needing to leave the country as quickly as possible. My parents and I dreaded returning to Kharkov: the absence notes from various doctors were no longer working, and the school director made it clear that my presence in the third grade was going to be mandatory. Gorbachev's reforms had put the country under great duress, and anti-Semitism was flaring up, as it always did when insecurity waxed. One month before coming to Estonia, Mom had picked me up from the last day of second grade. As she was icing the bruise over my eye, I asked her if it was possible to stop being a Jew. "We have to get out of here," Mom whispered to Dad that night, her hands trembling with helpless fury. "We have to, whatever happens, we have to get out of this inhuman country."*

Rita looked at me. I was getting too big to hide in my customary spot behind Dad's leg.

"Would you mind if my husband and I prayed for him?"

Dad hesitated. "Technically everyone's an atheist around here, but we're not even secretly Christian."

"We pray for everyone," said Rita. "You don't have to be Christian—that's not the point."

Dad glanced down at me, and I nodded. I wanted to be alone. Rita walked me over to Ben, her large skirt trailing in the wind. Darkness had fallen, and the sea wind whipped tree branches against the streetlamps, causing them to flicker. The Americans rested their hands on my head, Ben on my left, Rita on the right, and Ben started speaking with the air of someone who had an important, urgent request. Rita added her voice, and their disjointed murmurs blended together with the wind and the glimmer of the streetlamps.

And then it was over. The adults shook hands, Rita and Ben gave Mom and Dad their phone number in case we ever made it to America, and we returned to our rental apartment.

"Is that what religion is?" I asked Dad that evening as I munched on my nightly helping of blueberries.

"I think so," he replied. "It was my first time, too."

---

* "The things kids say," remarked Anna Konstantinovna when Mom confronted her. "I have no idea where Lev would get this from."

* * *

Arkasha was easy to spot—he was tall and lanky, and sported a fishing hat with big glasses poking out from underneath. He was fifteen and he knew how to read and write in Hebrew, a dangerous and dying skill pursued mostly by old people, the ones who had nothing to lose, as a widowed family friend once put it. But Arkasha knew more than a language. He knew *stories,* legends of Moses, and David, and Joshua, and other tales from mysterious Jewish sources. He quickly learned that I loved all kinds of myths and fairy tales and was eager to share those he knew with me.

We met Arkasha and his mother a couple of weeks before Rita and Ben blessed me. They were vacationing from Moscow, and every evening our two families met on the beach, a short walk from Pärnu's downtown. Giant sand dunes dotted the seascape. Most were covered with a scruff of reeds, as if the dunes themselves were on vacation and had decided to stop shaving. Every few kilometers an errant jetty waded into the sea, wet black rocks oddly stacked upon one another. Arkasha and I circled around the dunes, clambered over the boulders, or ventured out onto the jetties as he told me tales I'd never heard before, accounts of Jewish kings and prophets. Once in a while he would pick up a stick and draw on the ground to clarify a particular episode, and the Bible would emerge from the sand, just as it had done in the beginning, in Palestine, many centuries ago.

I journeyed with Abraham to the Promised Land, camped in the desert alongside the Twelve Tribes of Israel, waited for Moses as he ascended Mount Sinai. I would squat down to get a better look at the pictures in the twilight, and when I was crouched, watched over by Arkasha, I could hear the wind rustle through the dunes and taste the salty brine of the Baltic, and I felt both small and protected. Before we moved on, Arkasha would carefully scuff his foot over the ground, and the tale would vanish into the sand and a new one would begin.

"A man died once and the angels gathered to weigh his actions, to determine where he should end up. But when all his deeds were weighed, it turned out the man had done as much good as he had done evil, and the scales hung in perfect balance."

"So what happened to him? Did he go to heaven or hell? How did they decide?"

"The angels waited and then God sent him back down to Earth. God told him that if he witnessed one act of pure selflessness, he would be allowed to enter heaven."

"He came down? Like a ghost?"

"Not like a ghost. Like a *soul*—there's a difference. His *soul* went down and roamed the Earth, and after a while he came upon a Jewish man who lay chained in a dungeon. The man had been imprisoned there by people who wanted him to confess that Judaism was the work of the Devil. The man was brave, but he knew that if he was tortured there was a chance he would say something he would regret."

We reached the end of the jetty and stopped, listening to the tide gurgle through the black rocks. Everything, sea and land, was muffled by the twilight. The green of the wrack melted to olive; the blue sky dissolved into charcoal; the tan of the dunes faded to an indescribable ghostly hue. Off in the distance, I saw our families sitting on a bench. They were discussing their own issues and monitoring us to make sure we didn't get too loud.

"What did the captured man do?"

"He told the soul of his plight, and the soul flew around the prison until he found a sharp pin lying on the ground. He brought it to the man, and the man killed himself. He knew that he was going to die regardless, but he wanted to die on his own terms, to die as a Jew."

"What did the soul do then?"

"The soul picked up the bloody pin and soared with it to the gate of heaven. He told the angels what had happened and they agreed that he had fulfilled his task."

"And?"

"And he went to heaven. He went to heaven, and he was proud of helping a fellow Jew."*

During his last day in Estonia, Arkasha told me that his mother and he were moving to America in September. He promised to send me a package from Moscow with some of his old toy soldiers. I said goodbye, and we went home.

In Kharkov I eagerly waited. School began, fall began, I got sick again, I kept to myself in the apartment and waited. I didn't put much trust in people, but was sure Arkasha would come through. I wasn't the only optimist. My parents were delighted with my summer friendship. They'd talk to each other, with me well within earshot:

"Arkasha is so smart. Wouldn't it be great if Lev took after him?"

After a couple of weeks, the package arrived. Inside were twenty soldiers, medieval Slavic warriors made out of red plastic. The leader bore a large shield with a rampant lion on it. Two knights were mounted on horseback. They were the finest soldiers I'd ever seen. I examined the package, even turning it inside out to make sure I got everything. Arkasha knew me well: tucked under a crease, for me to find, were faintly penciled Hebrew letters along with the corresponding Russian ones. Next to them was written "Practice These." A spasm ran across my face. The

---

* Arkasha's story (or at least the way I remember him telling it) is an altered version of "The Three Gifts" by I. L. Peretz.

entire experience in Estonia—the sea air, the freedom, the safety of darkness, and the thrill of exotic tales under the twilight—all of it vanished and all I could think was *He's training me. He's training me to be a* zhid. I was furious for not recognizing Arkasha's trickery. Mom and Dad hadn't seen the secret note. I ripped it into fine pieces, then went to play with the soldiers.

*   *   *

I remember that September evening vividly, because while I was busy staging battles with my new red recruits, the old black rotary in Moskovskyi Prospekt 90, Apt. 5, rang, rang, rang, and rang like the Last Judgment was coming. Every caller had the same frantic news: "Did you hear? America is closing the border. The U.S. Congress will stop accepting Soviet Jews: anyone who's not registered in Vienna by December 31 won't be able to go to America. America is closing the border."

America is closing the border.

The rumor flashed through the city like a thunderbolt. "Go to Austria," the whispers rustled through the phone lines. "Go to Moscow, renew your summonses, get your exit visas, and head for Vienna. There's help in Vienna." Long after the soldiers and I had concluded the Siege of the China Closet, long into the night the calls continued.

"We're leaving," declared Mom; "we're leaving now!"

The next morning my father was on a train to Moscow.

$130, TWO SUITCASES, ONE PIECE OF JEWELRY, NOTHING OF VALUE

Kharkov, Ukraine, USSR, Fall of 1989

Mid-September, 3½ months to the December 31 dead-line to be in Vienna.

Dad's just returned from Moscow, where he spent the better part of a week standing in line to renew the summons—the looming deadline has every Jew in the USSR rushing to the capital to do the exact same thing. The next step is to obtain official permissions from Mom's clinic, Dad's engineering bureau, and Lina's Kharkov Polytechnic Institute to leave the USSR. All three institutions must sign off that my family knows no valuable state secrets that could harm the Soviet Union.

Running a totalitarian regime is simple: tell the people what they're going to do, shoot the first one to object, and repeat until everyone is on the same page. There's no need to bother with platforms, debates, and that inconvenient din of opinions that forms the heart of democracy. The Soviet behemoth sprawled across eleven time zones, swallowing up one-sixth of the world's landmass and scores of ethnicities, from dark-haired Chechens to blue-eyed Latvians. Holding this bloated cultural Franken-stein together was one rule: no one leaves. Moving to a town five kilometers over required governmental permission; expressing a desire to leave the country altogether was akin to a criminal act. The possibility of Jewish emigration cut to the source of the Party's power—denying its citizens options—which is why Washington kept raising the topic. The West realized that in its own symbolic way, the battle over Soviet Jewry was more dangerous to Moscow than that of nuclear weapons; self-determination is anathema to Communism.

And it had to be the Jews. America couldn't wrangle for Uzbek freedom, for example, for the same reason the USSR couldn't lobby Congress to let Texas secede: national sovereignty's a bitch. But the Jews were different. Until 1948, the Jews were one of a handful of people to not have a nation. But the creation of the State of Israel gave the Semitic citizens of the USSR a homeland to return to. This formed the lynchpin of Washington's argument, and that's what the West pushed for, meeting after meeting, summit after summit.

By the early 1970s, this relentless pressure made evading the Jewish issue unfeasible, and the Kremlin altered its course from flat denial to a more subtle strategy. Moscow conceded that there was in fact a Jewish homeland, and even established an official avenue by which Soviet Jews could apply for emigration to Israel. Built into this very process, however, were numerous hurdles designed to minimize (and preferably stem entirely) the flow of Jews out of the country. The goal was to exert indirect influence by turning emigration into a costly and often perilous gamble. As America soon learned, Moscow's *da* was just the beginning of a prolonged, at times outright bizarre cat-and-mouse game between the USSR and the West, with Soviet families caught in between.

The game commenced with a catch: the USSR would release only those Jews aspiring to reunite with family members living in

Israel. In other words, one could not begin the process of emigration without first having received a summons for reunification from a living Israeli relative. This was where the Kremlin drew the line, forcing the West to deal with the classic catch-22. Pyotr couldn't emigrate because his brother Pavel was also stuck in Russia, while Pavel couldn't emigrate because Pyotr was in the USSR.

Israel was thus presented with a dilemma: How does one get Jews out of Russia if there are no Russian Jews in Israel to summon them? It was an unusual problem, which forced the Israeli government to resort to an unusual solution. Jerusalem began by establishing an obscure little office known as the Family Reunification Department. On the surface it was a family-tree service, designed to help Jews, the perpetual wanderers, reconnect with long-lost family members scattered across the globe by migration and war. Its true mission, however, wasn't so much to locate people as to create them. That isn't as difficult as it sounds: as any good kindergarten teacher will tell you, anything is possible with a little imagination. So take a family such as the Golinkins, who want to leave Russia but have no known relatives in Israel. The Family Reunification Department pores over their history and discovers that the family matriarch, Faina Pevzner, lived in the Ukraine when the Germans invaded in 1941. Here's where the reunification workers put on their imagination caps and start asking questions: What if Faina had a brother (let's call him Isaak) who was separated from her during the invasion, evaded the Nazis, snuck across the border to Poland, and, after many trials and tribulations, found his way to the Promised Land? What if Isaak had an address, a driver's license, even a photograph? (Any old Jew playing chess in a Tel Aviv park will suffice.) What if Isaak took some time to locate Faina? And finally, what if he, now old and lonely, missed his sister dearly and wanted nothing more than to spend his golden years with her . . . and with the rest of her family stuck in the Soviet Union?

World War II left Eastern Europe a devastated, smoldering wasteland. Entire populations had been obliterated, to say nothing of the personal records of one insignificant Jew. The truth is, once he was created, there was no real way to prove that my great-uncle Isaak Pevzner *didn't* exist.

Late September, 3 months to deadline.

Mom's clinic signs off on her leaving with no issues. Dad's supervisor signs off, shakes his hand, and demands his bottle of cognac. Dad brings him two bottles the next day, just in case he isn't joking. Then Lina, a promising student at Kharkov Polytechnic, receives a letter from the dean. It states that the school (and by extension the Ukrainian SSR, and therefore the entire Soviet Union) has invested too much time and training in Lina to allow that precious knowledge to fall into the hands of our foreign adversaries. The irony is not lost on my sister. She never even wanted to become an engineer and now she shows so much potential that she won't be able to leave the USSR. Grandma starts cooking Lina's favorite meals. Mom does her best to shelter me from the stress of the entire autumn but even I can't help noticing and tone down Lina's prank regimen. Mom and Dad scramble for a solution. The family's not leaving without her.

The USSR quickly sensed it was about to lose a sizable chunk of its Jewish population, thanks to the thousands of Isaak Pevzners pouring out of the woodwork. It immediately clamped down on all outgoing communication with Israel. The Family Reunification Department in Jerusalem couldn't just concoct a person out of thin air; it required basic demographics, such as names, birthdays, birthplaces, parents' names, parents' birthdays, parents' birthplaces. Smuggling such a list out of Russia was tricky: phone lines and the mail were heavily monitored, and the few people permitted to leave the country were searched for any kind of documentation. People counteracted that policy by keeping the information concealed and encrypted.

Further measures were applied. All incoming mail from Israel was screened carefully for the large, bulky summonses. Thus, even if a relative was created and a summons mailed out, there was no way for the Israeli government to know that it reached its destination. This taught Israel to send summonses during Soviet holidays, when the postal system was inundated with mail, making thorough screening impossible. In 1974, Mom asked a trusted friend moving to Israel to smuggle out our list. For a few years my family heard nothing, until one autumn evening in 1977 when Grandma received a large, gaudy greeting card congratulating her on the "60th Anniversary of the Great October Socialist Revolution." Tucked inside was a thick sheet of paper covered with Hebrew. At long last, after forty years of separation, the prodigal great-uncle Isaak had returned.

Early October, 10 weeks to deadline.

One of Mom's old patients puts her in touch with a high-ranking administrator at Kharkov Polytechnic. A sizable package of rubles, cognac, and vodka (the Holy Trinity of Soviet bribery) is delivered to the administrator's apartment. Two days later, Lina's dean concludes that the faculty may have overreacted and that the loss of my sister probably shouldn't derail the dreams of workers and

peasants across the globe. Lina stops sulking. The pranks
escalate accordingly.

Back in the pre-Gorbachev era, receiving a summons was no guarantee of exit. On the contrary: it was where the process got terrifying. Once the precious summons was received and proper permissions were obtained, the candidate had to undergo a KGB background check. The Kremlin, which was engaged in a constant state of aggression with the West, asserted its right to deny an exit visa to any applicant who had been "exposed to information vital to the national security of the Soviet Union." What defined exposure to information vital to the national security of the Soviet Union? Pretty much anything. Living near a power plant (give or take a few hundred kilometers). Carrying a subscription to a scientific magazine. Having an aunt who lived near a power plant, or a cousin with a subscription to a scientific magazine. Reasons for refusal, which was irreversible, were rarely given, and it was impossible to predict who would be branded as un-exitable. Some people everyone thought were going to be detained had been released, while many bewildered applicants had been refused. The process was random, arbitrary, devoid of reason and logic, which, of course, was the whole point, and shortly after the first Jews had braved the application process, a new group of citizens emerged into being. They were called *otkazniki,* "the refused ones," or, as it was anglicized in the West, refuseniks.

The refuseniks couldn't leave the country, naturally, but that was only the beginning. They had attempted to emigrate with the assumed intent of disclosing "sensitive knowledge" to the West, thereby undermining the safety and security of the Soviet Union. Under that interpretation, the refusenik's decision to submit an exit visa application was a treasonous act that deserved punishment. And punished it was.

Most dissidents were arrested on the spot. Those who didn't vanish into the gulags found themselves trapped in a purgatory, a newly created subclass of people who existed neither inside the Communist society nor outside it. All lost their jobs. All were banned from ever working in their fields again. The lucky ones became janitors and night watchmen. The rest found their job applications summarily rejected, and after a period of several months they were imprisoned on charges of "social parasitism": shunning one's duty to Communist society by neglecting to work.

In a country where everything was owned and operated by the government—getting to a hospital, getting into a university, getting a driver's license, getting help from the police—the refuse-niks had the entire social safety net ripped out from under them. Sometimes, unfortunate accidents happened to their friends and family. Such was the case with one of Mom's coworkers, who was shipped off to Siberia without a trial. The following week, his fourteen-year-old son was snatched off the street as he was walking home from school. The son reemerged several days later, beaten to a pulp. Afterward, the boy and his mother never left their apartment.

Mid-November, 6 weeks to deadline.

Everyone in the family clears KGB background checks, to the enormous relief of my parents. Now we need photographs for the exit visas. Nobody knows what format the photos need to be in, except that the format in which we submit is not the right one. Typical USSR. Impossible to tell whether this is another nasty little obstacle or simple Soviet incompetence, both possibilities equally valid. We take profile, full face, ¾ view. All of the above with lots of space around head. All of the above with no space around head. Mom and I have to be on the same visa, so I'm on

Mom's left knee facing right, on Mom's right knee facing left, sprawled on Mom's lap facing forward. We see old, crotchety photographers with shaky hands, newer avant-garde photographers obsessed with umbrellas and lighting effects, nyet, nyet, not the right format, *and what began as an annoyance develops into a serious problem.*

Given the overwhelming deterrence against leaving, Mom and Dad (whose professions made them prime candidates for refusal) didn't consider applying for an exit visa until 1979, when the government was undergoing one of its more tolerant lulls. In the fall of that year, Dad approached his boss, Vassily Bonesco, with the paperwork for an exit visa. "We'll talk about this later," Bonesco said, and stashed the application in his desk. "I just got a call that the Kurgan plant is down; you're leaving tonight." Dad, who had spent two years working up the courage to go through the exit visa process, suggested that perhaps someone else on the team could assist the good comrades of Kurgan with their turbomachinery woes, but Bonesco was having none of it. Several hours later Dad was off to one of the worst jobs of his career.

The breakdown of Kurgan's hot-water plant turbine left the city with not only no hot water, but also no *heat,* since everything was heated by radiators. (Now is probably a good time to mention that Kurgan is in Siberia, and winter was around the corner.) Dad spent the rest of November and most of December on the job. When he wasn't working he would huddle with the rest of the town in the local movie theater, the only building besides the hospital with a separate generator. Six weeks later, after getting the plant back on line and catching up on a decade of Soviet cinema, Dad returned to Kharkov, just in time to learn that the Soviet Union had invaded Afghanistan and the border was closed.

"You screwed me real good," was the first thing he said after storming into Bonesco's office. "If you didn't send me to Kurgan I would've had my exit visa application submitted! Now I'm stuck here!"

"Idiot!" Bonesco stepped up to Dad, his voice furious but low. "If I had submitted your application, you would've been refused, and then I would've been firing you, not to mention possible imprisonment and other . . . unpleasantries. You think those bastards care if you applied before the invasion?"

Dad's anger was quickly eclipsed by comprehension, then terror. "I apologize, I didn't—"

"*You didn't* is right." Bonesco pulled Dad's application out of his drawer, carefully ripping it up. "You never asked me to fill this out. This conversation never happened. Do you understand?"

Dad stared past Bonesco's face and to the back wall of his office, at the plaques and Lenins and proclamations of loyal service to the Union. Dad had worked under the man for years. He knew his story. He knew that when Bonesco was still a boy, his father had been executed in one of Stalin's purges, and the young Bonesco, along with his mother, was exiled to a kolkhoz, a communal farm in Siberia. Bonesco spent the rest of his childhood operating a tractor; he had to carry a little stool with him to and from the fields, otherwise he couldn't see over the tractor's steering wheel. Years later, after Stalin's death, his father was posthumously pardoned, and Bonesco and his mother were allowed to leave the kolkhoz. The first thing he did upon returning to Kharkov was join the Party, the same one that had killed his father— he'd had enough of being on the wrong end of the Soviet Union.

"For now, get back to work. But one day, this Afghanistan shit will be over, and they'll reopen the border, and then I'll be honored to fill this out and help you get out of this blasted country," Bonesco continued in a whisper. "And one more thing: when that time comes, you'll bring me a bottle of cognac for Kurgan, because Kurgan just saved your ass."

Bonesco's prediction was right; shortly after the invasion of Afghanistan, détente was over, relations with the West froze, and everyone who had applied for an exit visa was rejected automatically. The refusenik population exploded overnight. There wasn't much hope that the border would open soon, so Mom and Dad decided it would be safest to let Isaak Pevzner's summons expire and not attract undue attention.

But by September 1989, almost ten years after Dad's (thankfully) aborted attempt, our circumstances had changed. There was Gorbachev, who had drastically slashed the numbers of refuseniks. There was also the rumor of the U.S. Congress closing the gate on Soviet refugees at the end of the year. And if that wasn't enough, another, more sinister rash of phone calls late in the fall gave Soviet Jews all the impetus they needed to get out of the country.

Glasnost wasn't just about singing in Estonia and peaceful demonstrations in the Caucasus. Gorbachev's reforms unleashed a wave of anger among those who felt the Motherland losing the Cold War, and many who took advantage of the new freedoms of speech and assembly weren't liberals. The anti-Semitic reactionary group Pamyat ("memory") was hard at work planning pogroms to cast off the *zhid* yoke and reclaim Mother Russia's glory. Pogroms. With recent massacres and expulsions against Meskhetian Turks, Georgians, and others, the word shook Soviet Jews to the core. My beatings at school had escalated, and the extended-absence notes were no longer accepted. "We are leaving now," Mom kept repeating, and every time I trembled at the thought.

Dad went straight to Moscow to renew the expired Isaak

Pevzner summons, which was now permitted, thanks to Gorbachev. The USSR had terminated all official relations with Jerusalem since the Six-Day War of 1967 (when the Kremlin labeled Israel a terrorist-sponsoring state), so Israeli interests in Russia were represented by a neutral third party, the Netherlands. Dad spent the next few days standing in line at the Dutch embassy with nervous Jews from Bukhara, St. Petersburg, and every place in between, hustling to squeak through before the gate got shut.

"If you make it out, there's help at the west train station in Vienna," instructed the clerk who renewed our summons.

"But then what?" pressed Dad. "And how will they, whoever *they* are, know who we are?"

"They'll know," said the clerk. "Next person, please."

Late November, 5 weeks to deadline.

Mom, Dad, and Lina finally hunt down a photographer with a good track record. We meet with the regional emigration official, who says our photos are acceptable but warns that there are exactly three secretaries who are responsible for typing up exit visas for the entire Kharkov region. Every Jew in the area is trying to get their visas processed, and the secretaries have other duties. The officer assures us the visas will be ready, but not before late January or early February. Our chances of going to America are hanging on a fucking secretary. Mom and Dad spend the night thinking.

Why Vienna? What did Vienna have to do with receiving Jews fleeing Soviet Russia? There was nothing special about the city. In fact, I have a strong suspicion it didn't volunteer to become the refugee capital of Western Europe. The role was bestowed upon it by basic geography. Refugees fleeing persecution in the Soviet

Union and ethnic cleansing in the Balkans traveled west, toward freedom. International aid agencies consulted a map, located the nearest metropolis to Eastern Europe, set up their processing bureaus, and just like that, Vienna became the gateway to the West. Word spread quickly; those who got out did their best to funnel information to friends and relatives left behind, and the moment the first migrant found shelter in the City of Music, the system propagated itself.

A tougher question is *Why America?* My family's summons, just like the summons of every other Russian Jew, was issued for relocation to Israel. So why did we accept Israel's invitation to leave the USSR, knowing full well that the moment we crossed the Soviet border we, just like the majority of our fellow emigrants, would immediately reject it and ask for asylum in the States? One would think that persecuted Jews would want to live in a country of, by, and for Jews. We would get together, spin dreidels, eat *matzah,* become doctors and lawyers, and everyone's happy. But that didn't happen.

Why?

In order to understand the desired destination, one must first consider the reason for departure. What exactly were we, Soviet Jews, fleeing from? The answer isn't as obvious as it appears, because the word "Jew" can mean one of two things. First, it can denote a follower of Judaism, which is a religion. In that sense, anyone can become a Jew and anyone can stop being a Jew, just as anyone can become Catholic or stop being Catholic. However, "Jew" can also refer to an ethnicity, a hereditary genetic makeup that's as immutable as the rest of the genome. In that case, a person either *is* a Jew or is *not* a Jew, just as one either *is* an Eskimo or is *not* an Eskimo. There's no way to convert in. More important, there is no way to opt out. To use the example of Italians, most ethnic Italians are Roman Catholic, but while an Italian can stop being Catholic, he can't stop being Italian.

We, Russian Jews, were persecuted *not* because of our religion but because of our ethnicity. We had no religion, spoke no prayers, and, aside from a few old superstitions and vestigial snippets of Yiddish, had little religious tradition. The existence of God or lack thereof never concerned me. Throughout my childhood I had never talked to God, or thought of God, or wanted a god, and the only prayer I ever had was a vague desperate wish to not be myself and shed the horrible, unalterable ethnic *zhid* features I spied in the mirror.

What my family and many families like mine desired was peace of mind, not a synagogue. We wanted freedom, the freedom to live our lives without trembling, and naturally we, like our innumerable predecessors, cast our gaze across the Atlantic. Israel may be a Western nation, but, as the Russian Jews who did immigrate there found out, it's also flavored with a bit of theocracy—if not governmental, then certainly cultural. Consider ham. A Russian couldn't imagine kicking ham off the menu. We were raised on boiled *pelmeni,* jellied *kholodets,* baked *zharkoye,* and *buzhenina* slathered with horseradish. We wanted ham, we craved ham, we wanted to live in a land where bacon flowed like wine, a land brimming with pork chops served in stores open on the Sabbath, and we didn't want anyone wagging their finger and informing us we were sinning. We'd paid our dues to our ethnicity; the Soviet Union had made sure of that.

Numerous reasons for declining Israel's invitation were provided: we couldn't tolerate the arid climate; we had a friend in America who could land us a job; we'd already started learning English and didn't want to waste it. Some of the blunter individuals said they did not want to reside in a land engaged in unremitting conflict, didn't want their sons and daughters in the army. But the one shadowy reason was that we didn't want to embrace an identity; we needed to cast off a stigma.

Early December, 1 month to deadline.

Mom uses her last resort. Thirty years of treating patients without taking bribes means there are many people in the city who feel that they owe her. Mom feels it cheapens her profession, but she puts out the call. Everywhere in Kharkov, from intelligentsia parlors to seedy living rooms in neighborhoods where other doctors wouldn't go, word spreads that Dr. Golinkin needs help. Assistance arrives in the form of an unsavory gentleman who shows up at the apartment claiming some sort of connection to one of the secretaries. The next day Mom walks into the visa bureau. The office is under audio surveillance, so Mom had been warned to say nothing. The secretary slides open her desk drawer and Mom drops in an envelope stuffed with more rubles than the secretary will make in two years. The secretary thanks Mom for her visit. During the ride home, the young Jewish cabbie puts on a tape by an ex-Soviet musician who is singing about life in Brooklyn. The song has been around for a few years, but it was recently removed from the list of forbidden materials. "America, America, you're so far away," goes the chorus, effectively summarizing Mom's mood, and both Mom and the cabbie hum along to the words.

During one of his trips to the Kharkov visa bureau, Dad ran into Sergei Kantler, a neighbor of ours who was leaving the USSR on a chartered bus from Kharkov straight to Bratislava on the western edge of Slovakia. Private bus companies hadn't even existed a few years earlier, but thanks to Gorbachev and *perestroika*, they were gaining popularity, and a handful of enterprising drivers had even obtained passes to cross the Soviet border into Eastern Europe. Sergei was looking for another family to split the fee, and Dad immediately agreed. The bus was extraordinarily expensive but money no longer mattered, because it was here that the final hurdle in the exit process came into effect. Because the Soviet Union was a Communist land, all of one's possessions technically belonged to the USSR and almost nothing would be permitted out of the country. Money didn't matter, because the rules were clear. Each migrant was allowed $130, two suitcases, one piece of jewelry, nothing of value.

Second week of December, 3 weeks to deadline.
    "You lucked out. Your visas are ready," says the emigration officer as he hands the documents to Dad. He glances down at me, peeking out from Dad's leg. I know the visas mean leaving and he must've caught the expression on my face. He crouches down under the obligatory portrait of Lenin hanging in his office and extends his hand. "Good luck, bandit." ("Bandit" is a slang term, like "homeboy," often used by criminals.) The man doesn't switch his voice to the obnoxious joyful squeak most adults use with children; he speaks in the same bored monotone as he does with my parents, which impresses me enough to venture out from behind Dad and shake his hand. He's one of them, but he's still human, thinks Mom, and we hurry home to pack.

Over the past several months Mom had been a hurricane, driving the family through every obstacle to getting out of Kharkov, and by this point she was spent. The Lina fiasco, the threat of pogroms, the desperate search for the secretary, the strain of severing herself from her world, the uncertain fate waiting beyond the border—a thousand things jostled and clashed in Mom's mind, and yet the image of me and the officer shaking hands, Lenin preaching to the masses overhead, took hold. Unbidden and inconsequential, that one moment has remained a vivid memory of her last days in Russia.

INTO THE STEPPE

The books vanished in droves. Eighteen bookshelves had lined our small apartment, filled to the brim with fat collectors' editions, rows upon rows of hardbound tomes, square little poetry anthologies, colorful travel guides, drab engineering manuals, and scraggly samizdat copies of forbidden works. Dad had waited in line for hours for some of those books. He hunted down volumes on the black market, paid through the nose for them, and once (as Lina told me in one of her scary stories) was detained by the KGB and almost wound up in prison for having banned material. My memory of the books stretched beyond consciousness. They were there when I first opened my eyes and began to identify things like "warm," and "house," and "bed," and while I didn't know about or understand the byzantine game of passports, imaginary relatives, summonses, and exit visas, it was the breakup of Dad's library that made leaving a reality. The books were the background of my little world, and seeing them carted away by friends and relatives was like watching someone dismantle the sky.

All the adults—Mom, Dad, Lina, and Grandma—were constantly hustling, saying goodbye to good friends, reconciling with old friends they hadn't kept up with, eating at their favorite places for the last time, and agonizing over what to pack. We were only allowed one piece of jewelry per person. Not that we had much treasure—a gold watch from one grandfather and a fat Austro-Hungarian coin from the other—but neither heirloom would be permitted to cross the border, so Mom brought them to a jeweler, the husband of one of her old patients. "Make something meaningful out of them," she asked the man. Two days later, she came home with a pair of necklaces, thin gold bands bearing intricately wrought *Mogen Dovidi* (Stars of David), a large pendant for me and a smaller one for Lina. A *Mogen Dovid* was not desirable in the Soviet Union and thus less likely to catch a greedy guard's eye; the symbol was also an apt reminder of the reason for our journey. The jewelry had to be worn by the emigrant who claimed it, and since Mom, Dad, and Grandma would be wearing their wedding bands, the *Mogen Dovidi* would have to be conveyed by Lina and me. I winced at the thought of having to wear a *zhid* nametag, if only for one night.

"Did they *have* to be those stars?" sniffed my sister.

Locating suitcases was a nightmare. We were permitted two suitcases per person, which made for a total of ten, but rumors of the U.S. border closing sparked a shopping frenzy, and not even a duffel bag was to be found in the stores. One of our neighbors, a surly mechanic who reeked of vodka and glared at me whenever I ventured into the yard, had a knack for ferreting things out on the black market and made a small fortune reselling large red-violet cases with metal frames, hideous but sturdy. The last four came the night of the move, when the neighbor dragged them upstairs. He counted the cash Mom paid him, twice, before carefully tucking the wad into his coat pocket. After some hesitation, the man turned back to Mom and handed her a worn pocket knife with the five-pointed Soviet star etched on the handle.

"What's this for?" asked Mom.

"Consider it a parting gift, doctor." He managed a grin, which still resembled a scowl. "It's always good to have a good knife. Use it to slash up the customs officers if they get out of hand."

The gloomy mechanic wasn't the only neighbor we saw that evening. All around the apartment complex, windows were lit long into the night. Mom and Dad tried to keep our date of departure concealed. There were many reports of refugees being hijacked in the lawless plains of western Ukraine, where bands of robbers, given advance notice by their urban scouts, lurked in the wilderness, ready to attack the buses. (Part of the reason the drivers charged so much was because they had to hire their own scouts to monitor the roads for bandits.) It was best to disappear without notice, at night, but moving was a rare occurrence in the USSR. People grew up, lived, and died in the same town, often at the same address. There was no such thing as a new family on the block or a new kid in school, and despite my parents' attempts at secrecy, the increased last-minute activity alerted anyone with eyes that departure was imminent. The neighbors kept a vigil to see what would be left behind. Every half-hour a thin woman with a black kerchief around her gray hair darted into the foyer to check whether we were done with the kitchen table. She had been promised that table, and she wanted to make sure she got it. Something about her quick movements, gaunt frame, and black dress made her resemble the scrawny birds that hopped around the apartment block's courtyard scavenging for food. Mom kept telling her to come back, and as the night wore on and the eager neighbor returned, an uneasy feeling washed over Mom—it was as if the bird-woman was waiting for us to die.

Friends and relatives rotated in and out in a mishmash cycle of legs from my perspective. I tried my best to stay out of the way, but my packing had long been completed. The most important thing was books: a collection of four stories by Gerald Durrell, *Three Men in a Boat* by Jerome K. Jerome, a new book of Moldavian fairy tales one of my relatives gave me, and a pocket world atlas I appropriated from the book boxes, so I would know where we were going. The rest of the backpack was taken up by ten elite knights and pirates (I tried to be fair but wound up recruiting heavily from the knights), a couple of shirts, a pair of pants, a sweater, socks, and underwear. Lastly, I went to my grandfather's old toolbox and fished out a little hammer and a couple of screwdrivers. After all, you never know when you'll have to take something apart. Backpack on my shoulders, my teddy bear (Comrade Bear) in one arm, my pillow in the other, and I was set. The supplies were all that mattered. Everything else, including our destination, was irrelevant: anywhere other than Moskovskyi Prospekt 90, Apt. 5, Kharkov, USSR, was fine with me.

Dad shook me awake around 4:00 a.m., and I trudged to the sink and lazily brushed my teeth, spitting out the rust-brown liquid that squirted from the faucet. Our itinerary may have been uncertain, but I had a feeling brushing was not going to be at the top of the agenda for the foreseeable future, and I liked that. I got dressed, jogged downstairs, and stepped out into the Russian night. Silence hung over the courtyard. A foot of wet snow blanketed the earth and the flickering streetlights cast a yellow glow on the mounds. Idling next to the apartment block was a bus surrounded with people examining suitcases, loading suitcases, and discussing the status of suitcases yet to be loaded. Eight crates of vodka were stacked on a nearby curb. These were going to be handed out along the way at inspection points and gas stations, to police officers and anyone else we might encounter. When it came to bribery, vodka was the surest form of currency in the volatile Soviet economy. Times were uncertain, exchange rates fluctuated, the ruble went up and the ruble went down, but the value of a good bottle of vodka never depreciated.

I climbed on the bus, took in the drone of the heater, the voices of the people, the smell of diesel liberally emanating from the tailpipe, and a peaceful feeling settled over me. I liked the rumbling, for some reason I also liked the smell of gas, and I certainly enjoyed watching the adults solve the suitcase placement puzzle. But all that was incidental: I was two months shy of my tenth birthday, yet I understood, fully understood, that I was never coming back (the thought would warm my nights for years to come). I had no one to say goodbye to. I hadn't spoken with Oleg since that afternoon with the mirror, Kolya and I had a strictly business relationship, and I barely knew the names of my classmates. Everything I needed was already in the gray backpack on my lap. I realized that I would never again walk through the parks, see Mom and Dad's friends and relatives, take the tram downtown, or quietly read in the bedroom. I also knew we were about to lose ourselves in the world, had no set destination, no friends, no rubles, and no plans beyond Vienna.

I realized it all; that's why I was happy.

However, after a few minutes of picturing the empty apartment I had explored for the past nine years, a strange itch crept over me, and I scrambled out of the bus, found Dad, and told him I needed to use the bathroom. He barked at me to hurry, and I scampered through the yard, up the stairs, past the padded black door, and stood, panting, in the apartment hallway.

Fifteen minutes had elapsed and already the place was picked clean. Gone was the furniture, carted away, gone were the little things like rugs and lamps, and all that remained were a few mangled boxes that could not be salvaged, bits of string, and a few trinkets on the windowsill. The trinkets, mainly tiny statuettes, were souvenirs from Dad's business trips around the Union. They had cluttered his bookshelves, much to my mother's annoyance, and as the shelves were emptied, the knickknacks had been tossed onto the sills. They were cheap, they could not be resold or reused as raw materials, and that's why they had been ignored by the scavengers.

I scanned the sad lineup. My eye fell on a small statue of a turtle. Dad had brought it from Uzbekistan, or maybe Kazakhstan— definitely one of the 'stans. I never fancied it; it looked more like a brown lump of clay than like a turtle. In fact, I can still recall the three turbaned wise men from Kirgizia, the Crimean alabaster ashtray decorated with monkeys, and several other attractive items I could've rescued. But the clock was ticking and the pathetic crawling turtle looked like it was doing its darndest to catch up with us. Without much thought, I grabbed it and ran back to the bus, and five minutes later we were rumbling through the dead streets of Kharkov, me wedged between Dad's brown jacket and my pillow, Comrade Bear on my lap, lumpy brown turtle clenched in my fist.

*　　*　　*

The ride lasted three days. Our drivers pushed the groaning engine as fast as the roads permitted, stopping only in trusted villages and only long enough for bathroom breaks and to check in with their scouts, who monitored the roads for bandits. I sat next to Dad, alternating between sleeping and staring. I cracked open the Moldavian fairy tales, the only book I hadn't read yet, and powered all the way through the first day of the trip. The next two days were spent staring out the window at country roads with nothing but fields surrounding us. The landscape was shackled with frost and all I could see were dead leaves interlocked with the frozen grass. Patches of trees hunkered down on the horizon. Every once in a while a thin line of them stretched to the road, dividing one field from the next. A field, a flash of bare branches, then the next field was all there was to see.

The Ukraine (*u-kraina*) isn't much of a name. It's just a word; it means "the land at the edge," and this was that edge. We had reached the outskirts of the Great Steppe, a vast sea of grass that stretches from Mongolia to Hungary. It was Eurasia's no-man's-land, a place called *pustyr,* or "emptiness," in Russian. For centuries, the steppe was inhabited by nomads, wild horsemen, skilled and dreaded archers. For centuries they rode out of the plains, sacking towns and ambushing caravans before receding back into the grasses. No one could predict the cycles of calm and strife: the nomads spoke their own tongues and lived by their own codes, with no discernible pattern or motif. Scythians, Pechenegs, Huns, Bulgars, myriad clans and tribes came and went through the steppe, leaving behind them only kurgans, hill-shaped barrows that concealed the bones and gold of their chieftains. To the Russian mind, the steppe was a symbol of the unknown, the primal, the wild. Thus it was in the beginning, and thus it had remained, even in 1989.

By the second day the trees thinned, shrunk, thinned some more, and finally ceded the steppe to the earth. The sheer amount of land was astounding. It unfolded steadily, relentlessly, ever expanding and never changing. At first I scanned the terrain as if it were a painting, looking for something distinct or hidden in a landscape composed solely of leaves and grass. After a few hours my eyes started hurting and I allowed them to lose focus and simply stare into the vastness. I thought of *bylini,* Russian folk tales I loved to read, stories of *bogatyri,* heroes who wandered into the steppe to test their mettle against the barbarians or the mythical monsters of old. For days the *bogatyr* would travel, sometimes for weeks. He'd ride and ride and ride and ride and suddenly it'd be a week later, and he'd be somewhere else. It used to frustrate me because the tales never divulged what took place during that time. *So what happened?* I used to lie in bed and wonder, *What did the* bogatyr *see on his journey?* Sitting on the bus, swallowed by the unending blur before me, I realized that the tales got it right. They said nothing because there was nothing to say—there was only the steppe.

Next to the drivers sat the Kantlers, the family who had chartered the bus. Although we'd lived in the same apartment block, we rarely interacted and heard about each other via the rumor mill that bubbled through the Jewish population of Kharkov. They were a family of five: two parents, two grandparents, and a teenage daughter.

Behind them were the Zhislins, the third family to share the bus. The father, Yura, was an engineer like Dad. He was short, with a wiry body and small, glistening eyes that gave him a perpetually curious appearance. At every stop, before the bus fully halted, he'd leap out and explore. He also jumped at any occasion to make a joke, laugh, lighten the mood, and his relentless humor spread through the bus, easing the tension. Yura's wife, Gera, was a tall woman whose quiet demeanor and graceful motions were a perfect foil for her husband. Their children, Igor and Vicki, both in their twenties, were leaving with them.

Our family sat in the back, behind the Zhislins but in front of the last two rows of seats, which were occupied by the vodka.

All three families were accompanied by trusted friends and relatives who were coming with us as far as the border. Additionally, each family had one or two young men to help haul suitcases and bulk up our numbers, in case we got boarded along the way. There were about thirty passengers in all, but the bus was hushed. People vanished beyond the border. It was forbidden to return, but many didn't even call or write. Long before my family left, the adults would gather for tea and muse about how if *they* left, *they* would never sever contacts, and how *they* would always stay in touch. But when our turn came, my parents and sister were so caught up they didn't say goodbye to many friends.

The adults were pondering leaving entire lifetimes behind them. The chaperones were preparing for an indefinite farewell to their friends and relatives. And everyone thought of the *tamozhnya*. With each westward mile the bus carried us farther from the Soviet government, but it also brought us closer to the border and the customs officers who waited there. Some families were rumored to breeze through the border, barely losing a necklace or a ring. Others got shaken down, left to stumble across with almost nothing. Still darker stories swirled around the border, stories of violence and detention and strip searches. Doubtless many were false. Doubtless many were true, and which were which, no one could tell, and that was the point. The reality didn't matter, because—as with the wild horsemen of the steppe, as with the refuseniks, as with most everything in the Soviet Union—uncertainty made the system work. Fear gnawed at the mind, fear permeated the bus, and the farther west we drove, the stronger it grew.

* * *

Uzhgorod, Soviet–Czechoslovak Border, December 23, 1989,
8 Days to the December 31 Deadline

An ominous haze covered the land as we filed out onto the plain. Nothing broke the frozen emptiness except the barbed-wire fence and the two-story rectangle of the Chop Border Post, which loomed at the end of the road. Our friends and relatives would not be allowed to enter the *tamozhnya,* so they did what they could, helping us unload suitcases before saying farewell.

The adults were getting emotional and I didn't want to stick out. Thankfully, the goodbyes lasted as long as there were suitcases to haul, which didn't take long. Everyone was on edge— quick hugs and quick good-lucks, that was all. The cases crunched on the dry gravel path, our relatives dwindled to silhouettes in the fog, and we were in the building.

The inside of the customs was as austere as the landscape: a large, bare waiting hall without so much as a bench or a trashcan. A small bathroom was at one end and a door leading to a separate examination chamber at the other. Several black-clad *tamozhniki* patrolled the hall. They said very little, and when they did talk, they kept their voices low. Mostly, they watched. They watched, and paced, and waited.

"First group," barked a female *tamozhnitsa,* and the Kantlers, who insisted on going first, disappeared inside the door to the examination room. The Zhislins sat with us on suitcases and no one moved—no one, that is, except Yura, who, driven by his insatiable curiosity, peeked into the bathroom. An older *tamozhnik* with yellow *makhorka* tobacco stains on his mustache lazily paced the hall. Lina and Vicki Zhislin nervously chatted about the toiletries and makeup they'd packed for the journey. *What will it be? What will we lose?* the adults wondered as they counted the minutes. The signs were good: after a mere half-hour, a new crew of *tamozhniki* took over, and their young shift captain called in the Zhislins.

One hour passed, then another. Then we heard the muffled sounds of things being flung against walls. I shared a suitcase with Dad, who was straining to hear as much as possible, and every few minutes I'd glance up to see his cheeks quiver, as if an electric current had passed through them. I didn't know it at the time, and I wouldn't find out for quite a while, but Dad had a very good reason to sweat. Under his long brown coat, beneath the layers of sweaters and the undershirt, nestled deep within his underwear, were eleven tiny metal disks, microfilms containing engineering patents, designs, and sketches of future ideas—three decades of Dad's work.

Many years, and much of Dad's savings, had gone into cultivating the contacts to create the films. Dad was no fool: he realized that the odds of an ex-Soviet engineer working in the States were tiny. He had full confidence in his acumen and in the value of his designs, but he would need to offer something tangible to American employers. He had no qualms about stealing the patents—they were his patents, and they'd been appropriated by the very dictatorship he was fleeing.

The only issue was whether he could smuggle them out.

The clamor from the examination chamber continued. Finally, Mom couldn't contain herself any longer and cracked open the door.

"There's a search going on—do you want to get arrested?!" A *tamozhnik* flung open the door. "Get back in the waiting room! Your turn will come soon enough."

Mayhem reigned on the other side: clothes, books, shards of porcelain were strewn everywhere, and anything that could've been broken lay shattered on the cement. The Zhislins had taken a chance on hiding a little gold; they had their family valuables melted down and spun into thin flexible wires, which an expert tailor had sewn into their clothing creases. Whether through bad luck or good searching, the *tamozhniki* found the gold and were now ripping everything to shreds. Yura was bent over a table, arms and legs spread, being frisked by a *tamozhnik*. Gera, Vicki, and Igor were lined up against the far wall, their faces expression-less. Panic struck Dad as all hope of a relaxed search vanished. A few grams of gold were nothing compared with classified power plant schematics. He was trapped inside the *tamozhnya* with items that could lead to arrests, imprisonment, denial of exit visas for the entire family. Witnessing the devastation of the Zhislins, the full ramification of Dad's gamble crashed into his mind.

The door to the examination chamber remained open for only one moment, but it was enough. Yura didn't know about Dad's microfilms, but many people tried to smuggle contraband through the border and he assumed Dad might have *something*. The little man twisted his head up from the table, his face assumed a sad smile, the dark, ferret-like eyes darted over to the far wall of the *tamozhnya,* and the door was slammed shut.

Dad waited a few minutes, coughing and rubbing his stomach, then asked the *tamozhnik* guarding us to excuse him. He made his way to the back left corner of the waiting hall to the bathroom, where Yura had been staring. It contained one toilet, no sink, and no trashcan. Russian toilets did not have standing water in the bowl and clogged up on the slightest pretense, so flushing the disks was out of the question. Dad jiggled the water tank lid but it was fastened shut. He was *certain* Yura wanted him to check out the bathroom, but once inside, he couldn't figure out what the man was hinting at. Dad stared at the bowl, about to try flushing the films in desperation, when a flicker of light interrupted his thoughts. Set in the wall above the toilet was a *fortochka,* a small ventilation window common to Eastern Europe, no bigger than a sheet of paper.

Dad craned his neck and peeked out the window. A lone *tamozhnik* sat on a crate off in the periphery, gazing over the shadowy steppe. The light he saw came from a fire blazing in a steel drum about two meters from the window. Dad snaked his hand out the pane and began tossing the metal disks one by one into the flames, keeping his eye on the sentry. The films popped as they caught fire, and he had to carefully sync his throws with the wind gusts. The timing had to be perfect: too long and he'd arouse the suspicion of the guards inside; too quick, and the rapid popping might alert the sentry. *Pop! pop! pop!* crackled the films, *pop! pop! pop!* went thirty years of painstaking labor for the very regime that had oppressed him. *Pop! pop! pop!* flashed Dad's chances of working again as an engineer, and with each *pop!* Dad grew more furious, and with each *pop!* Dad felt his family closer to escape.

It was already past three in the morning when our turn came. Whatever anger had possessed the *tamozhniki* to go berserk on the Zhislins had not abated, and they pawed through us and our belongings with a malicious zeal. They carefully ripped through the seams in my coat, perhaps because they thought we had gold sewn into our clothes like the Zhislins. Whenever they chanced upon something fragile they would hold it up as if to get a better look, then let it drop to the floor. Sounds of shattering were followed by flowery apologies as the officers rued their own clumsiness, lamenting, "I'm so, so sorry—you probably needed that. How awful!" Mom, who was always bad at masking her temper, seethed at the taunting, and Dad would periodically have to calm her down. At one point he lost it and began screaming at Mom to keep her mouth shut, and for the first time that night, the *tamozhniki* smiled.

Mostly the five of us stood against the wall like the Zhislins, like torpid sacks. Once in a while they ordered Dad to move a suitcase, and soon I began moving them, too, becoming engrossed in the task. Everything was suddenly simple. Existence had collapsed into itself, leaving me and ten red-violet-colored rectangles, adjusting, dragging, clearing out bits of broken pottery and glass, untangling shreds of clothes ripped up by knives and caught on suitcase zippers. The *tamozhniki* must've gotten a kick out of a little *zhidling* assisting with the destruction of his family's property. Dad, who would have nightmares about the border for years to come, remembered me tending the cases, and he would always speak with pride of how I helped him at the *tamozhnya,* but I didn't do it for Dad, and certainly not for those sadistic black-clad fucks. I was sick of being paralyzed by fear, there, at school, at the yard, everywhere. Moving suitcases was the only thing I could do, but it beat feeling helpless.

Thanks to Dad, our only real contraband had already disintegrated in the steel barrel outside. All they were able to find were a few minor items, like Dad's stamp collection and a pair of antique candlesticks, and as it dawned on the *tamozhniki* that there was nothing else, the tone of the search changed. They dropped the clumsiness charade and simply smashed what they could. The rummaging grew faster, more aggressive, and still they found nothing. The red exit door to Czechoslovakia was calling to us and we had begun to feel that soon, soon we must pass, soon we'll be on the other side, when suddenly the shift captain confronted Dad.

"Where are your documents?"

"I gave them to you the minute we walked in here," Dad said, taken aback. "They were right on that table!"

The documents in question were the complete record of our existence in the Soviet Union. According to the rules, all documents—passports, transcripts, my grade school report cards, birth certificates, death certificates, even official photographs—had to be surrendered at the border. The table Dad was pointing to was a small metal desk bolted into a side wall. Dad had watched the captain place the fat stack of papers on the desk when we first entered the examination chamber, but now the table was empty, its surface devoid of anything but dull metal. The documents were gone.

"You stole them!" the young *tamozhnik* captain bellowed. "You took them while we were inspecting your luggage! This is a goddamn criminal offense!"

I remember little from the next half-hour, but the few moments that remain are seared into my brain like a vivid nightmare. I remember clenching my jaw to the point where it felt like my cheekbones were going to shatter. I remember Mom's eyes flashing with unbridled hatred, Lina's lips uncontrollably twitching, Grandma collapsing on one of the opened suitcases, her face ashen. I remember the yelling, and I remember four soldiers storming out of a recessed side door and positioning themselves, one in each corner, feet apart, machine guns slung across their bodies.

Dad and the *tamozhnik* captain continued their recriminations until a groggy woman staggered out from the same door as the soldiers.

"What the hell is going on here?" The newcomer was buttoning her uniform as she shambled toward us, looking very much as if she had been roused from a deep sleep.

The *tamozhniki* hastily assembled. "These people have stolen their documents while we were examining their belongings, Comrade Overseer," the shift captain reported with a slightly annoyed tone in his voice. "I'm not sure how they did it, but I believe there is reason to suspect they're smuggling other contraband, Comrade Overseer. I recommend we put them on the pots."

Putting someone on the pots was a technique employed when a person was suspected of concealing something, usually drugs or diamonds, in his stomach. The prisoner was force-fed a potent laxative, such as castor oil, then locked in a cell with a large pot, where he would remain for the next two days, voiding everything in his body. Dad's heart dropped when he heard those dreaded words, and I don't know what would have happened next had the woman not reached out her arm and started groping around the empty metal desk.

"Are these the papers you're talking about?" In her hand, as if by magic, were the documents, neatly stacked together just as Dad had them when he had surrendered them to the captain. The desk had a secret compartment. A slight push in the right place and the metal surface tilted down, sliding its contents into a little niche hidden in the wall. This mechanism was a fail-safe, a pretense for the *tamozhniki* to detain those who had no real contraband. My father rushed over to the woman.

"Yes, yes! Did you see what he was doing?" Dad caught the dejection on the captain's face and launched into a full assault. "This is the kind of blatant Soviet criminal behavior that is broadcast all over the Western world. What is your full name? I have reporter friends waiting for me in Vienna—in a few hours your names and your provocative actions will be aired all over the Voice of America, Radio Free Europe, and the BBC!"

That was a lie, of course, since we knew no one beyond the fence. But it was a lie bolstered by reality. Every night, as it had for fifty years, the Voice of America crackled across Eastern Europe, broadcasting the crimes of the Soviet Union, and every day, human rights groups pressured the regime to end its abuses. The difference was that for the first time, the USSR was listening. A mere year earlier, the *tamozhniki* still had the power to detain anyone they pleased, for as long as they pleased. They didn't have to resort to rigged desks and cheap charades of vanishing documents. They could have done whatever they wanted. But in 1989 a strange thing happened, and a shift, long prayed for but never expected, took place. Earlier in the year, the country was stunned to read that a squad of policemen had been arrested on charges of prisoner abuse. During the summer, state media announced an official investigation into the Red Army Spetsnaz murders of the nineteen Georgian girls slain during the peaceful demonstration in Tbilisi. And on November 9, six weeks before my family stood at the border, a group of East Germans scampered atop the Berlin Wall and tore down the dreaded symbol of Communist power. And the culprits, these timid rodents armed with chisels and sledgehammers, they weren't shot; they weren't beaten or imprisoned: they were *photographed,* and the soldiers on the Wall were ordered to stand down and make way for the cameras. It worked—somehow, the leaflets scattered on American college campuses, the church petitions signed by midwestern housewives, the letters, the protests, the vigils, the boycotts, the countless irritating stings by countless little nuisances had worked, and Mikhail Gorbachev, the marked Mikhail, took away the Party's ability to destroy lives on a whim, and by doing so, he had destroyed the Soviet Union, and the old women's prophesies were fulfilled.

The *tamozhnya* overseer and her soldiers returned upstairs, leaving us with the wilted captain. "I apologize, it must have been some sort of a misunderstanding . . . We'll have to have that desk fixed," he mumbled. He rifled through the paperwork, fished out the pale green exit visas, which were the sole documents permitted to cross with us, and thrust the rest at a dour older subordinate. "Burn these," he spat, and waved his hand at us. "What are you waiting for? Gather your belongings and go across."

Before anyone—we or the *tamozhniki*—had a chance to exhale, Yura and Igor sprang into the room from the exit door and began scooping up suitcases and hauling them to Czechoslovak soil. The Zhislins had known us for less than a week. They could've been licking their wounds on the bus . . . they *should've* been licking their wounds on the bus. It would've taken a divine act to get me back into that cursed building. I certainly wouldn't have gone back for them. Instead, Yura and Igor remained in the hallway during the entire search, chomping at the bit for the chance to help get us out of there, and to this day, the fact that they came back for us remains the bravest, most insane thing anyone has done for me. Something inside gave me strength and I dragged the suitcases as best as I could, trying to keep up with the men. When I got to the bus, I saw Yura briskly tuck a bag into an undercarriage compartment. The little man looked down and gave me a wink, and it was only later, when we were already safe in Austria, that I found out that in the chaotic aftermath of the search Yura had managed to snatch the one bag that contained our books and Dad's stamps, petty contraband the *tamozhniki* meant to retain in Russia.

The examination chamber had no windows, and we had lost all sense of time during the search. It was already past six in the morning, and the first hints of light began to pierce through the fog. I would have been shocked at how long we had been searched, but my emotions were all tapped out, so I simply noted that it was dawn with an apathetic, almost bemused reaction. A wind gust whooshed by my hands, and I felt they were soaked with sweat. I squatted on the ground, reached down and grabbed a fistful of earth, and it felt good to run the cool, damp soil through my fingers. I was crouched in the no-man's-land separating the USSR and Czechoslovakia as two sets of silhouettes milled about in the fog. To my right, on the Soviet side, several *tamozhniki* were checking the area, making sure the gate was secured. To my left, in Czechoslovakia, was the box-like outline of the bus, with Yura, Dad, and Igor sorting and storing suitcases, trying to clean up the broken pieces of our possessions.

I remained where I was, crouched on the ground, waiting until they were finished. The driver turned the key, filling the air with the sickly-sweet smell of cheap gasoline, and we resumed our journey to Bratislava. It was only after I crawled back to my seat next to Dad that I realized just how exhausted I was. My knees were wooden, and I couldn't lift a finger, which was fine because I didn't want to move; I wanted to pass out and not think, or hear, or feel anything. My head felt stuffed to the brim with cotton, and for some strange reason, the story of the *Odyssey* kept swimming through my mind. I had read an abridged version of the epic many times, during days spent holed up in the Kharkov apartment, and I remembered how Odysseus spent ten years wandering from sea to sea, wanting so desperately to return to his native soil. I had just crouched on the ground at the very edge of the world that I had known, but I did not miss it, nor did I have another place where I wanted to be, and I remember thinking how Odysseus wanted to go home, and how I wanted to keep going, and debating whether that was a bad thing or not.

Dawn chased away the fog, and for a brief moment I caught the last few stars before they were snuffed out by the gray morning sky.

* * *

Back on the Soviet side of the border, the friends and relatives of our three families heard the coughing of the engine. They had not been allowed to enter the *tamozhnya* or even approach its territory, so they had spent the entire night huddling on the steppe, listening for the sound of our bus, which was the last communication they would hear from us. There was no shelter, so they took turns in the center of the group, doing their best to ward off the steady, unrelenting chill emanating from the plain. Six hours had elapsed, and at last they heard the engine, stretched out their frozen limbs, and set off on the hour-long hike to Uzhgorod, the nearest town with a train station. No one spoke. They knew that a long wait meant trouble with the *tamozhniki,* but beyond that there was no way of discerning what had transpired or which family had gotten the brunt of it. Once in Uzhgorod, they snagged some clothes on the black market to cheer themselves up and caught the next train back to Kharkov.

I'm not sure why the *tamozhnya* overseer saved us. Perhaps she was sleepy, or hungover, and did not even realize it when her fingers fumbled through the desk and grasped our documents. Maybe she was moved by the horror on our faces. However, it's difficult to imagine that the head of a *tamozhnya* would not be aware of the devilish intricacies of her own building. Likewise, as tempting as it would be to believe in her goodness, the fact remains that the majority of people who attained positions of power in the USSR had long been stripped if not of compassion, then at least of the desire to act upon it. The most plausible explanation is that what transpired at the *tamozhnya* had nothing to do with us.

The entire Soviet society, from rural cooperatives to the red halls of the Kremlin, operated on an intricate system of espionage. Graduate students spied on professors (Communist Party came before school). Workers kept an eye on the foremen (Party before work). Children, too, were encouraged to participate: every Little Octobrist and Pioneer learned the story of Brave Pavlik Morozov, a young Pioneer from the 1930s whose father was trying to subterfuge Stalin's cooperative farming programs. But Brave Pavlik was an exceptional Pioneer, burning with love for Lenin, and he brought his father's activities to the attention of the Party. Pavlik's father was promptly sent to the gulag (and eventually executed),

and the noble boy became a cult figure and inspiration for generations of Soviet children.* Party before family.

Nowhere was this spying more prevalent than in the Party
bureaucracy itself. Hungry young cadets, fresh from training and
ready to claw their way up the command chain, were recruited by
the KGB to report on their superiors. The cadets either found or
fabricated evidence of treachery and corruption, and the supervisors were executed or exiled to the gulags, and the cadets became
supervisors themselves, and new trainees were sent in to monitor
them. This was an old system developed and instituted by Stalin himself, who routinely purged the top ranks of the Party, the
Red Army, and the KGB. The mechanism was designed to sow
paranoia and ensure that no one could trust anyone, thereby preventing underlings from colluding against the dictatorship. The
tamozhnya overseer must have suspected (whether rightfully or
not) the young captain of being out to undermine her. So she
decided to embarrass him in front of the same *zhidi* he was ter-
rorizing. Ironically, the very factors that we ran from—anger, fear,
instability, paranoia—united to push us through our last, awful
night in the Soviet Union.

In the mid-1990s, after the USSR had fallen apart, my father
contacted the newly established Ukrainian Patent Bureau and
inquired whether, since the economy was now capitalist, he was
entitled to compensation for the dozen patents seized from him

---

* "Wanna know the rest of the story?" asked Lina the evening after Anna
Konstantinovna told me and my classmates about Pavlik Morozov. "Well,
some of Pavlik's relatives had escaped the Communists, and later on they
found Brave Pavlik Morozov and they slit his brave little throat. Because
that's what happens to brave little boys who inform on their families," said
Lina, and lightly drew a finger across my neck to underscore the moral.

by the defunct Soviet government. The bureau offered him the equivalent of six hundred dollars, but only with the stipulation that he personally fly into Kiev to accept the check. They wanted to make sure they awarded the right person, they explained. The whole thing was a joke, since the cost of the plane ticket was triple that of the reimbursement, and the bureau was well aware of it.

Dad's response was to send them a letter in which he declined their invitation but gave them his expressed written permission to keep the money, provided they shoved it, along with the patents, directly up their asses.

The Ukrainian Patent Bureau did not reply, and whether they took Dad up on his offer remains unclear.

Part Two

When you're traveling, you are what you are right there and then. People don't have your past to hold against you. No yesterdays on the road.

—From *Blue Highways* by William Least Heat-Moon

DOZENS OF SENTINEL GRANDMAS

Czechoslovakia, Late December 1989

The old Soviet bus creaked down the gray outline of a Czechoslovak road. Overhead, dark shades of gray reluctantly yielded to slightly lighter shades of gray. It was the dawn of Christmas Eve. The bus was silent. The *tamozhnya* had sucked the energy out of us, as if vitality, like our documents and valuables, was forbidden to cross the border. Now we were truly refugees. Back on Soviet soil we had belonged to a nation, however horrible that nation was, but here, beyond the fence, we were ghosts, drifters, entities with no recognizable destination or attachment. This awkward freedom of being beholden to nothing save for the mercy of others still lingers in my psyche and, I imagine, in the psyche of many ex-migrants.

The terror at the border made saying goodbye to the Soviet Union much easier for my father. Dad was about to turn fifty-two, and he had stockpiled his good moments, good memories—even the USSR couldn't steal those from him—but the *tamozhnya* had torched the nostalgia. Mom kept reminding herself that every passing kilometer was taking us farther away from them, the *tamozhniki*, the anti-Semites, the Communist Party of the USSR. She gazed out at rows of cottages perched on hills lining the road. Colorful garlands of gourds and dried peppers hung from their eaves, and something about the bucolic Slovak countryside made Mom believe that it was possible to establish a life beyond the border. I only remember that the bus was quiet, very quiet, and that we had distributed a significant portion of our dwindling vodka supply at gas stations and checkpoints along the way.

Dusk had fallen by the time our drivers pulled up to the sprawling gray Bratislava train station and killed the engine, which shuddered a few times before coughing up its life. This was as far as the drivers' permits allowed them to go. The workers loading crates onto freight trains ignored us; they'd seen Jews pass this way before. A few bored Czechoslovak policemen approached, punched our visas, and ambled away, vodka bottles in hand. Yura, Dad, and Sergei Kantler bought tickets to Austria. All three men had been told to head for the Westbahnhof rail station in Vienna, but no further information had been provided. People who left the USSR before us had embarked for the Westbahnhof; beyond that, our plans ran out.

Before the three drivers began the return trip, the head of the team pulled Dad aside. "Watch out for the Kantlers," he warned. "Five minutes after they walked into the *tamozhnya*, a *tamozhnik* came to the bus and went straight for where we kept the money you paid us. He left us only enough to make it back to Kharkov. They've done this before, at other border posts, but this bastard didn't even have to search. He went straight for my seat cushion. Now how would he have known that?"

Dad nodded. He'd noticed another driver carefully tucking bills into a tiny flap under the seat. ("It keeps my ass warm," the man told Dad when he saw him stashing the rubles.) The Kantlers' behavior had been strange from the start. Sergei had insisted his family go first, and they had waltzed through the examination room in half an hour. Several times before the journey, Sergei and his wife had asked us and the Zhislins what contraband we were packing, and then after the border, they kept to themselves. Maybe they sold us and the drivers out (they wouldn't have been the first family to do so), or maybe they just felt awkward for no other reason than that they were spared and we were not.

Dad's the only one who spoke with the driver at the Bratislava train station. Yura was in shock for a good couple of days after the border, and doesn't remember anyone warning him about the Kantlers. Mom thinks it's all bullshit and Dad's imagining things. Either way, the *tamozhniki*'s ministrations left both Yura's family and mine shaken and terrorized; the Kantlers, in the meantime, took a nap on the bus. Whatever the cause, Sergei and his clan barely spoke to us afterward, and we behaved the same toward them.

We boarded a standard, decrepit Communist train with two-bench cabins and an aisle running down one side of the car. The cabins' sliding glass doors made me think of the see-through cages for monkeys and reptiles at the zoo. Strewn inside our enclosure were the suitcases, members of my family interwoven among them. Dad, who up to this point maintained the red-violet luggage in regimented formation, was now too exhausted and temporarily allowed the cases to rest wherever they lay. Evening returned, and the black windowpanes threw our reflections back into the cabin, underscoring the fact that, as of now, all we had were our bags and our bodies.

As we lumbered across the Czechoslovak–Austrian border, a group of customs officers boarded the train. We were jumpy around men in uniform, but the Austrian inspectors were easy: a few quick glances, more stamps on the visas, and we were back to creaking through the darkness. The gloom was finally broken, first by small depots and then by the orange glare of Vienna's Westbahnhof station. The train stopped, the doors slid open, and we stepped out onto a platform teeming with refugees. Some must have arrived before us. Others apparently had shared our train—we hadn't even noticed. Porters dawdled by stairways, announcements buzzed over loudspeakers, and all up and down the concourse Soviet Jews squinted, stretched, and yawned, making the transition from motion to stillness, train to ground, Communism to freedom.

This sleepy moment was interrupted by a short, pudgy gentleman with glasses, a round, hoggish face, and a blue blazer. He strode among us, six or seven assistants in tow, all of whom were consulting paperwork and gazing around the platform as if whatever was written on their papers didn't quite jibe with what was in front of them. The short man nosed his way through the crowd, then spun around and yelled, in shrill English. "We need you to rapidly relocate to *this* side of the station. Do so immediately! Go now!"

"What's he saying? What does he want?" the grumbles began, and even once translated, the message had no effect. "What's so special about that corner? Where are we going afterward? Who are these people?" The pudgy man's eyes darted all over the platform, his lips wordlessly moving. Finally he launched into the speech once more. He had a strong voice for a small man, one that reverberated throughout the concourse; it was imperative to have us in *that* corner. We migrated slowly, individuals keeping in families, families gathering by cities, Muscovites here, Leningradians there, and so on. The man weaved in and out of the huddles, once in a while tossing a perfunctory glance at a visa. I misliked the porker at once. When Pig Face came near us, Dad overheard him muttering about terrorists being around the corner and needing to get us out of Vienna immediately. Dad made the mistake of translating the man's words, and some of the other English speakers must've done the same, because a restless murmur churned through the crowd.

It was Christmas Eve, and last-minute shoppers scurried around the platform, juggling parcels and packages in the rush to get home. We gawked at their clothes and strained to catch a peek of what they carried. Many Austrians cast surprised glances back at us, and at some point I realized that as exotic as I found the Westerners, *we* were the ones who didn't belong. My family wasn't alone in racing to beat the December 31 deadline for asylum in America: more trains arrived, disgorging refugees who'd gone through Krakow, Budapest, and Bratislava, and the crowd had swelled to over one hundred people. Each new batch was greeted by Pig Face's half-pleading, half-barking "relocate to this side" command. Judging by his exasperated expression, all the man wanted for Christmas was a few Scottish border collies, the ones that can corral sheep on cue. But time and again, despite his feverish prayers, the dogs would fail to materialize and he would sigh and start his speech anew.

A tall woman trotted back and forth between the platform and the street-level concourse at ten-minute intervals. She wore a long brown coat and had a tower of salt-and-pepper hair hovering over her head, and I can still recall the wind playing with her beehive and whipping the exposed ends of the paperwork clutched to her chest. Dad chatted to a group of Armenian Jews encamped nearby, reminiscing about the eateries he'd discovered on a trip to Yerevan five years back. I watched him, transfixed. Three days earlier he, like the rest of us, had jettisoned his entire life. He was a stranger in a strange land, stranded in an alien train station with no money and few possessions beyond some pots and spare underwear. The station was freezing, the food had run out that morning, his family was nervous, the Armenians were nervous, the Austrian shoppers were nervous, Pig Face was one violent sneeze away from a massive aneurism, and here was Dad, extolling the superiority of Armenian shish kebab over its Georgian, to say nothing of Azerbaijani, counterpart. That's who Dad was.

Bells ringing in Midnight Mass pealed through the city, the flow of shoppers died down, and one final train screeched in. Two hours later the woman with the salt-and-pepper beehive rushed down the platform steps, eagerly chattering to Pig Face. "There are buses located outside," he announced. "Load quickly—terrorists are here! Whatever cannot be placed on buses will remain behind. We must leave Vienna now!"

In a flash, I focused on the move. *Shove, shove, grab everything. Big suitcases and Grandma first. Up the stairs, to the long line of idling buses. Pick bus, leave suitcases by it, Grandma will watch them. Run back, grab more. Lina and Mom already moving toward Grandma. Count cases. Dad's behind me. Shove, drag, move to bus. Grandma's sitting on a suitcase and watching everything. Next to her is another grandma. Next to that one are more. Dozens of sentinel grandmas, all guarding suitcases. Load cases under bus. Count and load, count and load. Where are the Zhislins? Grab seats. Pillow's here. Dad's here. Mom, Lina, Grandma, Comrade Bear are here. Good.*

I don't know if they had prior intentions of sorting us or taking a census, but any such plans quickly disintegrated in the slapdash race to board. After making sure our bus was full, someone barked something to the driver, who slammed the shift into first gear and rumbled off. I never got to see the terrorists.

The pudgy man wasn't crazy. Western Europe had been reeling from the deadly onslaught of radical Islamic terrorism long before it reached U.S. shores. What's more disturbing is that some of the terror strikes were aimed directly at Soviet migrants. In 1973, the Austrian government intercepted three members of Black September, the Palestinian group infamous for the 1972 Munich Olympics Massacre, en route to bomb a Vienna hostel that housed Soviet refugees. Later that year, the as-Sa'iqa sect hijacked a Bratislava–Vienna train (the same corridor my family took) filled with migrants bound for the West: the terrorists' main demand was for Austria to close its border and refuse asylum to displaced Soviet Jews. And on December 27, 1985, merely four years before my family walked out onto the Westbahnhof platform, the Abu Nidal Organization made international headlines by executing coordinated attacks on El Al Israeli airline passengers in Rome and Vienna airports, which resulted in nineteen fatalities and 138 injuries. Terrorists lurking under train wheels was an exaggeration; the need to evacuate a huge crowd of Soviet Jews milling around an exposed platform was real.*

The bus wound through Vienna proper. It was late on Christmas Eve and the city slumbered under an enchantment. Rows of nutcrackers, puppets, candy, and chocolate beckoned from giant window displays. Christmas trees lit up plazas; garlands of snowflakes, crescents, exquisite ornaments, and intricate tinsel were draped across streets and twined around lampposts. It was bright, festive, varied, nothing like the anemic New Year's lightbulbs people hung up in Russia. And the roads shocked everyone, too:

---

* Why were Palestinian terror groups expending men and resources to target homeless migrant families in Austria? Well, if ten Soviet Jews moved to Israel, Israel gained ten soldiers, ten workers, ten more oppressors and occupiers, as the jihadists saw it. And in 1989, the Soviet Union didn't just have ten Jews—it had 1.4 million. We weren't homeless families; we were an army waiting to be unleashed. And, as we found out, the terrorists weren't the only ones who saw us that way.

the smooth pavement and lack of potholes felt like being in a land where people drove on butter. As Vienna faded into the distance, the glimmer of Christmas was replaced by the red-and-white glow of reflector posts that lined the highway. These also were a surprise to us, after we'd traversed the dark roads of Czechoslovakia and the steppe. The Austrians even splurged on side streets and parking lots. *How much light do these people have?*

The bus was warm, very warm, with soft seats and classical music on the radio. The music, the warmth, the gentle lilt enveloped us. For the first time since we had set out from Kharkov, we were no longer in control, and, paradoxically, that brought us peace. We had no choices, we didn't know when to stop or where to go; we couldn't even speak the language, but it didn't matter—we were safe and we were moving, and within a half-hour of leaving Vienna nearly everyone on the bus was fast asleep.

When Dad nudged me awake, we were idling in a lot illuminated by powerful spotlights mounted on a large building, the only structure in sight. Several other buses were parked nearby, and the people from the train station were already outside, making tracks in the fresh snow. Now that we were out of the city and confined to buses, the workers appeared calmer, a lot more confident. The pudgy man in the blue blazer carried on a discussion with a short bald man who somehow managed to sweat despite wearing just a thin white shirt and a tie, and no coat. After a few minutes he signaled to his assistants, who fanned out, each going to a bus. The tall beehive woman in the brown coat approached ours. The driver hopped out, unlatched the storage compartments, began tossing the suitcases onto the snow, and we sprang into action. It's amazing how efficient and ingrained the process had already become: *Dad and I haul from lot to building, Grandma watches*

in building, Mom and Lina watch in lot. Go back and repeat,
count and haul, count and haul.

Dad carried the suitcases whereas I dragged them, and by the time I deposited mine under the wary eye of Grandma he was already on his way to pick up another one. I took a few seconds to regain my breath. People scrambled with their belongings as the short bald man darted around in the snow like a matador dancing with fifty bulls. Rich, velvety darkness concealed the world beyond the lot. I inhaled, and the cold air stung my lungs. It was crisp, thin, and clean, and I liked it because it woke me up and made me concentrate on the cold instead of my hunger. A throng of migrants laden with bags pushed by, Yura Zhislin and his son, Igor, among them. Igor flashed me a smile though his thick mustache, and I ran to drag another suitcase.

Families coalesced around their belongings, each one staking claim to a little piece of the lobby. The tall woman in the brown coat positioned herself by the rear wall, in front of a line of men. The head of each family presented her with the only documents he had left, the pale green Soviet exit visas. These had several folded pages, which three days ago had been blank but had since broken out in a rash of seals, stamps, and scribbles worthy of an international treaty. The woman jotted down information on her clipboard, then directed the refugee to the bald man in the thin white shirt, who presided over a box of room keys.

Suddenly there was an epidemic of illness and obscure medical conditions as everyone in line angled for the best rooms. Someone had a blind mother; someone else was recovering from abdominal surgery. When our turn came, Dad, who was nervous about asking for handouts, started stammering. The man looked up at him, sharp blue eyes flashing from his flushed face. "Not worry," he rasped in a thick German accent. "You—I find rooms. It is okay," and in a few minutes a young blond woman approached us with two keys.

Before hauling anything, Dad and I went upstairs to investigate. The rooms were tiny, comprised of a single bed, a table, and a little closet, with not much floor space left over. "Two whole rooms—two beds—that's wonderful!" Dad mused. "Lina and Grandma will share a bed, and Mom will get this one, and the two of us—the *men*," he winked at me (Dad was extremely proud of my help with the suitcases), "we'll figure something out. If we get any food, we'll use the balconies for storage; in this weather, they're as good as fridges. Agreed?"

I was gawking at the floor. I was exhausted and starving, but still, I grew up on linoleum and didn't even know fully carpeted rooms *existed* outside of the *Arabian Nights*. "Agreed?" Dad repeated to snap me out of the shag-induced trance.

"Agreed!" I nodded, trying to sound as manly as possible, and we hurried downstairs to give the ladies the good news.

Once everything was heaped onto the floor you couldn't see much of the carpet. Mom and I reclined on the bed and watched Dad play with the suitcases. Mom suggested we wait until morning and I couldn't have agreed more, but Dad persisted and would've probably arranged everything if not for the young blond woman, who handed him a napkin with a number smudged on it and waved for us to come downstairs. There we joined the tail end of a line that snaked into a cafeteria. At the far end was a table with coffee, tea, and small brown rolls with dabs of butter on them. Each person received one cup and one crispy, hot roll. I forced myself to nibble at mine, because I remembered reading in one of my books that you shouldn't eat quickly when you're starving. Afterward, Dad gingerly folded the napkin and tucked it in his pocket. Others were already wrapping their rolls in pieces of newspaper, fudging the numbers written on the napkins, and getting back in line to try to sneak out another one. Quietly, effortlessly, life stripped to a bare hierarchy of needs. *Warmth? Yes. Shelter? Yes. Family? Here. Food? Got some. Not sure when there'll be more. Better change the number, get back in line, try to get more. Eat a little, save the rest. Save, save, save. Like a squirrel.*

*   *   *

I woke to the sound of the adults rummaging through suitcases for toothbrushes, towels, and soap. Lina stopped by to say hi and was off to find the bathroom. Russians were everywhere, milling around the hallways, yelling up and down the stairwells, lounging on couches in the lobby. I tagged along after Dad, who went downstairs to the cafeteria, following the aroma of warm bread and fresh coffee. I grabbed juice, Dad got coffee, and we walked outside, where the tracks from the night's bustle were dusted over by a fresh coat of snow. We were standing atop a hill, next to a road, the only road in sight. Down the slope to the left was a tiny village, so small one could easily walk to the farthest house. To our right, the road meandered through snowy fields, losing itself in a patch of forest on the horizon. A wavy line of small blue-gray mountains rested against the bright winter sky. The only mountains I'd ever seen were two grim black monoliths that rose from the Black Sea in Crimea. These looked different, clean and beautiful, and I instantly loved them. Behind Dad and me stood the white flat-roofed building, four stories of identical windows ringed by black balconies. More Russians stomped around the lot, smoking the remnants of old Soviet cigarettes. Three rows of black letters over the entrance spelled out "Hotel Restaurant Binder."

"What's that mean, Dad?"

"Well, the first two are clear: there's a hotel and a restaurant here, but I'm not sure about the binder . . . Lina!" he shouted to my sister, who poked her head out from the second-floor balcony. "What's a binder?"

"Bin-der? *I* Binder!" The short bald man who'd been handing out room keys earlier scampered outside. "*I* Binder," he repeated. "Hotel," he gestured toward the upstairs floors; "Restaurant," he moved down to the lobby; "Binder!" he ended with a flourish that clearly indicated he saved the best for last. "Inside food. Come."

While we munched on ham sandwiches and fruit salad, Binder gathered the forty heads of the newly arrived families in a circle inside the hotel's meeting hall. Waiting to address them was the pudgy man from the train station. He was seated next to a thick stack of forms, still wore the same rumpled navy blazer, and looked as tired as the migrants.

"Dear gentlemen, ex-citizens of the USSR, you are currently located in the town of Nondorf, which is two hours to the northwest of Vienna. My name is Oswald Prager, and I shall be the liaison person between you, Joint—which is the American Jewish Joint Distribution Committee—and HIAS, which is the Hebrew Immigrant Aid Society. Joint and HIAS are American-Jewish organizations. Joint will be providing sustenance for you while you are stationed in Austria and Italy, and HIAS will be overseeing your resettlement process."

Mr. Prager spoke in broken English, every so often reverting to German. Although none of the refugees knew regular German, some were fluent in Yiddish, an Eastern European Jewish dialect roughly equivalent to medieval German. Yiddish had been spoken in yeshivas and shtetls before Communism made such things obsolete. Afterward it was secretly passed down from father to son, and while diligent persecution greatly diminished its number of speakers, the language had survived among the older generation. The conversation with Mr. Prager was choppy: he'd utter a few sentences, the English and Yiddish speakers would translate, a short discourse over the meaning would ensue, and Mr. Prager would continue.

"I require you to take these forms. Please fill them out today because tomorrow morning, at six o'clock, there will be buses waiting to convey you and your families to the Israeli embassy in Vienna. Please understand that each of you was permitted to leave the Soviet Union and enter Austria at the request of the Israeli government. As of right now, each of your visas designates Israel as your final destination. Those who desire to be admitted to a country other than Israel will have to first approach the Israeli embassy and officially refuse its offer of asylum. That shall be step number one."

Mr. Prager didn't need to address what would happen to families who actually wanted to go to Israel. Those had already been pulled aside and put on a plane to Tel Aviv.

"Following that, the buses shall convey you to the Australian, Canadian, and American embassies. You will go to the embassy of the country you would desire to emigrate to and apply for political asylum. HIAS representatives will assist you with communication and paperwork. That will be step number two."

Questions erupted, just as at the train station. Russians are notorious fretters, and for good reason: they've been conditioned by their past to worry about the future. "How long will we be here? How will we eat? Will we get any spending money? Will America take us? How do you know for sure?"

"Live, you will live here," Mr. Prager ticked off the answers. "Your next transfer point shall be Rome, where you will receive linguistic, financial, and cultural training from HIAS and Joint.

Due to such a large spike in refugees, there is currently no room in Rome, and so you will remain here until space clears up or more space is created. I do not know when that will happen. In the meantime, please know that while you are in Austria, you are not permitted to work or to travel anywhere outside a fifteen-kilometer radius of where you're staying. Food, you shall receive twice a day. Additionally, everyone in your family shall receive a stipend of two and a half schillings per day."

"Only two schillings? People before us got ten!" A family friend stationed in Vienna just six months prior to us even stocked up enough money to buy a fur coat . . . or so he averred in a postcard mailed from Naples. The postcard gingerly made the rounds of Kharkov's Jewish communities, and the fur coat dominated the talk of the neighborhood for a week.

Mr. Prager spread his hands. "That was before the numbers of refugees went up. We no longer have the budget for ten a person. Dear gentlemen, I apologize, but I must do several more stops. Please fill the forms and be ready at six."

The questions only got louder. "But how long before we go to America?"

"You will stay until the appropriate agencies make the decision about your refugee status."

"What agencies?"

"The agencies whose job it is to make the decision will be deciding."

And on that philosophical note, Mr. Prager buttoned up his jacket, excused himself, and left.

Later, much later, experience taught me that Mr. Prager and the other human rights workers we encountered weren't being face-tious; they weren't lying or being evasive about dates, estimates, and explanations. They were in the refugee business, an occupation whose very nature was defined and governed by chaos. And the small percentage of those who didn't burn out or succumb to cynicism had been forced to learn to, as the adage goes, accept what they couldn't change and concentrate on what they could. What more could we have asked from them? But ask we did. We asked and we griped and we grumbled, and every fielded question spawned several more. Human nature, I guess.

As promised, the buses were waiting at six the next morning, and as promised, the first stop was the Israeli embassy in Vienna, and *it was awkward.* The Israeli clerks were well aware that we did not want to go to Israel, but they still extended the offer. "Israel is where Jews belong. Why live in crammed rooms in Austria and Italy? You could be in Israel in two days! We'll find you a place." Everyone rattled off their excuses: we couldn't deal with the hot climate, we've already started learning English, we had a friend in America who promised to get us a job, etcetera, etcetera, but valid or not, an ungrateful undertone seeped into the reasoning. Israel was a country bleeding on the front lines in the battle for Jewish rights, a nation without whose efforts we wouldn't have been able to leave Russia, yet there we stood, beggars choosing, telling Israel "Thanks, but no thanks."

Then it was our turn.

"We considered this extensively, and we want to go to America," my father avowed.

"Aren't you Jews?" prodded the young official.

Dad grew irritated. "Yes, we are Jews, and believe me, the Soviet government made sure that we were aware of that. Still, we would really prefer to go to America."

"Sign your denial here."

Once everyone endorsed the denials, Mr. Prager marched the group to the U.S. embassy, where he handed us over to his colleagues in HIAS. Mr. Prager instructed us to meet him by the buses at five, and amicably recommended that we enjoy Vienna's downtown after the diplomats were finished with us. An imposing array of clerks and tables waited inside the embassy, but we did little talking; HIAS representatives shepherded each family around the room. Although the U.S. government was familiar with the plight of Soviet Jewry, applicants still had to chronicle the specific abuses suffered under the Soviet regime in order to qualify for political asylum. HIAS knew the majority of families did not speak English; they also recognized that some were too proud to ask for help, and that others were not prepared to disclose humiliation and pain to complete strangers. This reticence could easily lead to trouble, since all an impatient clerk had to do was scribble "no evidence for asylum provided" and the shy family would be denied. HIAS workers hovered over us, acting as envoys between the two worlds, clarifying, encouraging, and ensuring that everyone got an opportunity to present their case to America.

My family was fortunate to be processed early, which left us plenty of time to heed Mr. Prager's suggestion and explore the heart of Vienna. Pillars and fountains decorated each wayward street and every plaza. Around one corner, we ran smack into a gorgeous imperial palace with seafoam-green domes and incredible statues, and Dad had to drag me away because I wanted to examine each one. In the center of it all rose the majestic St. Stephen's Cathedral, an enormous Gothic monolith whose spires soared over the downtown. The shops around the cathedral were overwhelming. Christmas was over, but the holiday spirit had not left the city. We saw bright decorations, shoppers with bags, and window displays brimming with *everything*. To people accustomed to waiting in lines and trying to predict which common staple would be the next to vanish from the shelves, this was another planet, a cornucopia, albeit with a hefty price tag. Someone quickly dubbed the area Millionaire Street, because from our perspective, anyone who could afford to shop there must surely be a millionaire. But then Lina and Mom stumbled upon an alley shoe store with winter boots on post-holiday clearance. My sister began to woo Mom, and shortly thereafter, a very happy Lina strutted down the cobblestones with a package of boots under her arms. She was trailed by my less-than-enthused father, who was shooting Mom dirty stares. Five minutes later we ran into the Zhislins, Vicki spied the package, and five minutes after *that* our party had doubled to two pairs of boots, two grinning twenty-year-olds, and two sets of accusing stares.

Oswald Prager was leaning against a pillar across from St. Stephen's Cathedral, squinting at the spires and sipping on a Vienna iced coffee—cold coffee with no ice and a dollop of ice cream floating on top. It was an unseasonably warm day, and my family and the Zhislins joined him in the afternoon sun. "Why were those people in the Israeli embassy so . . . not nice?" Vicki asked the Joint worker.

"Nobody likes 'no,'" he answered. "Besides, Israel requires men. There are many people, even in America, who want to get Jews out of Russia so they can make Israel become stronger. Some of those people apply pressure on Joint and HIAS because they think that you should have to go to Israel."

"And what do you think?" Dad inquired.

"I do not think much on that," Mr. Prager admitted. "Two more trains of refugees came last night. More trains will be tonight. American Congress just voted to continue accepting Jews in the next year. When Soviet Jews hear about this, more will come, and more. I will meet them, and work with them, find food and place. That is what I think. But if you ask me personally, if you desire to go to America, and if America desires to take you, there is no problem."

"Yes, yes, I agree!" Yura jumped in. "And if all those concerned Jews in America want people to go to Israel so much, they can always move there themselves. You're good at this." He gestured at the paperwork tucked under Mr. Prager's arm. "Maybe you can help those nice American Jews move to Israel."

"That is an interesting idea," yawned Mr. Prager, and a tired smile crossed his fleshy face.

WHERE PEOPLE HAVE NO NAMES

Nondorf, Niederösterreich (Lower Austria),
Late December 1989

Aside from eating and sleeping, there was little to do in the tiny village of Nondorf, and it was only natural for two hundred bored and penniless Russians to turn to the only available pastime: selling everything they had to curious Austrian locals. Back in Russia this activity was known as peddling, but we were in the West now, and to celebrate the new milieu, peddling was bestowed with a more dignified, Western name: "business." Business could be anything or anyone. One of our neighbors had brought a dog out of the USSR. It was a little white fluffball, a Maltese or a similar breed. The family treated the dog like one of their own, refusing to go anywhere without it, even toting it down to the cafeteria, and they quickly became known as the Dog People. The dog was pregnant, and Dog Man proudly told envious listeners that as soon as she whelped he was going to sell both the dog and the puppies and "make some business." That was the Soviet mind-set. The dog was more than a beloved family pet: it was an investment. It was business.

Word of the refugee-merchants spread through the area. Every night, Binder's foyer converted into a bazaar and the hotel became a hot spot, drawing Austrians from local mountain hamlets and as far away as Vienna. Some made getaways out of it, skiing during the day and shopping at night. They pulled up, had a few drinks in the lounge, and strolled around, inspecting both the goods and the merchants. After all, we were denizens of the dreaded USSR, the Evil Empire, a land as forbidden and unknown to everyday Austrians as the West was to us. The Westerners were mesmerized by all things Soviet, even products of dubious value, such as Belomorkanalki, our cheap, noxious cigarettes that were basically filterless garbage with a few tobacco shavings tossed in for flavor. But the red stars and Cyrillic characters on the wrapper transformed their acrid smoke into a testament to the rustic hardiness of the Russian people. The Austrians choked them down with gusto. Belomorkanalki sales were so profitable that many businessmen sold them by the cigarette, to ensure maximum yield.

Austrian women bought *matryoshki* (the famous Russian nesting dolls), decorative plates, and spoons splashed with mushrooms, leaves, and berries in the bright reds and yellows that define Russian folk art. Others purchased hand-knit shawls as well as brooches, pendants, and ornate jewelry boxes lacquered with fanciful renderings of *bogatyri,* firebirds, snow maidens, and *troiki* of Slavic folklore. The men were drawn to Soviet military paraphernalia, especially the prized officer's watches awarded to various ranks of the Red Army and the KGB. The buyers brandished these like trophies of a feared adversary, lion fangs safely extracted from the jaws of their original owner and set in a benign bracelet.

But there was more than knickknacks to be had at Binder's, because the little mountain hotel housed two kinds of refugees. The first, like my family, came from Russian cities like Moscow and Leningrad or from eastern Ukrainian industrial centers, such as Kiev and Kharkov. The second group hailed from the towns and villages that dotted the enormous expanse of western

Ukraine. Life on the periphery of the Soviet empire granted these *Zapodentsi,* as we called them, a certain degree of independence.* The Party's authority waned the farther one got from the cities, because its tools of control—surveillance, informants, the secret police—operated best in dense, urban environments and were less suited for remote outposts. The *Zapodentsi* were, simply put, more Jewish than us: they spoke with flavorful Yiddish accents, bandied about little Jewish anecdotes, and were familiar with customs which for us, city dwellers, had already become faint memories. Most of the *Zapodentsi* were blue-collar workers, smiths and seamstresses, but what they lacked in formal education they made up for in other ways.

The little *chachki* that we, city folk, brought to the marketplace paled in comparison with the mind-boggling selections of the rural Jews. Some *Zapodentsi* families huddled in crammed rooms, the floors hidden by rolls of antique rugs. A woman in her thirties whom everyone called the Hat Lady (her dream was to open a hat boutique in Brooklyn) boasted a vast array of paintings, some dating back to tsarist Russia. Comrade Diamonds, the Hat Lady's fiercest rival, advertised a Zales-sized inventory of the gems, loose, set, fake, and real.† Of course, jewelry, artwork, and rugs weren't permitted to leave the Motherland, but that didn't deter the *Zapodentsi.* Their proximity to the border gave them years of practice smuggling contraband from Czechoslovakia and Romania into Russia, and when the time came to emigrate, they drew upon that expertise to move product in the opposite direc-

---

* *Zapodentsi* literally means "west folk."
† Dog Man, Hat Lady, and Comrade Diamonds aren't nicknames I invented to protect these people's identities—it's how they were referred to among the refugee community at Binder's. Many in the hotel were reluctant to disclose anything personal, and when people introduced themselves, quite a few replied, "Pleased to meet you," and left it at that.

tion, out west. They did what their background and resources enabled them to do, and while Dad memorized English and bribed clerks to create his microfilms, the *Zapodentsi* hoarded antiques and paid border guards to look the other way.

Some of the younger Austrians ventured to Nondorf to meet and greet the Slavic girls. My mom remembers one particular affair between a Leningradi teenager waiting to rejoin distant relatives in San Francisco and a Viennese fellow who took such a liking to her that he vowed to get her Austrian citizenship, even if he had to personally lobby the federal chancellor. The admirer clearly was a millionaire, because he drove a Mercedes, and to us, the model automatically indicated a seven-digit income. The infatuated couple held hands and wandered around our tiny hamlet or necked among the snow-covered evergreens that ringed the hotel. The girl beamed, and for good reason: she'd nabbed herself a foreigner. Everyone was awfully jealous and thought that it was all very romantic.

The girl's father was ecstatic—he had fled Russia with two daughters and now he strutted around the halls telling anyone who'd listen, "Well, I'm going to have one girl established in Austria, and when we get moved to Italy I hope to find a nice Italian millionaire for the other one, and then the wife and I will fly to San Francisco with no baggage!"

He was the happiest businessman in all of Nondorf.

*　　*　　*

On New Year's Eve, Binder threw a party. It wasn't much of a party, but there were three meals instead of two, and part of the cafeteria was cleared away to make a dance floor. Someone wheeled in an old tape deck with speakers, and the lobby Christmas tree was converted into a New Year's tree (aside from the name change, no other conversion efforts were required). Almost everyone danced. They danced because they were penniless, homeless, and out of Russia, and out of Russia was good. The Hat Lady danced because she was going to open up a hat store in Brooklyn. Some of the *Zapodentsi* danced old Jewish country jigs left over from the days of the shtetls. Sergei Kantler danced with Gera Zhislin, the aftermath of the *tamozhnya* temporarily forgotten. Dog Man danced with Mom, Lina, Gera, and Vicki, fortified himself with bread rolls and mineral water, and came back for round two. The *babushki* did what *babushki* always do—monitored the activity from the fringes of the dance floor with the dignified and somewhat disapproving expressions of chaperones at a middle school formal.

Dad and I didn't dance. I hated dancing, and Dad saw no point. "We're not in America, and we're nowhere near settled," he stared around in disbelief. "What the hell are they celebrating?" Shortly after the music started, he collected some leftover English-language newspapers from the lobby and retired upstairs to catch up on reading comprehension. I helped myself to an extra cup of tea and was amusing myself by watching the *babushki* watching everyone else, when Yura approached me.

"Why aren't you dancing?" he asked, interrupting teatime with two of my least favorite things: talking to strangers (I was starting to get used to Yura, but anyone other than family was a stranger) and having to explain my actions to anyone, family or strangers.

"Because there are no presents," I said, and somewhere in his tomb, Lenin shuddered. Less than a week out of the Motherland, and another member of the proletariat, lost to decadent materialism. I was thrilled to be out of Russia, but New Year's Eve meant presents, and dancing was for girls and people who drank too much vodka. I couldn't justify doing something that awful unless tangible incentives were involved.

"So if you'll get presents, you'll dance? Promise?"

"Yes," I said. Yura wasn't about to produce gifts on command; the Zhislins lost even more at the border than we did. I started squirming for a way to end the conversation, except that Yura had vanished. My *"da"* still hung in the air, and he was gone.

He reappeared five minutes later, panting and dripping with sweat, with a giant yellow marker and a slightly used coloring book. A chubby kid was diligently constructing a sand castle on the back cover. On the front, partially colored in by the book's previous owner, was the Happiest Dog in the World. This dog looked ecstatic. It was as if it had been moments away from being euthanized when someone burst into the shelter and said that there'd been a terrible mix-up, and that it was going to a loving family with a big yard and lots of tennis balls to boot. To this day, I have no idea what Yura traded for the book and marker, or where he found them. He insisted they came from Grandfather Frost, and when I said that Grandfather Frost was stupid and only kids believed in him, Yura just laughed.

I started flipping through the book, only to be interrupted by meaningful stares toward the dance floor. "But, Uncle Yura, I only promised you because I didn't think you would get any gifts!" I exclaimed, even throwing in the "Uncle," which children used to address grown-ups they were fond of. I was certain Uncle Yura would understand the situation.

Uncle Yura did not understand the situation. Uncle Yura convulsed with laughter.

"Well, it, it looks like someone, looks like someone learned an important lesson today," he finally managed to get out. Unfortunately, Dad's maxims about a real man *always* keeping his word, drilled into my head during strolls in the lilac park, picked the worst possible moment to kick in. I drained the teacup.

The rest of the evening found me bouncing up and down on both legs, big yellow marker bobbing in one hand, the Happiest Dog in the World flopping around in the other, my mind analyzing the possibilities. *I have yellow. Dad has pencils that can produce both regular gray, when used lightly, and blackish gray, when pressed heavily. Sometimes Austrians lose pens in the lobby couches . . . They're usually snatched up by the businessmen, but if I pay attention I should be able to score blue, maybe even red. What's the best way to steal Lina's lipstick, which will yield a lovely shade of coral? Does Binder have anything at the front desk? It's been ten whole minutes: Can I stop hopping around like a jackass? Happy New Year!*

Midnight came, and with it the dancing was over. Before going upstairs, the businessmen made sure to clear the lobby for the next day's bazaar. It was a new year, and there was plenty of business to be done.

*   *   *

Dad hated business. Hard, no-cutting-corners work was the foundation of his world, and he had always shown contempt for people ferreting pennies out of life. Hearing other refugees brag about their latest sales made him smirk. "Idiot! He just sold a thirty-schilling bottle of champagne for twelve schillings and he's crowing about it. What a schmuck!" Nevertheless, Dad still packed a suitcase of trinkets, mainly *matryoshki*, a few jewelry boxes, and several pairs of opera glasses, which folded into a palm-sized case. (I'm still confused as to what led Dad to believe that collapsible, low-magnitude binoculars were a hot commodity in the West, but I'm sure he had his reasons.) Dad's original intent was to hand these out as thank-you gifts to friendly locals we might encounter along the way, but the ceaseless commotion around us finally got to Mom and one night she declared that there was no reason our family shouldn't be doing business, "just like everyone else."

"Go ahead, peddle away," Dad grumbled, so Mom grabbed a pair of binoculars and a *matryoshka* and walked down to the bustling marketplace. The lobby was tense as seasoned business-men swarmed to potential clients and communally glared at incoming competition. Mom had paused by the staircase, unsure of what to do, when Binder flew up to her in a flash of white shirt and glistening baldness. He yelled something to three elderly Austrians, who seemed as taken aback by the ferocious sleeve-tugging as Mom was. Binder escorted them over, and, after a lot of hand-bargaining and "You, how much sell?" "You, how much pay?" the trio took both the dolls and the glasses. For a few moments after the transaction, the parties remained in place, Mom appraising the Austrians, the Austrians staring at Mom. Binder positioned himself off to the side, looking every bit like a UN diplomat presiding over a cultural summit. He smiled at Mom, and Mom returned to our room, proud of her sale.

Otto Binder was a decent man. He grew up in a working-class household in post-*Anschluss* Vienna. Agnes, his wife, was born in Croatia. She was just a child when a squad of soldiers raided her village, looting crops and raping women. When they burst into her family cottage, Agnes and her siblings literally shielded her mother. As soon as the soldiers managed to pull off one child, another scrambled up and desperately hung on, until eventually the men gave up and moved along. Soon afterward, Agnes and her older sister escaped over the Karavanke Mountains to Vienna, where she met Otto.

The young couple opened a small bakery on the outskirts

of the city; in the winters they'd stay after hours to serve bread and soup to the homeless. Years passed; Otto and Agnes saved up a few schillings, moved to the countryside, bought a hotel. Things were better for Binder, and although he was plagued with the usual worries of a small-business owner, he was certainly far from where he started. And yet he didn't forget. Binder understood why a former doctor was trying to peddle *matryoshki* just to feel like she was doing something productive. When Joint first approached him about turning his hotel into a refugee camp (obviously a deal no sane hotel owner would go for), Otto not only agreed; he offered Joint a group discount.

Binder's busiest time was in the dead of night, when a hushed rapping would come at his door. Years of living under a dictatorship had bred in Russians a pervasive distrust that was somehow equated with survival. No one wanted to disclose anything, especially any weaknesses, so petitioners crept up to Binder's room past midnight, when the hallways were empty. Otto would answer and, using a mixture of gestures and rudimentary English, figure out what was the matter and how to solve it. When people fell ill (as happened to me after one of my teeth rotted through), he arranged for transportation to local doctors whom he had convinced to treat the refugees at a reduced rate. During disputes, which were frequent given the diverse mix of cultures and backgrounds, he reconciled the conflicting parties, reminding everyone that the end goal was safety in America, not detention in Europe. More than seventy families were stationed at the hotel at peak times, and the knocks kept coming. Shortly after the first refugees had arrived, Binder resigned himself to the fact that he was not going to get a full night's sleep for the foreseeable future. He simply slept in his clothes and waited for the knock.

Of course, my family didn't know any of this at the time, and it was only when I returned to Nondorf seventeen years later that I was able to sit down with Otto and Agnes to learn about their backgrounds and their memories of our stay. In 1990, Binder was a foreign entity, a man unlike us: someone with money, and options, and a home. All we could do was rely on instincts, and instincts told us that Otto Binder was a decent man.

THE FORESTER

Niederösterreich (Lower Austria), January 1990

Peter the forester had rather disproportionate tastes for a man of his occupation. Other Austrians putzed around the cheaper things at Binder's hotel—shawls, *matryoshki,* Red Army watches—but not the forester. The forester would march into the lobby, black boots and long green coat caked with pine needles and mud, ignore the trinkets, and head for the costly goods. He bought handmade crystal and antique jewelry. He carted away caviar by the caseload. But his real penchant was for rugs. Peter *loved* fine rugs—Russian, Armenian, Persian, Turkish—and although he was a reserved man, a hungry glimmer crept into his pale blue eyes when they happened upon a quality piece.

He did not like to linger at the hotel, opting instead to deal on the road, in the privacy of his midnight-green military-grade Mercedes jeep. The seller would hop in and Peter would circle around the local countryside until he arrived at a price he deemed satisfactory. He was a tough customer who haggled for every schilling, but he didn't think twice about spending considerable sums of money on a worthy investment. What he *did* with those investments was anyone's guess: he'd carefully load his purchases into the Mercedes and return the next day, the jeep empty, ready for more.

The vendors quickly discovered that, unlike other customers, Peter had a profound understanding of the eras, history, norms, and art movements of our ex-homeland. Businessmen who embellished or tacked on a few extra decades to an antique learned never to try it again. Conversely, no one knew anything about Peter, and he seemed to prefer it that way. "I am a man who tends the local trees," he'd remark, and nothing more. He didn't interact with the other Austrians, the other Austrians didn't approach him, and even Binder remained silent on the matter. Terseness, privacy, and an inexplicable knowledge of Russian culture swirled around the pale red-headed man, shrouding him in mystery. A favorite post-bazaar pastime at Binder's was trying to figure out just who or what he was. "An agent of the Austrian secret service" was the leading theory. "No, that'd be too obvious; he spies for the CIA," held a rival contention. "That's stupid. He launders money for an international crime syndicate—why else would he buy all those rugs?" The debates ranged long into the night.

The one gap in Peter's formidable Russian acumen was language: the man didn't speak a lick of Russian, which was an issue, because the peddlers didn't have a good enough grasp of English to field Peter's detailed inquiries. The businessmen needed to locate a single common translator, someone who not only spoke English but, more important, wouldn't disrupt the sale by hawking his own goods or swaying Peter toward another deal. They settled on Dad because he was notoriously anti-business and didn't charge for the translation services, merely wanting to practice his conversational skills. He was harmless, which made him the perfect translator.

Every day after dinner, Dad climbed into the front seat of Peter's Mercedes to join him and the sellers for a spin around the neighborhood. One sleety January evening, as business was wrapping up for the night, Dog Man (the peddler with the pregnant Maltese) requested a meeting with the forester. Once in the jeep, the trader fished a little cloth bag out of his pocket. Inside was a set of four or five diamonds of astonishing quality and size. According to Dog Man, the gems came from the personal collection of Tsar Nikolai II himself, Nikolai the Bloody, the last tsar of Russia. Peter perked up his ears. The fate of the fabled Romanov jewels has been inspiring myths and conspiracy theories since 1917, when the Communists overthrew the tsar. Lenin and the Bolsheviks may have despised the aristocratic bloodsuckers, but they had no qualms about pocketing as much tsarist treasure as they could get their hands on. The idea was to redistribute the wealth to the proletariat, of course, but somewhere in the redistribution process many of the jewels simply vanished; over the next seventy years some resurfaced in rather improbable places, places as strange as, if not stranger than, the back mountains of Austria. Needless to say, Dog Man had Peter's attention.

The forester shifted course and drove to a house in a tiny village the size of Nondorf. Peter disappeared into the sleet, returning with a man carrying a flashlight and a set of loupes. The newcomer peered at the stones, turning them this way and that, switching lenses for various magnifications, then said something in German and ran back indoors. Without a word, Peter returned to the road, flying *past* Binder's and to the larger town of Gmünd, careening the jeep into a lot next to a one-story building. The forester spoke to Dad while staring at Dog Man in the rearview mirror.

"Please inform this whoreson that the man who examined his garbage was an expert jeweler who said that they are well-crafted fakes. Inform this bastard that I do not like getting fooled. Inform him that we're in front of the local constable center, where he will learn what happens to people who sell fake diamonds in Austria."

Over the next five minutes Dad's translation skills were tested like they'd never been tested before as he struggled to convey the barrage of pleas, apologies, and explanations pouring out of the backseat. The whole thing was an awful, colossal misunderstanding: Dog Man was the real victim in all this, he'd been victimized *twice,* in fact, first when he was ripped off by that vile, lying scumbag from Minsk—may he go to hell!—and again for looking like he was trying to con Peter, a respectable Austrian gentleman whom Dog Man would never, ever take advantage of. Peter must realize that he [Dog Man] didn't know the tsar personally, of course, so it's not as if he could verify the source, and above all—

"Let him go," Dad asked. It was less than a month after the night at the *tamozhnya,* and the horror on Dog Man's face was too familiar. "Maybe he isn't lying."

Peter brooded with barely controlled fury as the wipers lashed across the windshield. He gave Dad a long look, then a nod, and spun the jeep around. Both Dad and the forester ignored continued appeals for clemency during the return trip to Nondorf. As soon as Binder's lobby emerged into view, Dog Man extricated himself from the colossal misunderstanding, grabbing his diamonds and taking off into the downpour as if every constable in Austria and the ghost of the tsar were on his heels.

"Would you like to stay for a while?" Peter asked Dad, who was about to follow Dog Man. "We can talk and drive around, since it is nice outside."

Dad stayed, and their cruises became a nightly post-business ritual. The two men chatted about politics, literature, and history. Both shared a healthy distrust of government, both had a quirky, somewhat immature sense of humor. They got along well.

Peter revealed himself slowly, via innocuous remarks sprinkled into the conversation. "I work as a forester, and I work for the man who lives in that house," he mentioned one day, pointing to a large stone castle that towered on a hill over a nearby town. "He is a baron, and all of these lands belong to him," Peter clarified on another pass by the castle. Several nights later Dad learned: "I also live in that house, with the man who owns the forests." The whole situation was strange, but Dad valued privacy and didn't press for answers.

One January afternoon, Mom, Dad, Lina, and I were stomping home from the grocery store. Nondorf had no shops, and the nearest village, Hoheneich, was an hour's walk away, but the commute was an almost-daily ritual, since the adults were hesitant to use an entire week's stipend to stock up on groceries. I was usually excluded from the Hoheneich excursions, because the road had no shoulder and Austrian drivers didn't believe in things like swerving or slowing down to avoid pedestrians. But being cooped up in the hotel was making me antsy and I had already turned my attentions to pestering Lina, so Mom bundled me up in one of Dad's sweaters and permitted the trip.

By the time we picked up the bread, cheese, and orange juice and began the crawl back I was regretting it. At the border, the *tamozhniki* had ripped through the seams of my warm rabbit fur coat (perhaps the border guards thought Mom and Dad were using me to smuggle out gold), and it was starting to disintegrate at an alarming pace. The icy trudge accentuated every little pine needle, each clump of snow, peeling off the landscape's magic and exposing the monotony underneath. Fields fell around us, brimmed by hoary pines, and each one took a decade to traverse, thanks to the snow and ice and the uniformity, broken only by small groups of other refugees drifting by.

The rumble of a heavy car carried far up the road, giving us plenty of time to leap into the safety of the snow banks (the practice had quickly become instinctual). Stomping through the snow was futile and so was trying to hitchhike, so we stood by and waited for the car to pass. Instead it rolled to a halt, and out hopped Peter. He scooped us up into the warmth of the jeep and turned to Dad, a mischievous grin on his face. "Would you like to stop by that house where the man who owns the forests lives?"

"Is that possible?" Dad asked the forester.

"Yes," Peter shrugged. "He is my father."

"He wants to know if we want to see where he lives." A confused Dad polled the backseat, and we agreed. Well, we would've agreed if we had time to, but scarcely had the offer been translated than Peter threw the shift into first, the engine's idle grew to a deep, satisfied purr, and the pines and fields, so clear to discern as we'd shuffled past, became a blur. We zoomed past Nondorf, into another town, and veered off the road and over a bridge spanning a small moat with a thin coat of ice floating on the bottom. Peter heaved the jeep up a sharp incline, through a portal in a massive stone curtain wall, and slammed on the brakes, scattering frozen white pebbles from under the tires.

We stood atop a hill in the middle of the town, with a commanding view of the surroundings. Two lean hunting dogs trotted up to the jeep, received pats and affirmations of being *gute hunde,* and returned to patrolling the premises. To our right was a low stone barrier. Little statues of grimy cherubs were scattered beside it like displaced garden gnomes, curly heads and manicured wings poking through the snow. "Late Romanesque, manufactured shortly before the Renaissance," Peter muttered to Dad. Beyond the barrier, a twenty-foot drop-off led to a field, which in turn sloped away to a distant forest. To our left and behind us squatted several ancient buildings hewn out of thick stone. The nearest one appeared to be the medieval version of a multi-car garage, since it had only three walls and an interior separated by massive dividers carved right out of the stone supports. "That's a stable, that's a stable, Dad!" I yelled, illustrations from our old *Ivanhoe* book flashing before me. "Stable, yes," agreed Peter. "Cows no, horse no, but stable yes."

But we caught only a glimpse of the landscape before our gaze was snared by something else. Next to the stable and obscuring the town below rose "the house," a four-story castle complete with a belfry, balconies, and twin ten-foot gateways with flanking towers, all made out of crumbling gray stone.

"How—how old is this place?" Dad stuttered.

"It was originally constructed in the twelfth century, but"— Peter nodded toward a gray satellite dish peeking out from a corner parapet—"we have made certain modifications to the original design."

I'll never forget watching Peter fumble through his key chain in front of the giant oaken gate, just as ordinary people fumble through ordinary key chains in front of normal doors. "Let us go," he waved. "Let us go inside."

A murky passage led to an inner bailey that cut through all four stories up to the icy gray sky. Grim stone walls were interspersed with three rows of balconies. More statues watched from the terraces, and other unknown objects lurked in the shadows. The bailey was silent; nothing disturbed the chilly gloom. Once again, we barely had time to orient ourselves before we were ushered up a winding staircase. "This way, please." Peter unlatched another door and showed us in, carefully locking it behind him. "These are my apartments," he said, visibly relieved.

On the other side of the door lay the answer to the fate of the rugs—Peter's floors were covered by an exhibition of the history and craft of carpet weaving that stretched into the distance. We halted, unsure of how to maneuver through the expensive and colorful patchwork, but Peter marched right across in his boots.

Dusty paintings and antique vases were strewn on floors and

chairs. Cabinets and curios stuffed with everything from ancient Greek pottery to cheap Soviet perfume crouched in the corners. A long glass case running the length of one wall housed an extensive collection of firearms, beginning with medieval muskets and culminating with a high-power sniper rifle.

"Don't touch, Lev," Dad warned when he saw me eyeing the guns.

"Touch is not a problem," interrupted Peter. "But do not depress the trigger."

"They're loaded?" Dad asked.

"Why would they not be?" Peter raised an eyebrow, and Dad's frown banished all thoughts of hands-on contact from my head. Peter's apartments bristled with enough weapons to stock a Hollywood studio. Ceremonial officers' daggers from armies Western and Oriental, ancient and modern, were mounted along the hallways. Racks of pikes, poleaxes, halberds, morning stars, and other cruel and unusual implements of battle hung from the walls. The man took the defense of his castle seriously. I was impressed.

Our host disappeared into the eclectic labyrinth, returning with a set of teacups. By the time he fetched the kettle, the adults had regained the ability to speak and were eager to learn about Peter's noble lineage, but the baron was quick to dismiss their romantic notions. "It is silly, the whole 'nobility' thing. In 1919, when Austria became a republic, the government abolished most aristocratic privileges, and I fully support that decision," he said. "Who you are should have nothing to do with who your father was. Who you are should be determined by what you do and nothing else. Please sit down."

I hovered near an array of fanned-out swords above a mantel. Mom and Lina browsed through a small chest bulging with photographs of dignitaries at galas, receptions, foxhunts, and other dignitary affairs, and while they noticed several men who resembled Peter, none of the photographs were actually of him. Peter led Dad through his vast antiques collection. No object existed in a vacuum: each one had its own tantalizing historical context, as well as a record of how and where Peter had purchased it. Viennese auction houses, Dutch bazaars, Bulgarian flea markets—he fondly recalled all the locales where the hunt had taken him. And it was the hunt, more than the actual trophies, that appeared to hold true meaning for Peter.

Mom spied a large bed draped in black sheets with three black pillows resting on top. "Why three?" she asked.

"My two children attend school right now, but sometimes they get afraid at night and they come to me," Peter explained. Mom smiled. She'd dealt with nightmares aplenty, with Lina and me both, and the notion of little barons and baronesses scampering to their father for comfort made the suddenly giant-sized Peter more human.

At the end of the visit we were hustled out of the castle and dropped off at Binder's. Peter asked Dad if we would be interested in taking a tour of the Austrian countryside the next day. Dad hesitated. "The rules say we can't go farther than fifteen kilometers from the hotel."

"Idiot rules made by idiots," Peter snorted, but, noticing that his assessment didn't allay Dad's concern, he turned to address us all. "I can go anywhere I want. Tomorrow, when with me, you are my guests; that is so. Be ready at seven."

*   *   *

For more than sixteen hours, the dark green Mercedes roared across Niederösterreich, the northernmost Austrian province. Peter was truly a man of the land, intricately familiar with the region and its people. He drove us around forests and past peat bogs, up mountains or through them via giant tunnels. There were castles—a castle on every hill, it seemed—some renovated, others just piles of stones left to brood over the past. We stopped at gorgeous abbeys with musty libraries and saintly relics, lone towers jutting out by the roadside, factories of Bohemian glass-blowers who crafted some of the world's finest crystal, lush vine-yards whose keepers stirred aromas and spices into secret recipes passed down for generations. Our host knew them all, vintners and craftsmen and monks, but even more intriguing was his abil-ity to retrace his own history far down the corridors of time.

"Dagger makers; my ancestors were dagger makers. They had traveled down into this area around the fifteenth century, and made a living fashioning weapons for local townspeople. Later, they became sailors and fishermen, transporting goods in central Europe. When they became barons in the 1800s, they got the right to create a coat-of-arms, and they applied an anchor on one side and a smith on the other. Anchor and smith, fishermen and dag-ger makers, yes, that is so." Of his immediate family, Peter said little. He touched on his grandfather, who'd served as the Austro-Hungarian Empire's ambassador to the United States, mentioned he had three sisters and that his father was once in the Austrian army, and nothing more.

We listened with fascination, Dad speaking to Peter, Lina translating for Mom and me in the backseat. Lina, a sucker for medieval romances, would toss in needless literary references and annoying fashion commentary, and I, wedged between her and Mom, would lean forward into the gap between the front seats, preferring to be in the unintelligible-English company of Dad and Peter. The baron was an aggressive and skilled driver who flew down the autobahns at breakneck speeds. He would hunch over the steering wheel, hauling himself up toward the windshield as if trying to merge with the road. Dad, always bent on getting a head start in America, mimicked Peter's movements, trying to learn how to drive. Peter hits the gas, Dad's foot taps down on an invisible pedal; Peter shifts gears, Dad's hand twitches. I'm not sure how much Dad picked up, but he did this during the entire trip.

"Mom, want to know a secret?" I asked during a stopover late in the day. We were west of Binder's, where the mountains grew taller, at a roadside restaurant clinging to the side of a peak. Peter, Dad, and Lina were finishing dessert; Mom, who loved people-watching, cradled her coffee at an outside table. My secret wasn't much of a secret, but I wanted to check out the mountains, and with the cold winds rising I felt like I had to open with a hook before Mom shooed me indoors.

"Peter doesn't like standing still," I said. What I meant was tough to describe. Peter wasn't uncomfortable, quite the opposite: the stout, red-haired man moved, talked, walked, and drove with an arrogant surety that comes with nobility. I wanted to explain that he grew pensive when we were still, and no matter whether we were exploring a ruin in a forgotten valley or dining at a restaurant up in the clouds, Peter always seemed happier to be in motion.

Mom tugged on my coat, coaxing the torn rabbit pelts into some semblance of a unified garment. "Maybe you noticed it because you don't like standing still either." She smiled, and she was right. My favorite thing about going to Estonia was *going* to Estonia, curling up on the top bunk of the train cabin and staring out the window, getting lost in the bliss of being in neither one place nor the other, just dissolving into a particle in transit. When you're standing you have time to think, worry, contemplate; when you're a blur, you can relax.

We would go on several more trips with Peter, and while I

enjoyed the places we visited, driving was always my favorite. I still tailed Dad during sightseeing, but when it was time to leave I'd be in the vanguard with Peter, ready to get back into fifth gear.

*   *   *

The refugees at Binder's were suspended in diplomatic limbo in the mountains, but Dad's mind was already on the other side of the Atlantic. He thought about work, which was nothing new: he was always thinking about work. Work defined him, shaped his life, gave him purpose, and no matter when we'd get to the United States, no matter where we'd wind up, Dad was determined to be an engineer once more.

That was a problem: he was already past fifty, he knew no one, and his school transcripts and records of professional achievements had been confiscated and burned at the border. Even if he had them, they would've been worthless: decades of Cold War secrecy had left the USSR and the United States with mutual contempt. Employers in the West knew nothing about Soviet professionals, not to mention Kharkov's good ol' Central Design Bureau. After destroying the microfilms, Dad realized that American companies would have to hire him on faith alone. But Dad was not a man of faith—he was a man of statistics, and statistics dictated that old immigrants who came to America ended up delivering pizzas and driving taxis. And *that's* what consumed Dad; that's what he turned over in his mind, parsing, speculating, analyzing, attacking. *How to beat the statistics. How to get a job.*

One day Peter asked Dad what was troubling him, and Dad told him, and Peter got Dad a job interview. Well, technically it wasn't an interview, since Austrian law barred us from seeking employment. Technically, all Peter did was draw on his contacts to arrange a scheduled, one-on-one conversation between Dad and the director of an engineering firm in Vienna. "There is no harm in discussion," Peter reasoned. "You are two grown men, you can talk about whatever you want. If you decide to talk about the beautiful Austrian mountains, that is up to you. If you decide to talk about turbine engineering, that is also up to you . . . Austria, too, is a free country."

Dad and the director passed on the mountains and cut straight to the turbines. They made a whole day of it, the director probing Dad about turbomachinery on the other side of the Iron Curtain. By the end of the session the man was cautiously showing Dad some of his company's designs, inquiring about ideas for innovation. The sun had long set by the time Peter's Mercedes pulled into Binder's parking lot and the baron faced Dad. "I go to Vienna two times a week for business. You shall come with me, you shall spend your time with them, and you shall return with me. They cannot pay you money because it is too risky: you will work for free, that is so, but if you do a good job, they will write recommendation letters to use in America." Peter gave Dad a thumbs-up. "I thought you would fail, but you did not. You impressed them."

The money didn't matter to Dad; reputation was everything. "Work hard for your reputation, and then your reputation will work hard for you" was a favorite saying of his, one I'd heard time and again during walks in the lilac park behind our apartment complex back in Kharkov. I didn't know what Dad meant by it, but I knew he loved his profession, and I was thrilled when he strutted into our room and proudly announced that he was going to work again.

WAKING THE NOMADS

Nondorf, Niederösterreich (Lower Austria),
Mid-January 1990

By mid-January, the mood at Binder's had soured. Every family in the hotel knew people who had crossed the border before us. And every one of those forerunners had spent no more than one week in Austria before being sent on to Italy and then to the States. We had been stuck in the back mountains of Niederösterreich for a month with no explanation and no end in sight. *What's happening? Is there trouble with going to America?* Questions grew in the hallways, took root in the lobby, spread to breakfast and the late hours, but Mr. Prager continued to provide no information and Binder claimed he knew as much as we did. The one group who would have the answer was HIAS, the Hebrew Immigrant Aid Society, which was overseeing Jewish resettlement into the United States. And by January 1990, HIAS had a problem.

In 1987, a total of 8,155 Jews had been permitted to leave the USSR. The following year that number grew to 18,965. In 1989, the year my family left, 71,000 had been granted permits. And in 1990, this spiked to a staggering 200,000 people.[*] These numbers

---

[*] Howard M. Sachar, *A History of the Jews in America* (New York: Knopf, 1992), p. 929.

meant various things to different parties. For the U.S. government, this was another small triumph in its struggle with Moscow. For the American Jews, the ones who paid attention, it was cause for rejoicing, the payoff from three decades of lobbying, rallying, and fund-raising. But human rights workers, the people on the ground, are always the last to celebrate. HIAS's joy was tempered by the fact that every digit represented an individual in need of housing, and food, and political asylum. Running refugee camps in Europe wasn't the immediate issue, since these were funded by Joint, which had just thrown open its coffers. The problem was getting people into America.

Every refugee had to have a sponsor, a person or organization to vouchsafe housing, medical care, education, and employment. The U.S. Congress made it clear that *if* it was going to pressure the Kremlin to release its Jews, *if* America was going to raise its annual refugee admission quota, then HIAS would have to provide its refugees with sponsors. In part, this sponsorship requirement was meant to ensure that the new arrivals wouldn't be left to fend for themselves in a foreign country. But Washington also sought to protect itself as much as the refugees, and understandably so—laissez-faire immigration can take a heavy toll on health care, welfare, and all sorts of social services. In the interests of everyone, sponsorship was a must.

In years past, when the refugee flow out of Russia was merely a trickle, this had not been a serious obstacle. HIAS enjoyed long-standing relationships with urban immigrant communities, such as the ones in New York, Chicago, and Los Angeles. Many refugees were going to reunite with family members already interwoven into the fabric of these hubs. Those who left Russia without any kin in America were taken in under the auspices of grassroots Jewish organizations coordinating with HIAS.

But with the immigrant numbers exploding from thousands

to tens of thousands to hundreds of thousands, the seemingly infinite capacity of the cities had suddenly reached a limit. Individuals who were already supporting relatives were forced to refuse sponsorship for other family members who had counted on them. Organizations that had planned their budgets for several families were now bombarded with nonstop sponsorship requests. Neighborhood by neighborhood, New York, Chicago, and L.A. began telling HIAS to slow down, to give them time, to hold the refugees in Europe while they cleared space and resources. And yet every day more trains pulled up to Vienna, disgorging new families seeking shelter in the West. The camps, HIAS's pipeline to America, were suddenly faced with a massive influx on one end and a bottleneck at the other. The system was strained to the maximum, and HIAS needed to address the crisis immediately.

HIAS had to free up the camps to make room for the incomers. The only way to accomplish that was to move those already in the camps into the States. And to do *that* HIAS required a fresh supply of sponsors, a suburban network that extended past the overtaxed enclaves of the cities. This went beyond asking someone to sign a petition or mail you a check. HIAS would have to convince random American Jews to take legal and moral responsibility for complete strangers, to accept entire families of refugees into their homes. First came recruitment, making local communities aware of the pressing need for sponsors. Then there was fund-raising. And training. And preparations. All for one family. There were thousands of families.

*　　*　　*

Two thousand years of roaming the world are enough to humble any nation, or what's left of one. Two thousand years of fleeing an oppressive homeland, only to be oppressed in the next one, have etched into the Jewish mind-set a keen memory of traumas past and a nervous premonition of traumas to come. We are reminded of them when we dine on Passover, and build huts on Sukkoth, and hear family stories of persecutions of the past. To this day, the Jews will tell you where they're from, and where their family escaped from to get there, and where they ran from before to get to that place, and so on. From the Exodus to the Holocaust, the Jews remember.

The defining moment in Jewish history was the Exodus, the flight from a hostile land ruled by a hostile people who "knew not Joseph." Everything from that point on has been, for the most part, a series of exoduses, a series of escapes. Some, such as the waves of immigration to America, have been massive. Others, accounts of a few families moving here this year, running there the next, are smaller but no less painful. The Exodus was there in the beginning and the Exodus has remained, manifesting itself over and over to become a part of nearly every Jewish family.

One consequence of this collective pain has been the development of the idea that every Jew is responsible for the welfare of every other Jew, because you never know—tomorrow may be your turn to run. This undying vigilance is such a part of the Jewish psyche that it might as well be genetic. Nomads we are, and nomads we remain. Cars replaced caravans, tents calcified into houses, yet the wanderings of old course through us, simmering under the surface. The suburban network HIAS sought had been there all along, mowing the lawns, driving the kids to soccer practice, renting movies on the weekends. Seemingly wispy and disjointed, isolated and oblivious, it was nevertheless capable of extremely rapid mobilization. All it needed was a stimulus.

Nobody recognized this better than HIAS. As Valery Bazarov, the HIAS director of location and family history services, and himself an erstwhile Soviet refugee, told me, "We were always good at keeping records, and we are not shy about reminding people of their roots. Say someone needs to come to the U.S. but has no sponsor. So we go to someone who we assisted years ago, or whose father we assisted years ago, and we say, 'Look, you came here and people helped you and you're successful, and now it's time to help someone else. This person needs a sponsor. Let's bring them in.' And it works; it worked in the past and it works now, and it works very well. That's part of what HIAS does: it unites people through generations. We were all strangers at some point, and it is important to remember that."

In the early months of 1990, an urgent reminder went out to synagogues and Jewish centers across America. Phone calls, faxes, groups of young ambassadors fanned out from New York, visiting cities, then towns, then suburbs, all of them bearing the same message: *We fought for the release of our people; now they are free. They are waiting in Vienna. They are waiting in Rome. They need our help. Let's bring them in.*

PENNIES AND PEACH SLICES

Nondorf, Niederösterreich (Lower Austria),
Late January 1990

I was playing with my soldiers in an upstairs stairwell when I heard that Lina and Mom had been arrested. "Watch him!" Dad barked to Grandma, who grabbed my arm, and he scrambled down the stairs, joining the throng of Russians spilling out into Binder's parking lot.

The businessmen had gotten too greedy. By the end of January, the novelty of ex-Soviets living in the midst of Austria had worn off, the flow of gawkers to Binder's bazaar had diminished, and the traders decided to gain wider exposure. Down the hill from the hotel, the road took a tight curve over a little bridge, where passing cars had to slow down. The peddlers armed themselves with *matryoshki* and cigarettes and started camping out on the bridge, setting up a hybrid roadblock/drive-thru boutique. They had some initial success attracting new customers, which only emboldened them to crowd in on motorists, almost *forcing* them to stop. These new tactics quickly attracted attention of a different kind.

In 1990, the Austrian countryside was not a land of immigrants; it was a land of Austrians. The influx of noisy strangers who didn't speak German, tried to haggle over set store prices, and attempted to hitchhike where normal people drove must have been jarring. Some of the locals in Nondorf and Hoheneich were friendly to the migrants (my parents fondly remember a Hoheneich woman who invited them to warm up over tea during an especially frigid shopping trip), but many viewed our presence as undesirable. Every refugee at Binder's had long grown used to the angry honks and stares during the daily slogs to buy groceries. The businessmen's bridge activities ratcheted this tension to another level, until one late afternoon a squad of police cars screeched up to the overpass. Mom and Lina, who sometimes took a *matryoshka* or two to the bridge, were among those detained.

The peddlers had done more than create a dangerous road hazard: they had violated a key condition of their refugee status by engaging in work, and the Austrian police wasted no time lining everyone up and asking for identification. Binder flew outside the moment he heard the cops gathering names, and for a good hour the little bald man circled from officer to officer, arguing, pleading, throwing out one hand, then the other, all the while anxiously glancing up at the sky. And it's a testament to Binder's reputation with the local authorities that he managed to stall the cops long enough for the sun to set, until the distant mountains blurred into the twilight, bazaar time neared, and the dark green Mercedes pulled into the hotel's parking lot.

It wasn't easy to read Peter's face as he crossed the police cordon toward the terrified crowd that included his favorite sellers, as well as Mom and Lina. Dad, Grandma, and I stood to the side, watching with the rest of the refugees. Peter shouldered past Binder, pulled out his wallet, and began lazily flipping through little rectangular cards, occasionally pausing to show one to the officer in charge. He could have been a street magician entertaining a tourist. Peter kept shuffling his papers and muttering to the cop in clipped, bored sentences, until the officer took a step back and let out a sharp whistle. Suddenly, his men began packing up. Peter remained in the lot, hands in the pockets of his mud-stained coat. Mom and Lina collapsed into the arms of Gera and Vicki Zhislin, and the baron shrugged and drove away without saying a word.

Binder immediately announced that business was finished, both inside and out. Everyone caught selling on the bridge was fined 100 schillings (which put a significant dent into the $650 my family had been allowed to bring out of Russia), but no names were taken and no one was reported to immigration.

"Let's go," said Grandma, and trudged to the cafeteria, where an anxious Agnes Binder and her workers were keeping dinner warm. Not much fazed my grandmother. Dad may have spent years planning for emigration, but Grandma had survived the evacuation of Kharkov, grabbing all she could carry and jumping on a train with my infant mother hours before the Nazis stormed the city and killed every Jew they could find. We'd eaten breakfast this morning, supper was waiting, tomorrow's meal forecast looked promising, and Grandma was doing all right.

Grandma ate up, but I claimed I had a headache and snuck outside. The raid petrified everyone; not even the smokers were out that night, and I had the grounds to myself. I circled the snowy arbors by the hotel, the ones where the Leningradi girl kissed her love-stricken Austrian who was going to lobby the federal chancellor to get her citizenship. I started breaking off branches from Binder's pines, snapping them into smaller branches, then twigs, then kindling. My stupid bunny coat picked this time to fall apart for good, but I barely noticed the cold. It was clear that the cops viewed the migrants on the bridge as not just reckless asses (which, to be fair, they were) but trash. I terrorized Lina to the best of my abilities, but she was still a good person, a student who giggled at silly things and read books and told scary stories. And Mom, only a month ago (in what already felt like another life), Mom was as respected as Binder, maybe more. Mom, who couldn't eat at restaurants without some old patient stopping by the table to say thank you. Mom, who walked through bad neighborhoods because criminals didn't touch her, and now *she* was a criminal. *To the cops they were* vermin. I did not feel the frost, or the pine splinters pricking my fingers; I felt nothing but unbelievable, blinding rage and in that cocoon I floated, neither thinking nor feeling for most of the evening.

Thankfully Mom was too exhausted and didn't even ask when I threw away the now-useless coat in the hallway trashcan.

* * *

The loss of business had a profound effect on Binder's. We had too much time and not enough purpose. Every day was the same, and every day was long. There were few children staying at the hotel, for which I was grateful, and no school to cower from. It was a wonderful life for me, especially compared with nine years of being caged up in the sooty Kharkov apartment. Our daily diet consisted of chunks of wax-wrapped cheese, and every morning I'd carefully peel off the red casings to fashion soldiers with. I mounted sieges and went on raids with my wax platoon, read and reread my books, strolled around the hotel, walked to the store once in a while, and was at peace. The only eerie part was, I felt old. There's no such thing as a young refugee; every migrant has a past they've fled from, and how can you be young when you already have one life behind you? I felt old when I passed by local Austrian children flinging snowballs and building snow forts, but it didn't bother me. It was worse for the adults.

People unearthed dignity wherever they could find it. Some of the older women took to waking up an hour early and shuffling down to the kitchen to help Agnes Binder and the cooks prepare breakfast. Agnes remembered the women being wary, and only approaching the kitchen if she was there herself. She didn't need their help or ask for it, but she began assigning small duties like cutting bread and setting dishes on the tables. Agnes rewarded each *babushka* with a little cup of peach slices for her efforts, but old Russian women don't eat much fruit as it is. They didn't do it for the peaches.

Our travel companion Yura had once visited his brother in Nashville, an experience that qualified him to become Binder's in-house economist. Every morning he would collect the newspapers abandoned in the lobby, check on the latest schilling-to-dollar exchange rate, and try to predict when it would favor the dollar. "Today, dear comrades," he'd proclaim, "today is the day we triumph over the Capitalists!" and the heads of families, *Zapodentsi* and city folk, would start bundling up. Nondorf had no bank, of course, and neither did nearby Hoheneich, so the men made the ninety-minute trek to the town of Gmünd, which boasted two banks. (Yura, the inveterate jester, proposed that one of the banks relocate to charming Nondorf, even going so far as to hand out Binder's hotel brochures, but the tellers didn't bite.) Once in Gmünd, the men tinkered with minuscule transactions, using refugee stipends and *matryoshki* proceeds to ply the exchange rate and squeeze out a few pennies. They would make the return trip, triumphant, pant legs caked with ice, breath pouring out in puffs, bank slips tucked deep inside their coat pockets. Twice a week the men tackled the Gmünd circuit. It was a hell of a slog in the middle of winter for such a small payout, but then again, it was the work involved that gave the payoff meaning.

*

Learning English trumped every other concern. It took only a few days in a foreign land to hammer home the crucial role of language. No matter whether we were talking with Binder or with HIAS— English was the difference between impotence and empowerment, and the race for verbs and nouns had begun. Informal classes were held in the lobby day and night, where anyone with a new scrap of English to share was mobbed by anxious students. For expediency's sake, lessons focused exclusively on basic conversational skills: phrases, questions, and answers. Grammar was considered irrelevant.

Dad was busy poring over Austrian power plant schematics from the job Peter had gotten him, but Lina and Vicki were among the teachers. Vicki patiently tutored an old pensioner who had left the USSR by himself. He was something of a pariah, prone to complaining and inciting arguments, but studying with Vicki transformed him. He would sit with her on a couch in a corner of the lobby, intensely mimicking her facial gestures, wrestling the new syllables into submission. *Ha-u aRR yuuuu, aRRR yuuu, yuuu? Mai nay-eem eez Vadeem. Vat eeeez yoRR nay-eem?* he'd growl. Vicki was fiercely protective of her pupil, and one look from her was enough to forestall any snickering. Besides, we were all in the same position—the cantankerous old-timer just made it more obvious.

My attitude toward English was conflicted. When I was in second grade, Mom and Dad, America on the forefront of their minds, enrolled me in an English class at school. It was a disaster. Tamara Alexandrovna, the teacher, was a graceful woman with long, dark hair. The good thing was, she didn't tolerate beatings, although whether this policy stemmed from compassion or from simple expediency (it's difficult to conjugate while prone on the ground), I don't know. But the downside was that Tamara Alexandrovna considered herself the guardian of and ambassador for the English language, and as such, she demanded the utmost commitment from her pupils.[*]

Our pre–first class homework assignment (Tamara Alexandrovna went balls-out from day one) was to memorize the English alphabet. I barely glanced at it. I hadn't even bothered learning Ukrainian, a language so ridiculously similar to Russian that the two are mutually intelligible. No, I had enough trouble in regular classes to justify paying attention to a language I would never use.

Monday morning, Tamara Alexandrovna glided into the room and leafed through the roster. Her dark brown eyes brightened upon reaching my name. "Lev Golinkin. Lina Golinkin's brother, correct? Jolly good. Kindly go up front, Lev, and show us how to recite the English alphabet." Lina was once Tamara Alexandrovna's star pupil. The teacher mistakenly assumed that diligence and a strong work ethic ran in the family, and wanted me to go first to set the tone. Her disillusionment would be swift and brutal.

What do I know about the English alphabet? I thought during the slow march to the chalkboard. I vaguely recalled that the beginning was similar to the Russian one, except that the third letter was C and not V, and I even felt comfortable enough with the first few letters to rattle them off together.

"A. B. C."

Tamara Alexandrovna shone with an encouraging smile. Life was good.

"D."

---

[*] And when I say "English" I mean *English,* because Tamara Alexandrovna taught strictly British vocabulary and phrases, proclaiming all else to be a corruption of the noble tongue of Merrie Olde England. This had hilarious consequences, because after we came to America it took my sister a good two years to weed all the greengrocers, letterboxes, knickers, and bangers out of her lexicon.

I paused, trying to remember whether the next letter was also the same as in Russian. I didn't have many alternatives, so I kept going.

"*E.*"

And that was it. I knew that after *E* the two alphabets split. Russian moved on with *Ë,* a letter not to be found in diacritic-free English; English had something else, *K* perhaps, or that weird snake-shaped letter, I wasn't sure. Two alphabets diverged in my mind, and I, I knew not which to travel by, so I just gave Mrs. Tamara a satisfied nod and returned to my seat.

The guardian of the English language stared, appalled, into the void by the blackboard. I had just taken the beautiful English alphabet, the building block of Shakespeare and Joyce, Tennyson and Yeats, and I had truncated it from twenty-six unique and essential characters to five. This assault on one thousand years of linguistic development would not go unanswered on Tamara Alexandrovna's watch.

"*F,* Lev. *F* is the next letter. Do you know what *F* indicates in English? It means 'fail,' a concept you will become quite familiar with in the future. It means you don't know anything. It means you don't belong in this class."

I cried and I cried, but I couldn't wait to get out of there. I hated English and I hated Tamara Alexandrovna.

Now, at Binder's, I was forced to concede that those lessons may have been useful after all. Over and over, I muttered the alphabet, chewing on the acrid feeling of being wrong. But after a little effort, the ABCs came easily, and I was just starting to think that maybe English and I had gotten off to a bad start when I ran into my nemesis. *Th* is the most frustrating sound in the world for a Russian. We can't pronounce it. Most of us accept our fate ("it's tree o'clock"), but even if we contrive to say *th*, it still feels unnatural. Now, I will acknowledge that I, as a native Russian speaker, should keep my mouth shut when it comes to judging other tongues. I understand that at some juncture in the development of my language my ancestors decided to save a little money and not buy any vowels. People attempting to learn Russian have compared the experience to trekking through a barren wasteland of consonants without the respite of any vowel in between.* Maybe the inability to say *th* is just well-earned payback, but an appreciation of karma doesn't make pronouncing the awful sound any easier.

I overheard the adults discuss that a good way to learn *th* was by practicing "one, two, three." I dedicated a good week to that, playing with my red wax commandos while diligently reciting my threes:

"One, two, tree, one, two, tree,
one, two, shtree, one, two, thtree,
one, two, tree,
tree, three, thshtree, one, two, tree."

"Are you going insane?" My head jerked up and I saw Lina leaning on the doorframe. "I didn't think it'd happen so soon . . . bravo!" she smirked.

"I'm not going insane, stupid. I'm learning English. I'm practicing the *th* thingy."

Lina perched on the corner of the bed, the laughter beginning to squeak out of her. "Learning English, huh? Practicing the *th* thingy? [Of course, Tamara Alexandrovna's pet said it perfectly.] How's that working out for you?"

---

* My favorite example is *vzbzdnyt*, an archaic word that means "to back out of a situation due to fear." V-Z-B-Z-D-N—in a row! *I* can't pronounce it. My parents, lifelong Russian speakers, can't pronounce it. I'm not even sure if it's anatomically feasible for the human larynx to create the word.

"Not good. It sounds like I have a lisp. I've been working on it for a week, and I still can't move my tongue right."

"A week?" asked Lina. "One, two, three—that's what you've been doing for a week?! At that rate . . . You know what?" She grabbed a napkin. "I'm going to teach you two sentences right now."

Ai do-unt un-der-stand. Pleez speek slou-er, she scribbled phonetically.

"Get good at saying them: you'll be using them a lot."

"Wait, so if someone says something to me, then I should say 'I don't understand,' right?"

"Correct. Then you wait for their response, and then you say, 'Please speak slower.'"

"But what if I still don't understand them?"

Lina shrugged. "Just go back to the first sentence. Keep alternating. Eventually you'll get somewhere."

She ducked out of the room, giggling, and I returned to my troops. "Ai do-unt un-der-stand. Pleez speek slou-er. Ai do-unt un-der-stand. Pleez speek slou-er" softly echoed around the room.

* * *

February 7 finally gave us something to look forward to. It was Gera Zhislin's birthday, and our two families had a little celebration. Yura and Dad went to the balcony fridges and dug up the last sardine cans they had brought from Russia. Someone, Vicki I think, conspired with Agnes Binder to bake a cake. Gera arranged the Zhislins' suitcases in the middle of the room, stretched a bedsheet over them, and we had a dinner table. Afterward, the adults were sipping tea and I was curled up in the corner with my coloring book, when Yura's neighbor rapped on the door. "Samuel, they're looking for you."

"Who's looking for me?" Dad asked.

"HIAS. They're waiting on the phone," the neighbor replied, and Dad bolted downstairs, Gera's party frozen.

Dad returned shortly, looking disturbed. "We need to pack right now—we're going to Vienna."

"Vienna?!" Yura jumped up. "I thought they were sending us to Rome."

Dad shook his head. "No, *you're* staying. Everyone else is staying here for now. But we, just our family, are being moved to Vienna."

"Why?"

"They didn't say . . . They just said to be ready at six," Dad replied, and the birthday party ended, or rather transformed into a moving party, one that lasted long into the night.

As Dad was packing, he decided to make up a bit for the loss of the hundred schillings Mom and Lina had to pay at the bridge by selling Binder a tea service we had hauled out of Russia. It was an amalgamation of chipped cups, plates, and saucers that used to belong to my grandmother. Much of the service didn't survive our night on the border, but Dad had salvaged what he could and stored the pale green remnants, carefully wrapped in shawls and shirts, in a suitcase. During our emigration, and for many years afterward, it boggled my mind to think that of all the things to lug through the border, Mom and Dad had elected to bring a cumbersome and unnecessary tea service. It would certainly not make my list of survival items. What were they going to do, host a refugee social?

What I knew but didn't understand was that everyone in Russia, regardless of ethnicity or income, owned a tea service. Tea was mandatory; tea was the common denominator. From Siberia to Uzbekistan, no matter who came to your door or when they arrived, they were always offered a cup. A tea service was more than a set of cups and saucers: it represented a meal, which represented a home, which represented a life. As impractical as they were, those faded green teacups held the hope of once again having friends and entertaining guests, and it was hard for Dad to part with them. His one consolation was that the service went to the Binders, a family who had already demonstrated their abundant hospitality by welcoming some two hundred refugees to their remote mountain hotel.

HIAS's bus was punctual as always, and for once we were grateful for the early departure time. Everyone else was going to Italy but for some reason our family had been singled out, and we didn't want to share our situation with anyone, since that would only have amplified our worries. The Zhislins were an exception, of course. Although our two families had known each other for less than two months, we shared a trust forged out of our ordeal at the Soviet border. Their room at Binder's was a safe haven for us, and vice versa, and it was hard to say goodbye. The Binders and the Zhislins were the only ones who knew about our departure. Igor and Yura helped us load the suitcases in the predawn haze.

A LAYOVER IN PURGATORY

Vienna, Austria, February 1990

Thick fog enveloped the road during the ride to Vienna. A handful of families were already on the bus, and by the time we reached the capital we had swung by a few other hamlets and picked up more. No one spoke. It was as if the anxiety that is such an integral part of the refugee makeup just waited for us in Binder's parking lot, counting down the days until we would step through the lobby, ready to latch on to us again. At the outskirts of the city, the bus stopped at a shabby apartment building, the driver yelled out a name, and a family got off. Several stops later, we rumbled through a dilapidated neighborhood and idled in front of a large white house surrounded by a cast-iron fence, and the driver called out "Golinkins."

Dad and I dragged the bigger suitcases through a withered garden and into a shed, where they joined a colony of other luggage, then made our way to the front atrium, where our arrival was greeted with a loud chorus of groans, gurgles, coughs, and farts. The first floor was a single giant room diced up into little compartments by bedsheets draped over outstretched ropes. These curtains, together with the cacophony of bodily noises, gave off the look and smell of a makeshift field hospital. Shortly after our entrance, the sheets started pinching and rippling as their inhabitants shambled out to get a glimpse of the newcomers. The watchers were old, and none looked healthy. The house itself had seen better days. Judging by its vast size and location, it could've originally been a villa for a minor lordling or a wealthy merchant. But now the paint was peeling, empty niches with long-gone statues gaped from the walls, and high above, crusty wires for what must've once been an enormous chandelier curled down from the ceiling. The vestigial luxury, the decaying garden and decaying people, cast a melancholy gloom over the ex-villa.

"Welcome. I'm Nadya." A heavyset *babushka* with a thick braid wheezed up to us. "Your room is upstairs." The second floor consisted of a hallway with about five rooms off it. A modest kitchen occupied one end, a large communal bathroom took up the other, and across the hall from the bathroom was our new home. The attic room had a small window, a table in the middle, and a cot in each corner. Sloping ceilings slid down on us, making it impossible for the adults to stand anywhere but in the center. We tossed the bags under the table, and each person claimed a cot; Dad and I, "the men," shared, as usual.

Nadya, like those people we saw on the curtained-off first floor, was stationed in the villa on account of health problems. The curtain dwellers were migrants deemed too infirm for relocation to the crammed, filthy shelters of Rome (*two* families per room was the norm in Italy). Expediting them straight to America was also out of the question, since HIAS first needed to find sponsors who'd guarantee health care coverage. Joint's only option was to retain them in Austria, out of the way, yet close to a hospital. The old villa, Nadya explained, became Joint's purgatory, a place to keep her and those like her until something changed.

A chronic heart problem and shortage of breath didn't stop Nadya from serving as purgatory's unofficial manager. By the time the day was over, Mom and Dad were enrolled in Joint-run

English classes, Mom in a beginner's course, Dad in an intermediate one. Dad also signed up for what could be called Living in America 101 seminars, where volunteers culled from U.S. synagogues and Jewish centers lectured on topics such as credit cards, civil rights, customs, and résumés.

He continued to work for the Vienna engineering company that Peter had introduced him to. The firm wasn't comfortable with allowing him to take home schematics (and Dad didn't want to risk being caught with them either), so he kept the designs in his head, writing out calculations on napkins and newspaper margins at the villa, then returning to the plant. Mom's old profession also came in handy, and she could rarely walk down to the first-floor curtains without encountering someone waiting for a consult. She monitored vital signs and dressed wounds, and it seemed that just the notion of having an in-house doctor, even an ex-doctor, provided the villa residents with comfort.

But Lina hit the jackpot. As soon as we presented ourselves at Joint's Vienna office to receive our weekly food stipend, the beleaguered clerk caught Lina's English and immediately conscripted her to work for Joint.

"Isn't that illegal?" asked Lina. "I thought we can't work in—"

"Yes, you can," the clerk cut her off. "Joint's exempt from the ban on employment. Here's your bus pass. See you at six-thirty tomorrow."

"One moment, please." Lina turned to us and switched to Russian.

"What?" snapped Dad.

"I'm not sure I want to do it," Lina dithered. "I'm afraid."

"Afraid of what?"

"I'm afraid they're going to kill me!"

"They" were the five heavily armed gentlemen at Joint's guard post who looked as if they considered anything short of violence

163

to be a waste of their time. Rumor had it the guards were Iranian Jews, but years later when I asked a Joint member about it in one of my interviews, they refused to comment on the subject. What I *can* say is that the fierce, bearded men who loomed behind the desk looked like promising young jihadists plucked fresh from a terrorist boot camp. Joint's security measures were born out of a grim reality—Islamist terror cells were targeting Soviet Jews in Austria, and nothing shouted *Bomb me!* like a small foreign office staffed with American Jews. But Lina wasn't thinking about potential terrorists somewhere out in the ether; she was concerned with their comrades standing ten feet away from us.

"Let me see if I understand," said Dad. "You're afraid that the guards—Joint's own guards placed here to protect Joint workers—will kill you?"

The jihadists were studying us, pensively stroking their Uzis. Lina emitted a series of squeaks.

"You're taking the damn job," Dad sighed. "And try to remember that your idiocy reflects on us all."

"Take the job, dear," encouraged Mom, and suggested that Lina view this as a wonderful opportunity to gain valuable Western work experience, all while helping other refugees in need.

"Definitely take the job, *dear*," I piped in, and asked Mom if I could have Lina's cot in case she was detained. I was tired of bunking with Dad.

Joint's newest employee glared at me during the entire walk home.

After a few days of not being murdered, Lina came to enjoy her work. Joint operated several other purgatories similar to the one we resided in, and my sister spent her days zipping all over Vienna. She visited the elderly, consulted with doctors about treatments, assisted people with paperwork, translated for incoming refugees, delivered food, mail, and stipends, and on one occasion helped coordinate an effort to get a young Bosnian refugee a kidney transplant. She even charmed the guards . . . to a degree. They still stared at her with hopes of bloodshed, but once in a while one of them would throw what could be interpreted as a non-hostile grunt in her direction.

The one question Lina, or any of us, did *not* ask HIAS or Joint was why our family had been singled out and moved to the villa in the first place.

* * *

Life in the house was quiet. For the first time since those chaotic months leading up to emigration, things calmed down, and the initial gloom we felt upon entering the villa quickly dissipated into a welcome sense of routine.

The old folks took it upon themselves to maintain order in the house. The more mobile ones swept the floors and scoured the downstairs kitchen. Once March came around, they migrated outside, and soon enough the once-withered garden had orchids and alpine roses, attracting hordes of insects and little birds. Property lines didn't mean much to the *babushki,* who ventured into neighbors' yards to trim shrubs or water the plants. Others (including Grandma) entrenched themselves in the main foyer, monitoring the front door. Any resident entering or exiting the villa had to first run through a gauntlet of questions—*Where are you coming from? Where are you headed? What's in that bag?*— the standard, annoying old-people interrogations we were used to back home. These daily inquisitions were nothing compared with what befell strangers. Any outsider attempting to enter the villa found himself unceremoniously detained and prodded by a throng of old women until someone provided a reason (a *plau-*

sible reason) for his intrusion. One spring afternoon, Mom, Lina, and I had to rescue a very confused and incapacitated Peter from being ruffled and poked at in a dusty corner of the downstairs atrium.

"Why," the baron panted, once extricated to the safety of our room in the attic. "Why are your elderly women so angry?"

"They're not angry," Mom explained, as she helped Peter smooth out his suit. "They're doing their job, making sure strange people don't enter the house. It's part of their nature, to protect."

A familiar image of grim, frozen Russia is the *babushka,* the old woman, hunched and determined, head wrapped in a scarf. Her gnarled face stares out from old Ellis Island photographs and modern cable specials, and never fails to elicit *awww*s from concerned Westerners who'd love nothing more than to hug poor, helpless Granny and tell her that everything's going to be all right. That is misguided, and potentially hazardous. Women who had survived long enough to become grandmothers by the 1980s were Russia's rocks. Their generation had a hard life, even by the unforgiving standards of Mother Russia. Forged from the crucible of wars, famines, and purges, the *babushki* had witnessed entire populations of husbands and sons vanish into the grave. These women were instilled with a fierce matriarchal instinct, the notion that they were responsible for the welfare of all society, not just their kin, and underneath their kerchiefs the *babushki* watched, and listened, and remembered, and commanded.

Peter may have found some comfort in knowing he wasn't the only Westerner to learn who was truly in charge in Mother Russia. Paul Christensen, my Boston College professor who traveled to the USSR in 1989 to research post-*glasnost* labor movements for his doctoral dissertation, never forgot his first meeting with a *babushka.* Christensen recalled landing in Moscow, dropping off his bags, and strolling to the subway to explore the Evil

Empire. Moscow's cavernous metros are deep underground (they were designed to double as fallout shelters) and accessible by immense escalators, so long that Christensen's ears popped on the way down. Stationed at the bottom of each escalator was a *babushka* with a bullhorn, there to ensure everyone acted like a decent Soviet citizen. Christensen had just hopped onto the platform when: "Young man! Yes, you, young man, come here!" the bullhorn blared at him.

For a few long moments, Christensen squirmed as the *babushka* stared, twitching her lips as if she'd just swallowed something vile and Christensen was to blame. The Russian commuters coasted by like wayward students slinking past a hall monitor. Two trains screeched up to the platform, brakes echoing off marble walls festooned with mosaics of peasants farming and Lenin preaching to attentive workers. Unwelcome images of half-starved prisoners hacking at frozen boulders in Siberia began to flicker through Christensen's mind when the *babushka* finally broke the silence.

"Young man: the streets are cold and windy. Where is your hat?"

Christensen gazed around at the sea of fur bobbing past him. He was the only one with a bare head. "My hat is . . . at home?" he said, half asking the woman.

"Well. Turn around, go back, and get it," snapped the *babushka*, blocking Christensen's path into the station, and leaving him with few options. "Faster, young man," the bullhorn echoed up the escalator shaft, "before you get sick!" and Christensen found himself running. Up to the street he ran, and to the nearest store to purchase a hat, one that remained firmly on his head for the duration of his stay.

Paul Christensen was a smart man, a PhD candidate, and it did not take him long to absorb a crucial lesson of Soviet survival: never cross a *babushka*.

EVA

Vienna, Austria, February 1990

The first time I heard the rumor about the house with the red door was the day after my family had been moved to the old villa, when Nadya caught me sneaking outside in just a sweater. "Go to the house on Schüttelstrasse, the house with the red door," the stolid caretaker told my parents after corralling me indoors. "It's where people receive free clothing."

"I thought the Joint guy was making some sort of American joke when he said all you have to do is ring the doorbell and this crazy woman named Eva will give you whatever you need," said Nadya's husband, Vova, in the awed voice of the converted. "But I swear it's true." Mom and Dad looked skeptical. Nadya, who appeared used to this response, waddled up to the nearest first-floor curtain.

"See?" She plucked at a European sweater triumphantly worn by a shriveled old man. The geezer sat up, spitting out a glob of phlegm. "And these shoes, and that coat." Nadya moved down the row. "Where else would they get them from? All from Eva, and she has children's stuff, too!" The grinning geriatric models, together with the prospect of a warm Western coat for me, con-vinced Mom it was worth at least a look.

Suspicion was an appropriate reaction from people bred in the

168

Soviet culture of survival. To be sure, families and close friends looked out for one another, but this was different. "Take," not "give," was king in the land of constant deficits, so the idea of a person freely giving out perfectly good clothes seemed . . . unnatural. But the temptation was too strong, and we set out to find Madame Eva's on a frigid February afternoon after my parents' English classes and Lina's workday with Joint. We walked along the Danube Canal, in the older part of the city, on a path bordered by stone, the concrete barrier of the canal to our right and rows of stone houses on the left. The walk was long, around a half-hour. The wind blew mercilessly. Vienna's wind is impulsive and brutal. It comes from the east, gathers strength over the Hungarian Plain, then rips through the city, flaring up then dying down or changing direction in an instant, pushing, piercing. *A woman who gives out free clothes.* Our doubts were strong; the gusts were stronger.

I was desperate to be warm. Life in the city was less sedentary than at Binder's in Nondorf. It required walking, which I used to love—before my rabbit fur coat had disintegrated. My only other jacket was too small, and I was constantly contorting my hands into the tiny pockets that hovered around my rib cage. It was a purely symbolic gesture, anyway, since the jacket was designed for light autumn strolls, not life in the February wind tunnels of Vienna.

I didn't want toys, or food, or a home, or anything like that: I wanted to walk outside without shivering. That was everything. Madame Eva's house, the house full of clothes, beckoned. The closer we got, the stronger the urges rang, and the more I couldn't stop myself from hoping. *Get warm, get warm, walk around, be warm, go anywhere, play outside, be warm.* I shoved the thoughts aside and concentrated on counting the street numbers passing by in the twilight.

*

The house blended in with the rest of the massive stone façades. A huge metal gate opened into a drafty tunnel leading away from the canal. On one side of the tunnel, recessed into the concrete and barely visible in the fading light, was the door. Thick layers of maroon paint covered all but a small yellowing sign: EVA. We shuffled our feet in front of the sign, wondering how exactly individuals asking for free clothes should introduce themselves. I tried hiding in my usual spot behind Dad's leg, but I was almost ten and couldn't quite pull it off.

"What if it's the wrong house?" Mom whispered.

"I don't know," Dad said.

"What if we need documents?"

"I don't know."

"Maybe they make you sign a paper saying you'll pay them."

Dad rang the doorbell and the questions died down.

A young woman peeked out and escorted us into a small vestibule. She spoke in a calm stream of English. "They will help us shortly," Dad said. "They are helping another family right now, and they only work with one family at a time." I craned my neck, listening for what the other family sounded like, but heard nothing except the rustle of Mom's renewed questions.

After a few minutes, the young woman led us past several doors, through a modest kitchen, and into an enormous wooden room. Blouses, pants, shirts, sweaters swung from racks and huddled together on the floor. Several more women, all young, thin, and blond, guided Mom and Lina to different sections of the room. I tagged along with Dad and watched him try on black shoes to replace his worn-out ones. Mom and Lina were sorting through blouses, with attendants advising them on sizes and styles. The girls smoothly navigated the piles of clothing with a sincere desire to find exactly what their "customers" wanted. It felt like shopping in a store but without a register waiting by the exit.

Dad found shoes he liked, carefully tucked the old ones under his arm, and was walking around getting acquainted with the new pair when suddenly I felt someone touch my shoulder. It was a different woman, very young, no more than seventeen. She pointed to a door recessed in the far corner, approached it, and waited, her face calm and expressionless. Mom was busy and Dad didn't appear concerned, and so I followed her into the small room on the other side.

I froze and stared at the pile of children's jackets. A thrill rushed over me, washing away everything else from my mind. Here it was; here was *warmth*. I rifled through the heap, searching, grasping, trying one on, then the next, and then I found it: a padded black bomber jacket with golden zippers that flashed down the wool lining and across two outside pockets. I scrambled out of the pile. In front of me was a window that faced the canal. It was already dark outside and the unlit water transformed the glass into an enormous jet-black mirror. I took in my jacket, marveling at the fit and its absolute, undeniable coolness. The left arm had a tiny zippered pocket on the elbow. I had no idea what it was for or what I would put in it, but I loved it, because somehow it was that extra zipper that made everything authentic, made me believe that I was cool and tough, like a real pilot. The wind shifted direction, flinging itself against the windowpane. Listening to it, I squeezed the chest and arms of my jacket and knew that warmth was all around me, inside and out.

Suddenly I was aware of the girl behind me, her image captured in the blackness of the window. Her hands were resting at her sides, her blond hair falling on her black blouse. She was smiling. She had one of those faces that was subtly lit by a smile. Panic poured over me, bringing me back to my senses. *Is she laughing at me? People don't give out clothes. What if she takes the jacket away?* I shrank inward, spun around, and shot her a glance full of hatred. I wasn't going to let some girl amuse herself by staring at a refugee kid dancing around like a crazed marionette. I reverted to what I was: a migrant, a thing in a room full of things.

The smile vanished. For a split second she looked surprised, and then her face cleared, assuming the same emotionless mask she had worn before. I followed her out to the main room, jacket zipped all the way up, fists clenched, face twisted into the meanest, nastiest grimace I could assemble. Mom crouched down, hugging me and feeling my jacket. I begged her to leave. I told her I had a headache.

A BLEAK, MAN-MADE HORIZON

Oberösterreich (Upper Austria), April 1990

Upstream from Vienna, the Danube takes a sharp westward turn, meanders through the vineyards of Lower Austria, flows past Dürnstein Castle, where Richard the Lionheart was held captive on his way back from the Crusades, and winds around the industrial city of Linz before heading up to its source in the Black Forest in Germany. Right near Linz, where the water marks the boundary between the provinces of Upper and Lower Austria, the E55 Autobahn runs across the river, offering two options to the passing tourist. If the traveler remains on the Danube's north bank, he will soon hit a small market town called Mauthausen; if he crosses the river, he will arrive at place called Sankt Florian. Both towns contain eponymous, albeit very different landmarks. Mauthausen houses the Mauthausen-Gusen complex, once a dreaded concentration camp, today a monument to Nazi atrocities, preserved for the world, and Austria, to remember. Sankt Florian is home to the famed St. Florian's priory, devoted to the patron saint of firefighters.

It was during a sunny April Saturday on the E55 Autobahn that Peter offered Dad a choice: visit Mauthausen or Sankt Florian. Dad chose the camp. My father's always been eerily drawn to the Nazis. Maybe it was because his earliest memories were of escaping the German invasion of the Ukraine and spending the next several years huddling in a hole (literally) in the Ural Mountains, precisely to escape winding up in such a place.* A similar fascination seemed to hold sway over Peter, who had set a course for Mauthausen long before asking Dad's opinion.

We veered off the highway and drove past a small town with little houses with red roofs that looked just like the hundreds of other towns nestled within the valleys of Lower Austria. The road swished around a bend, left the cottages behind, cut across a patch of forest, and ambled through a field, terminating in front of a series of elongated buildings separated from the field by a dull gray wall that stretched far to the left and right like a bleak, man-made horizon. There was no beauty to the endless rectangle, only functional, harsh geometry, and the crudeness of it jarred the eye. It had neither the opulence of Vienna nor the quaintness of the countryside, and one was tempted to think that the ugly gray compound was misplaced, meant perhaps to be a communal apartment complex in Poland, or an industrial warehouse in Vladivostok, not a concentration camp in the sleepy hills of Oberösterreich. But Mauthausen *was* in Austria; it had been constructed, staffed, and operated by Austrians, and neither the magic of the countryside nor the majesty of Vienna could budge it from its home.

I didn't require the customary briefings given by rabbis and schoolteachers to children visiting the National Holocaust Museum or viewing *Schindler's List*. I didn't need to travel to

---

* Dad and his family were evacuated to Nizhny Tagil and put up in a *zemlyanka* ("earth thingy" in Russian)—dig a hole large enough for cots and a fire pit, throw earth and tarps over the hole (for camouflage in case of air raids), leave an opening for entry and a smaller one for smoke ventilation, and you're home.

Austria to walk through a Nazi killing ground; I'd played in one every day back in Kharkov. The war was the War, not just to doddering old soldiers, but to my parents, my neighbors, to the crumbling mortar holes on our balcony wall and monuments to the fallen throughout the city. Every family, Russian and Jewish, had at least one ghost relative who either perished or vanished in the War (Uncle Yasha was mine; he vanished). Neither I nor any other child in the Ukraine could escape learning about the Nazis.

I didn't feel much. It was a rather nondescript place, and I really remember only the Stairs of Death and the gas chamber. Mauthausen was initially slated to be a labor camp: "the Stairs of Death" was the name given to a steep, rail-less staircase embedded into the stone quarry deep inside the complex. The inmates were forced to haul giant slabs of rock up the 186 stairs, and every day malnourished bodies plummeted to the bottom. That was part of the quarry's design, harnessing gravity to weed out the exhausted.

As the war unfolded, Mauthausen's mission shifted from death by labor to a purer, more streamlined extermination. The camp's gas chamber was a large, tiled room, outfitted much like old showers in high school gyms. The walls were covered with little slashes haphazardly scattered throughout the room. At first I thought the marks were a natural part of the material, but upon closer examination I realized they were grooves, hundreds of tiny grooves etched deep into the dirty yellow tile. I pointed them out to Dad, who consulted a nearby curator and then explained that the grooves had not been there when the place was built. They were added later, by the dead, who had clawed at solid tile with their fingernails, leaving their last and only mark on Mauthausen. I traced the nearest groove with my finger, trying to estimate how many emaciated hands it took to carve it. After a while I decided it was better to pretend that the grooves had been there in the beginning, artistically added by the Nazis.

We walked out of the grayness and back to the jeep, welcomed by the blinding sunshine and the bright green field. Peter, who had not entered the compound, looked more tense than normal. Something in his eyes filled me with dread. I was fine with Mauthausen. The dead didn't bother me, especially not dead Jews, but looking at Peter I suddenly sensed it, the feeling of being stuck in a movable trap that goes wherever you do. Peter was a demigod—he did what he wanted, went where he wanted, didn't hide or apologize, and wasn't afraid, not even of policemen. Yet there it was, like an echo or a nasty memory, the same thing that lived in our old apartment, in Oleg's mirror, in the hallways of Kharkov's School Number Three. I feared it above everything else, feared it so much I never mentioned it to Dad or anyone, and to meet it again in Austria, especially in Peter, was unsettling.

"Do you think it is possible for the Jewish people to ever forgive the Austrian people?" Peter asked Dad as the concrete horizon dwindled behind us. Mom was quiet and Lina was crying; Dad made soothing English noises and I said nothing. I respected Peter's incredible knowledge, which was why his question struck me as thoroughly dumb. From the day my family came to Nondorf I could walk out of a room without being afraid, which was unlike anything I'd experienced before. I'd take Austrians over Russians and Ukrainians any day. We were right across the Danube from Sankt Florian and Peter asserted we still had time for a quick tour, but my parents insisted on returning to the villa. I assumed Peter would simply veto the adults like he always did, but this one time the baron yielded and we began the quiet ride back to Vienna. The adults were silent for their own reasons. I sulked because I wanted to go with Peter to his favorite monastery, and eventually I would get a chance to do so, but not for another seventeen years.

Late that evening, after Lina and Grandma were asleep, as I lay on the cot sandwiched between my father's back and the pillow, I overheard Dad whisper to Mom about Peter. Peter's father was a mid-level Nazi officer who was captured by the Allies at the end of the war and spared the noose only in deference to his noble bloodline. The man was quietly tossed in prison, which left Peter, who was still a boy, in the care of his grandfather. The grandfather (the one who had been the Austro-Hungarian ambassador to the United States) reared Peter to be a Western-minded, democratic thinker. By the time Peter's father had served out his prison term and met his teenage son, the two were worse than strangers. *"Vorwærts in Treu und Wahrheit"* ("Forward, Faithful, and True") read the motto emblazoned on the family coat-of-arms, and the old baron did not disappoint. Unlike many ex-Nazis who repudiated their past (or at least had the decency to keep quiet about it), Peter's father remained staunchly loyal to the Führer. He was unrepentant, a man defeated but not deterred, and he loathed his son with bitterness at once ideological and personal. Peter did not lie when he introduced himself as a forester—a forester he was, living with his father in service of his estate, tending the thousands of acres of pine trees that were their hereditary source of income.

Peter attempted to carve out an identity of his own. The man started a family, which left him with two children whom he adored. He defended a doctorate degree in forestry, wrote a thesis on the heritage of local castles, dug into the history of his ancestors and Niederösterreich, grasping for something redeeming about his family and homeland. He collected antiques, traveling to all those exotic locales he told my dad about . . . but no matter where he turned, he still felt his father's past. When Peter heard about the Soviet Jews at nearby Binder's he decided to drive over and take a look. Doubtless he was intrigued by the fire sale of antiques, but why he spent so much time with my family, we aren't sure. Maybe he intended to pay back some Jews for his father, or maybe he wanted to pay back his father by helping some Jews. Perhaps he just wished to enjoy a few day trips with people who wouldn't judge him. It could've been any of those, or all, or none; Peter was never an easy man to read. In any case, a bond formed between us and for one reason or another, the baron-forester kept returning to our room.

New York, N.Y., May 1990

At times, Amir Shaviv, the Joint worker who had met Rabbi Adolf Shayevich in Romania, felt as if the flurry of activity at Joint's Manhattan headquarters could rival that of the New York Stock Exchange. International phone lines from the Vienna and Rome field bureaus rang nonstop, fund-raisers cajoled sponsors and benefactors, and interns scurried between offices as the creaking of fax machines noisily announced new problems and fresh developments. There were plenty of both. Shaviv's premonitions from his 1988 trip to Bucharest had materialized into reality: Gorbachev's reforms were rapidly gaining momentum, and Jews were fleeing Eastern Europe in droves. By the late spring of 1990, the wave of refugees had broken through.

Unlike the émigrés of the 1970s who had embarked for America with relatives and addresses in mind, many of the current migrants had neither. They had left because they felt compelled to leave, and they had no fixed destination other than a resounding "not the USSR." They knew to come to Vienna, and so to Vienna they came, by the trainload, by the hour, bringing with them an explosion of questions. HIAS was overseeing the resettlement process, but the sustenance of displaced Jews on foreign soil was Joint's responsibility (and has been since its inception in 1914, when the group began aiding impoverished Jews in the Ottoman Empire). And since Joint operated the camps, it fell to them to deal with the ground issues. Who's supplying the food? What about transportation, medicine, beds? How do we process them? Refugees come with bags, not CVs. Many (including my family) didn't even possess birth certificates, for those had been seized and burned at the Soviet border. So who is a criminal? Who is a *real* criminal, not someone saddled with bogus charges such as "participation in subversive Zionist machinations"? Who is a danger to himself? To others? Who knows?

All this demanded a rapid escalation of capital and personnel, and there was no time for a fund-raising campaign. Joint reacted by tapping into its budget, diverting all resources and incurring what would eventually become a $19 million deficit, which is an astounding number for an institution that relies on public donations rather than a fixed stipend.

* * *

I first learned of this when I sat down with Amir Shaviv in New York in 2006. On my way to the interview, I couldn't help but note certain similarities between Joint's U.S. headquarters and its high-security Vienna bureau, to which my family had gone for stipends during our emigration. Both places were difficult to find: the Vienna office had been completely unmarked, and although the New York headquarters was in a Manhattan skyscraper, I was unable to locate a physical address until Shaviv provided me with one two days prior to our meeting. Downstairs, the lobby was similar to that of many skyscrapers, with a security desk, visitor passes, and turnstiles, but once I stepped out of the elevator onto Joint's floor I was immediately faced with the familiar bulletproof glass and buzz-door. The one welcome difference was the elderly secretary behind the glass, who was a far cry from the grim, Uzi-toting guards of Vienna. I even managed to elicit a smile out of her, and if Granny was packing heat, at least it wasn't overt.

By the time I interviewed Shaviv, I had already been involved with several fund-raising efforts for student organizations at Boston College, as well as a community revitalization group in New Jersey. Admittedly, none of those budgets ranged anywhere near eight digits, and it was hard for me to absorb the multimillion-dollar figure Shaviv threw out. Put simply, I couldn't comprehend taking an operation, spending all of its funds, and then spending $19 million *more*.

"I may be thinking on a provincial level, but that seems like an awful lot of money," I said.

"It was," Shaviv replied. "It certainly was."

"Didn't that decimate you? You're a nonprofit, you rely on donations, you have to answer to board members and stakeholders. How did you inform the trustees and convince the donors?"

The tall, beefy man leaned back in his chair, eyes scanning the room. Shaviv's office displayed an austere functionality, which matched its occupant's demeanor. It was clean and uncluttered, without all the extraneous coffee mugs and paperweights, the only exception being a smattering of unframed photographs tucked about the room. I noticed Shaviv's eyes lingering over the photos, and it was here that my pre-interview Wikipedia-ing paid off. Next to the printer I recognized an off-centered shot of enormous camps in Sarajevo; Joint was there before the camera crews had arrived. Peeking out from behind a stack of forms was Operation Solomon, a massive airlift of fourteen thousand Jews from Ethiopia to Israel in the wake of a civil war. Moses brought his people through the Red Sea; Joint flew them over it. There were other scenes: the Middle East, Africa, Latin America, tanks and camps, black-and-white and color, natural disasters and disasters man-made. Post-Soviet deployments were there, too, and I gazed upon volunteers triaging survivors in Darfur, and the devastation of the 2004 South Asian tsunami, and more locales I couldn't pinpoint.

Shaviv crossed one leg over the other, European style. His face assumed the expression of a college professor feeding a rather obvious answer to an obtuse freshman. "The role of Joint is to help overseas Jews in need. That is our mission, the *reason* for our existence. What was the point of having money sit in the bank when it was needed immediately? There were Jews in need, massive amounts of them, so the pressing question was, 'Let's help them now, and we'll worry about the budget afterward.' And that is what we did, Lev. That is what we did."

I'm not a fan of cities—in fact, I hate them—but I had an hour to kill before the next bus to Jersey and decided to walk for a bit. I wandered around Times Square and Rockefeller Center, glancing at landmarks and constantly pausing to wait for tourists snapping photos. An odd feeling gripped my chest, swelling and ebbing as I walked. It wasn't an anxious or bad sensation, just new and uncomfortable, something that shouldn't be there, and walking had always helped me deal with strangeness. I swung by the Empire State Building, edged around Central Park, reviewing Shaviv's remarks, thinking of follow-up questions to e-mail him, transcribing the interview in my head. Eventually the courtesy wore off, and I started walking through tourist photos like the New Yorkers do. I missed the afternoon bus and the evening ones as well, and it wasn't until I was on the late bus on the New Jersey Turnpike that it hit me that for the first time in my life I was proud of being a Jew.

THE BOSNIANS DON'T COME
OUT AT NIGHT

Vienna, Austria, May 1990

One sweaty May evening, a strange new family appeared at the villa. They were accompanied by the blue-blazered Mr. Prager, the human rights worker we knew from the train station when my family first came to Austria. It was a large family, with a father, a mother, and four or five children. The father wore a long robe, and all of the women had their heads wrapped in scarves. It was hard to catch their tongue, since they spoke little and in whispers, but the snippets we overheard sounded like nothing Slavic. Consensus was that they were Muslims who fled Yugoslavia because their lives had been threatened by Serbian Orthodox militias. Dad guessed they were Bosnian, but they could have been from Croatia, or Serbia, or somewhere else in the Balkans—there was plenty of carnage to go around. One thing was clear, though: wherever they had come from, they must've left in a hell of a hurry, because not one of the people huddled together in the downstairs atrium carried a suitcase, or a sack, or a bag, or anything.

I don't know how Joint found them or how they found Joint, because Mr. Prager wouldn't address questions from the agitated old folks until one adamant man shouted, "Why are you dealing with these Muslims?!"

"Joint aids refugees, and not just Jewish ones," Mr. Prager

snapped back. "This family *will* be living upstairs, and they *will* be left alone. May I remind everyone that you're living in Austria under a *refugee status,* which would be seriously jeopardized by any cross-cultural incidents." With that, he ushered the Bosnians to an upstairs room down the hall from us, gave Dad a nod, and left the villa.

The children and their father disappeared inside. The mother, together with her eldest daughter, sat on the hallway floor, leaning against the hard white plaster, and there the two of them remained for the evening. After some deliberation, Mom and Dad inventoried our sleeping supplies, and Dad pulled me aside. "I want you to give these to the women." He pointed to a pillow and three wool blankets.

"Why don't *you* do it?" I was habitually shy around strangers; emigration didn't change that.

"Please stop complaining," Dad said. "Your mom and I already had to deal with Lina over giving these up. You're the least threatening one of us." Dad forestalled any further protests by piling the blankets and pillow into my arms, and in short order I was hauling the bundle down the hallway. "Go."

The women didn't move at all. I peered at them from around the bundle until my arms grew tired, then set down the bedclothes, crouching in front of the mother. *These—you—to sleep, these— you—to sleep,* I explained with lots of pointing. She didn't glance at me. She just kept staring at the floor, as if that one patch of old linoleum contained something so mesmerizing, so incredibly beautiful that she couldn't look away. I knew I should leave, but nosiness got the better of me and I got down on my knees and craned my head to intercept her gaze. The scarf wound around her face set off her features in an ivory oval. Her eyes were big and dark brown, slightly elongated, pretty, and dead. Whatever she saw when she last used them must've been awful. Her vacant stare chased away my curiosity, and I slowly backed down the hallway, leaving her with a few apologetic gestures to cement that the bedding was hers to keep.

"Everything all right?" Dad asked.

"It was fine," I lied.

"Did they take the blankets?"

"I think so. They didn't say anything about giving them back."

"Good," Dad summed up. "You did good."

Several more Bosnians arrived the next morning. The young men were visibly less shaken and more defensive, and shot challenging looks about them, ready to fight. They also found shelter in the upstairs corridor, and our two groups, ex–Soviet Jews and ex–Yugoslav Muslims, wound up being housemates for a few weeks. I'm not sure who first took to posting men in the hallway while the women and children were using the communal shower, but as soon as one group began the practice, the other followed suit. In time, an unspoken routine was established in which we and the two other upstairs Jewish families cooked in the evening, while the Bosnians cooked in the morning (all the Bosnians, including the young men, were reluctant to leave their rooms after nightfall). Otherwise we barely interacted, but as the Joint worker pointed out, cross-cultural incidents were greatly undesirable, and so no cross-cultural incidents took place. We didn't hold hands and dance around in a circle; we didn't negotiate a solution to the Middle East crisis. We walked in separately and we walked out separately and we only caught each other in glimpses in the hallways, but we felt safe.

Around mid-June, HIAS informed us they were close to finalizing negotiations with a U.S. community that had offered to sponsor us. The worker said that we were to be relocated to one more place before flying out to the States, and once again we woke in the pre-dawn hours to meet HIAS's van. By this point packing and moving suitcases was so efficient that we were loaded in a flash, and since we were running a few minutes ahead of schedule, Dad asked the driver to wait and hustled upstairs to make sure nothing had been forgotten.

As he scanned the empty attic room in the dim morning light, Dad felt a hesitant touch on his shoulder. He spun around and saw the Bosnian woman we gave the blankets to standing in the hallway. In her hand was a tiny cloth bag.

The woman signed, alternatively pointing at Dad and the bag, which Dad cautiously opened. Inside was a handful of hard, glossy seeds.

Many Bosnians displaced by the Yugoslav Wars had been subsistence farmers who lived off what they could grow on the land. This family, whose sudden flight precluded them from packing even basic supplies, must've grabbed their most portable, vital possession: seeds for future crops. The small, oval flecks were their version of a tea service, hope for someday replanting their lives in a newer, more fertile land.

Thank you, I can't. Dad smiled and shook his head. My father explained that he didn't know how to farm and didn't want the seeds to go to waste. I don't know how much he got across, since he used only gestures, and the van driver started honking. Dad cinched the bag shut, returned it to the woman, and trotted downstairs, and that was the last we saw of the Bosnians.

*   *   *

Our last stop before being shipped out to America was a tiny, one-room apartment somewhere in Vienna. We were there only a few days; I have no idea why they even bothered moving us in the first place, and I remember little of it, not even where it was. The suitcases remained packed in "battle readiness," as Dad called it, and there was nothing to do but wait for the phone call and wonder where we would be going.

On the third or fourth night in the apartment, a young HIAS worker swung by to tell us that our destination in America was a town called Lafayette. Suddenly, an idea hit me, and while Mom, Dad, and Grandma were intoning the name of our mysterious new home, I asked Lina to see if the worker could lend me an atlas. The tiny Soviet version I brought out of Russia wasn't very helpful. It had detailed maps of Eastern Europe, Central Asia, and Vietnam, but only one page dedicated to the entire New World. According to it, everything in America was colored pink, and the country had three cities called New York, Philadelphia, and San Francisco, a cluster of impressive lakes in the north, and a sad pink wasteland everywhere else. Lina translated, and much to my joy the worker retrieved a giant American atlas with two pages per each state from his van. ("Leave it in the room when you're done . . . or whatever," the man said. "There are so many refugees pouring in, I'm not going to be stateside anytime soon.") I retired to the apartment's closet, which I had claimed as my room, opened the atlas, and settled down on the blankets, only to jump up a minute later.

"I found it! Louisiana! Lafayette in Lou-i-si-ana!" I screamed, announcing our new home to the apartment building and nearby pedestrians.

Dad was so impressed he didn't even yell when I slammed the book onto the table. Mom and Grandma began discussing the best ways to deal with the balmy southern weather. Dad tried to recall if any of the books he'd read had mentioned the state, and Lina was already scouring the surroundings for universities. It was my finest hour, better even than helping Dad haul suitcases at the *tamozhnya*. Everyone else had been putzing around wasting time while I, I delivered our latitude and longitude, in a minute flat! "Remember, *I* found it," I told Lina for the tenth time.

Self-adoration kept me aloft for a good half-hour before doubt seeped in. A fat atlas with many pages, and I just happened to flip to the correct spot? It seemed too easy, and I reclaimed the book from Lina.

"I found Lafayette . . . again. There's another one in Tennessee," I announced, quietly this time.

The apartment was silenced. "Are you joking?" asked Lina. "How can there be two?"

There couldn't be two . . . at least not in Russia. Each town had its own name, and if someone said he was from L'vov, or Dnepropetrovsk, or Sevastopol, then that's where he was from and there was never a need to ask "Which one?" It was a ludicrous concept; it'd be like having the same word for a monkey and a giraffe. Yet there it was, right at the top of that stupid, long state, snatching away my triumph.

I took advantage of the confusion to grab the atlas and Comrade Bear and slink away to the fourth-floor landing, where I could concentrate and began with Alabama. The first ten or so states were combed through in expeditious fashion. By the time I reached Massachusetts the sun had set, leaving me to deal with the flickering yellow lightbulb over the landing. Pennsylvania was both big and dense, which necessitated a short break for tea, especially after big, dense Ohio. Everything post-Utah was a slow trudge, since the town names started jumping around the pages, but by that point I was committed. After a total of four hours, Comrade Bear and I staggered back into the room.

"What the hell were you doing?" barked Dad.

"Reading." I held up the atlas.

"You read an atlas?" smirked Lina.

"Are we going to Louisiana or Tennessee?" asked Grandma, as if the book somehow showed a flashing GOLINKINS LAND HERE sign over one of the towns.

"I don't know. My head hurts. I'm going to bed. Good night." I went to my room in the closet, wrapped myself in blankets, and tried to shut out the world. They were everywhere. I found them in the mountains, I found them on the plains, I found them tucked into little forgotten corners. Ohio had *two*—in the same state! *How do these people function?* My head was pounding, pounding, pounding, my eyes were watering and I hoped they wouldn't fall out, and I silently cursed the Americans, who couldn't even be bothered to come up with a new town name.

There were seventeen Lafayettes in the continental United States.

A SIMPLE REQUEST

Vienna, Austria, June 1990

We saved seeing Peter until the very end, when HIAS warned Dad that our departure was imminent. The baron came to the apartment the next evening. The goodbye was similar to the ones the adults had exchanged with friends and family back in Russia: a true goodbye, indefinite and lasting, where you say "farewell" because you don't know when, if ever, you will see the person again. And after six months of floating through towns and villages, it felt wonderfully painful to say goodbye to someone. When first we became refugees it seemed that an exotic parade of human rights workers and clerks, border guards, Austrians, and policemen was marching by our lives. But after enough days of being stamped and processed, honked at and waved along, it began to feel like *we* were the ones trapped in some strange, wispy procession drifting by the lives of normal people. It was good to have Peter, to know that our path had intertwined with at least one person who would miss us, one person who was anchored in the world.

For several minutes the adults sat on crammed cots, sipping cheap Austrian tea Mom had brewed in a borrowed teapot. Dad was saying something to Peter, who replied with a series of quiet "no"s. "What's going on?" I poked Lina.

"Mom and Dad really want to have a picture of Peter or with him. Dad keeps asking if we can go somewhere to take one before we leave."

"And?"

"And he refuses." Lina listened, then translated some more. "He says that we don't need a picture of him . . . that he hates being in pictures, he doesn't even *have* any of himself, and that if we want to remember him then we'll do so in our minds, and we won't need a photograph . . . and if we don't remember in our minds, then . . . then a picture would be useless anyway. What a strange man, huh?"

Eventually Dad gave up and the conversation shifted to meaningless goodbye chatter.

We went downstairs and walked Peter out. Peter didn't do hugs, so he just shook our hands. He gave Mom a forlorn smile and said something in English, and then, with a sharp pivot, strode across the street to the jeep. We barely caught a glimpse of him, green jacket, red hair, and it seemed that by the time we heard him start the engine he was already gone. He had left us as he had met us, of his own volition and on his own terms, a baron and a forester, a man deeply in love with and deeply ashamed of his nation, a conflicted and inexplicable man whose complexity was as profound as his kindness.

"What did he say to me?" asked Mom.

"He said there are some good things about Austria, and he hopes you won't forget them," Dad said, after a pause. "I still don't understand why he wouldn't take a picture: he's done so much for us, and it was such a simple request."

The adults returned upstairs and I sat down on the outside steps. I realized that I was going to miss Vienna, which was passing strange because I'd never missed a place before. Estonia was lovely, with its unkempt dunes and queer twilight, but the Estonians were so protective of their little country that it was obvious that guests were welcome, but only as guests. Even I understood that. Nondorf, too, had its charms. I loved the castles and the gray-blue mountains, but we were reminded that we were different at every turn. Vienna, though, Vienna was so damn beautiful it didn't matter what you were or what language you spoke. There were churches, old façades, public gardens, and fountains, none of which charged admission. Twice, Dad and I snuck into the city's Kunsthistorisches art museum, when attendance was slow and the guards looked the other way. It was so easy to get lost in the beauty; no one pays attention to your clothes when you're standing next to a van Eyck.

I was a little upset, too, upset with my family because I didn't like photographs either and felt cornered along with Peter. I wished Dad hadn't pressured him. Evening fell, the late buses rumbled by, and for a long time I sat on the steps, clenching my jaw, staring at the city and at the empty spot where the Mercedes had been parked. I desperately wanted to remember him; I wanted to prove to Dad that Peter was right, that you didn't need a picture to trap someone's image, that you only have to want to remember him and that would be enough.

* * *

East Windsor, N.J., June 2007

"Ah, so, you are returning to Austria." The casual, accented voice crackled through the receiver. Seventeen years had passed before I contacted Peter, telling him that I was planning a trip to Austria and asking if he would mind meeting with me. "Yes, you can come," he acceded. "Telephone me when you purchase your tickets." I informed three of my friends, Jeff, Steve, and Kyle, that I was traveling to Europe and making a sojourn to a castle to stay with a baron; they graciously offered to come along.

Peter met us on the hilltop outside the castle. I was nervous about seeing the man after a very long hiatus, especially with three strangers in tow, but Peter calmly shook everyone's hands and began to supervise the unloading.

My friends disappeared inside, and I approached the baron. "How are you?"

"Well, my father died shortly after your family left Austria, and now I am in charge. I am doing good," he replied.

I smiled. "My dad wanted me to become a doctor but I said no, and I'm writing a book instead. I am also doing good."

"Ah yes, that is so. I have done a lot of remodeling—come inside."

Having thus caught up on the past seventeen years, I followed Peter through the giant oak doorway.

The first thing we ran into was Kyle, frozen in the center of the courtyard. My normally impassive friend gaped at me. "I don't think you described this . . . place adequately."

I took a long look around. No one could've described the remodeled interior of Peter's castle "adequately." The best thing (the only thing, really) I can say is that it was a cross between the Metropolitan Museum of Art and Applebee's. Bright yellow paint warmed the indoor bailey. Gone was the cold opening to the sky, covered with a paned glass roof, and a tiled floor lay over what was once bare rock. Chairs and couches were arranged around tables. Green ivy draped the walls, and clean, restored cherubs, the ones that had once been scattered under the outside barrier, greeted the visitors from the courtyard balconies. And all of it—walls, floors, ceilings, alcoves—was filled with incongruous, seemingly incompatible items juxtaposed against one another.

Triptychs and wall hangings mingled with rusty novelty plaques. A marble pedestal featured a lava lamp lovingly nestled between two 2,500-year-old Greek vases. Overhead, a grinning Beanie Babies devil dangled from a crystal chandelier. I turned to Kyle.

"I told you he was a baron and he lived in a castle. There's the baron," I pointed to Peter, "and here's the castle. Plus, I was a kid back then; I mostly focused on the weapons." I walked up to two jewel-encrusted Moroccan daggers mounted under an animal skull. "Didn't I tell you he had lots of daggers?"

"Daggers? He has a Louis XIV bedroom set! I saw it upstairs, when we brought up the luggage."

"Okay." I yawned, making a mental note to Google what a Louis XIV bedroom set was.

"But he has medieval tapestries just hanging there like they're dorm posters, which he also has, by the way. He has an entire room paneled with Byzantine icons! He has Renaissance paintings. He has paintings, painted in the fucking Renaissance . . . and a lava lamp!"

"He's a baron. He can do what he wants."

I walked up the back staircase, giving Kyle the time to acclimate and leaving faint murmurs of "Renaissance" and "lava lamp" behind me.

Peter took us on a greatly curtailed tour of the interior (a full one would've required a day). My friends may have laughed at the junk, but Peter gave it as much attention as he did to the relics. "Amethyst, Brazil. It's really the best kind—the ones from Europe aren't as deep in the color. License plate, Montana. Usually the metal is . . . not flat, but this one is in very nice condition. I was pleased to find it."

We ended the tour at the main library, a beautiful room with provincial-blue walls overlaid with bright gold stenciling. "There is an identical study area at the Kaiser apartments in the winter palace of the Austro-Hungarian monarchy," Peter remarked. "And that is a seventeenth-century book of maps." He'd caught Steve hovering over an antique tome resting on a table. "Go ahead, you can read it."

"Really? But—" Steve was working on a way to approach the atlas when Peter picked it up and handed it to him.

"So where's the secret passage?" Jeff asked.

"It is right here." Peter unlatched a glass door protecting one of the bookcases and grasped the edge, easily swinging it open. The bookcase turned out to be a panel skillfully painted with trompe l'oeil books, so that only a close inspection revealed them to be fake. Our host permitted himself a little dramatic flair as he gestured toward the gaping void in the wall. "When you were last here, Lev, I was not with my wife, Gabi, but now we are back together. This door is very useful, especially when you're having an argument and would like to get away for some time." He pointed to a bookcase across the room. "There is another passageway over there, but that shelf contains actual books, not painted ones, so it is difficult to move," he said apologetically.

I nodded. I had long ago ceased to be amazed by Peter. In fact, if the sci-fi writers are correct and somewhere on this planet is a portal to Narnia or to John Malkovich's brain, I'm certain the gateway lies in a forgotten corner of Peter's castle, and if he ever shows it to me, I'll just nod. My friends were cracking up. They, too, reached the threshold at which you accept that things work differently with Peter, and all you can do is smile and be glad you're with him.

The next morning the baron loaded the four of us in a new, yet still midnight-green Mercedes jeep and took off on a tour of local towns and monasteries, just as he had done with my family years earlier. Our first stop was Freistadt, a remarkably preserved medieval fortress encircled by ancient battlements and a moat. Peter steered toward the cobblestone plaza in the center of town and calmly parked the jeep next to a PARKING VERBOTEN sign. It was a bright day, and the square was alive with cafés and tourists.

"I shall stay with the car, and you take a look. It is a very old town, and very nice—enjoy." Jeff, Steve, and Kyle ambled off to explore the local church. I kicked around the plaza for a bit, then made my way back to the jeep. Peter was inside, arm leaning out the window, methodically munching on an ice cream cone. "I saw all of this before; you go and look."

"I'd like to stay here for a couple of minutes, if that's okay." I lit up a cigarette, just to have something to do. A long, branching chain of causes and effects streamed through my mind. *What if Peter hadn't rescued Lina and Mom from the Austrian cops at the bridge? What if we'd gone to Brooklyn? What if he didn't get Dad a job in Austria and then Dad wouldn't have gotten one in the U.S. and would've probably joined the 97 percent of foreign engineers who wind up driving taxis or delivering pizzas, and then I couldn't have gone to a good college, and . . .* I shuddered. All that aside, here was a man who'd taken interest in us when we were at our lowest point, who somehow managed to make refugees feel like welcome guests in his land. How the hell do you say thank you for that? Expressing emotion wasn't my strong suit, and if memory served it also wasn't Peter's, but I wanted to say something, as a migrant and a writer, about the role he had played in my life and in my plot.

"I just want to say I really appreciate you having us over," I began. *Me, my friends, my family.* "And—and spending your time with us." *Both now and back then.*

Peter slowly polished off the remnants of his cone. "That is fine," he shrugged. "It is not a problem."

After Niederösterreich we headed to Prague, and Peter was kind enough to drive us across the Czech border to the nearest train depot. My friends occupied an empty cabin, and I was about to head for the ticket counter when Peter cut me off.

"The tickets are here—go." He shoved four tickets into my hand and, before I could protest, reached into his suit and began producing photographs, which he laid atop the tickets, one by one. "Maybe they will help for your book. Here is the castle, the town, ah yes, a nice lake, another one of the castle." Finally he tossed one more rectangle onto the pile. It was a photo of him, taken from behind someone's back, a candid shot and not a great one at that.

I beamed. Peter glanced up at me. "I still do not like photographs taken, I do not like it at all, but Gabi managed, and you can show it to your family. They have asked me for one a long time ago."

"Board now!" yelled the conductor. I mumbled "Thank you," and leapt aboard the train. The last I saw of Peter, he was straightening his suit and arranging his hair, a bemused little smile on his face. I put the rest of the photographs in my suitcase. The one of Peter I tucked into my passport, which, along with my interview notebook, never left my side.

The Czech Republic must've updated their tobacco laws: the train was non-smoking, which forced Kyle and me to scout out a deserted cabin so as not to disturb the conductor. We slid down the window and split a Marlboro, and stared out at the pine forests and peat bogs passing by. Crossing into eastern Europe was creepy. Public smoking rules may have Westernized, but time stood still in the backwoods of old Czechoslovakia. Every so often, a cluster of Soviet-era apartments broke through the pines, brick boxes with all the dull functionality of Communist architecture. Laundry lines hung between balconies, birds pecked around for crumbs, and an occasional *babushka* waddled by, sacks of groceries in hand. I could almost *see* the parades. My forearms and knees started tensing up, sometimes visibly twitching, which I hoped Kyle would ignore or, better yet, not notice. Reality was, I was a twenty-seven-year-old American tourist visiting a European country with all the protection of the U.S. of A. at my back. The other reality, just as real, was the vague sense of panic pulsing through my body, screaming at me to get out, go somewhere, America, Austria, Japan, doesn't matter, anywhere other than this land that was no land, where bad things lived and bad things happened and nobody stepped in to make them stop. Shit, harmless dinosaur bones still quicken the blood of the caveman in us, and a few kilometers across the Czech–Austrian border was all that it took to wipe away seventeen years, planting me back in Kharkov. I was grateful my friends were with me.

I spread my feet wide, like I used to when I rode trains as a kid, and tried to concentrate on something pleasant. My body rocked with the cabin's lazy cadence, and I smoked and thought about the past few days with Peter. I noticed that the baron wasn't as eager to be in motion. He drove markedly slower than he used to back in the days when he would tear through Austria with my family. Perhaps I was too young back then and all speeds seemed fast; perhaps age slowed him down, or maybe they finally started enforcing speed limits on the autobahns. I hoped those weren't the sole reasons. I'm not a fan of tacking undue fluff onto a situation, but after listening to Peter, watching him around Gabi, marking his driving, I felt comfortable enough to hope, very much hope, that he had reached some acceptance, had finally found a bit of peace.

Part Three

Those who cannot remember the past
are condemned to repeat it.

—George Santayana

THIS AIN'T ELLIS ISLAND

New York, N.Y., June 1990

The three women from HIAS were enjoying the air-conditioning at JFK's international arrivals hall, quietly waiting for the afternoon's cases to land. The women spoke Russian. Like most HIAS greeters, they themselves were recent newcomers to the States. HIAS recognized that the best person to relate to a refugee was an ex-refugee; hiring Russian speakers also circumvented the language barrier. The first case on June 19, 1990, was the Golinkin family, file #90-2212, arriving on flight TW749. An hour later, a family from Naples would land, followed by two more from Rome. For the four families, June 19 would become a milestone, a unique holiday to celebrate down the road. For HIAS, it was just another day in the mission. *Welcome the stranger. Protect the refugee.* The Hebrew Immigrant Aid Society has stood at America's doorstep since 1881, before Ellis Island opened its gates or Lady Liberty first gazed over New York Harbor. "We used to wait in harbors; now we wait in airports," Valery Bazarov, one of the directors at HIAS, told me. "Little else has changed . . . Refugees are refugees."

I don't remember seeing the Statue of Liberty or the famed Manhattan skyscrapers; I remember badges, clipboards, and fear. Passing through customs was simple, since we carried little physical baggage, but immigration was another story. INS workers drilled us to verify that we qualified for political refugee status, and then sent us to quarantine. In reality, these were formalities: HIAS would not have flown us out of Austria without assurance of asylum from Washington. But standing in line while strangers in uniforms decided your fate was too similar to the *tamozhnya*. Inspectors in lab coats circled around us, consulting chest X-rays and pathogen reports performed by American physicians at the U.S. embassy in Vienna. *Head down, don't attract attention, avoid eye contact.* Old habits I didn't remember learning kicked in. Just as at the border, or with Kolya and his stash of illegal coins when the *druzhinniki* swept through the yard, the paralysis around people in uniform had followed us to America. The quarantine room was so clinically sterile there was nothing to focus on but the floor, and all I saw were the inspectors' legs, white coats, and a white hand that seemed to move on its own accord, lifting up my shirt to expose my chest. After a moment's pause, the hand dropped down, the legs moved on. We passed.

The curly-haired young man weaved the yellow minivan through Queens, zigzagging toward LaGuardia Airport. As he drove he spoke, and as he spoke his right arm mimicked the motion of the van, haphazardly jerking around the cabin. "I came here from Costa Rica, got here a few years ago— Fuck!" He swerved to avoid a collision with another taxi. "This ain't Ellis Island, so don't buy into the old 'stand there and look helpless' garbage. Everyone's an immigrant here, and don't let no one tell you— Fuck!" Another yellow blur screeched by. New York had a lot of taxis.

"What's 'fuck'?" I tilted my head toward Lina, who sat alongside me in the back of the van, feet propped on suitcases.

"'Fuck' is a great word," mused Lina. "You're going to love

it. For starters, you can use it to draw attention to what you're saying, so if something's really great, it's *fucking* great, or when it really sucks, it *fucking* sucks. It's kind of like the Swiss Army knife of English: you can use it in so many ways." She paused and her eyes scrunched together. "Just be careful, because *some* people . . ." She glanced at Dad, blithely talking to the driver. "Some people might not appreciate it."

Lina'd previously taught me many Russian words, the sound of which made her giggle and Dad glower. Russian is a fantastic language for cursing, with obscene variants to the most innocent words, and intricate tiers of insults that allow one to tailor a slur to the desired level of humiliation. Lina had invested a great deal of time helping me navigate the maze of profanity, and I was excited about continuing my education in America.

"Got it." *I don't understand. Please speak slower. ABCDEFG. Fucking. Fuck. My English is growing!*

* * *

Unlike LaGuardia and O'Hare, Purdue University Airport in West Lafayette, Indiana, was not equipped with gates, so the little puddle jumper from Chicago simply taxied to a standstill in the middle of the tarmac. A hundred yards away sat a brown one-story building, and in front of the building, separated from the tarmac by a short chain-link fence, waited the crowd. There were children, a couple of babies, plenty of middle-aged couples, and one ancient, bearded rabbi. Several photographers hovered next to the fence, twisting and tweaking their lenses. Two women tapped on microphones connected to cameramen. A large paper banner made on a late-eighties dot matrix flapped from the overhang above the crowd. Lina translated the gray, pixilated letters: WELCOME HOME. The only thing missing was the marching band.

I'd love to know what went through the heads of our fellow passengers when they realized that the five nervous strangers whispering in an odd language were actually goodwill ambassadors, or foreign dignitaries, perhaps even an "international delegation." As soon as the stairs folded down, everyone, including the flight crew, evaporated from sight. "Just close the door on your way out," mumbled the pilot as he squeezed past Lina.

"Now what?" I tugged on Dad's sleeve as the two of us surveyed the scene from atop the stairs.

Dad took in the banner, the crowd, the bright summer sky, and I watched his fingers pumping and flexing around the suitcase handles, getting the blood flowing, the way he always did before charging into an important matter. "The sign says 'Welcome Home.'" He nudged his glasses against his face. "So we go home." We traversed the tarmac to the buzzing of gnats and the drone of another plane taking off, strode up to a gap in the chain-link fence, and paused. Somehow I wound up in front; perhaps Dad decided to commence the introductions with the cutest family member. The crowd was silent. The photographers lurked.

Across the gap towered a mustached man in a checkered beige sports jacket. His thick glasses reminded me of Dad's, which put me at ease. The man extended a long beige arm, I shook it, stepping across the gap, and suddenly everyone moved. Rapid shutter clicks burst through the air. The women in suits jostled toward us, tugging on cameramen and chattering into microphones. I heard the faltering rumble of Dad's English mingled with the surer stream of Lina's. The wizened old rabbi began speaking to Grandma, others approached, and handshakes flew everywhere as we were engulfed by Americans.

A kid cautiously edged his way around the crowd. He was tall and skinny, with black hair, black eyes, thick black eyebrows, and a black T-shirt with a shark on it. I tensed, anticipating the upcoming greeting; my handshake with the tall man with glasses had been limp and nervous, and I didn't want to mess up the next one, especially not with someone my age. But the kid looked like he was no expert either. He swung out a lanky arm in an awkward arc, and we shook. "Aaron," he coughed in a low quiet voice.

His name is Aaron. I nodded. "Lev."

Aaron nodded. *Good.*

"Um, *English English*," the kid launched a jumble of words. "*English English English, English English English.*"

"I. Fucking. Don't. Understand," I enunciated, and proudly grinned up at Lina, chatting with one of the journalists.

After a half-hour of milling around and interviews, we drifted toward a van, which took us past clusters of large brick buildings with large parking lots (this was Purdue University, the heart of West Lafayette) that were soon replaced by little streets with rows of houses, lawns, and garages. I'd never seen a suburb, and the individual houses with separate walls and driveways astounded me. I kept a wary eye out for nagging *babushki* and skulking bullies, and to my relief, I saw neither. Just a few Americans walking with their dogs, or their kids, or by themselves. *Please, please don't be an apartment,* I prayed, harder than I'd prayed before, harder than I thought myself capable of. *Please be one of those houses. Please, please, please.* Apartments were beatings. Apartments were communal yards full of danger, watchful eyes, ready to report you, drunk men in dark places, "Crush the Jews, Save Russia" scribbled on foyer doors. *Please God, let it be a house.*

To my great relief the van rounded a few corners, then pulled up to a gray ranch house whose lawn was bustling with people from the airport. The tall man with the thick glasses slid open the van's door, grabbed a suitcase in one hand and Grandma in the other, and headed up the driveway. Grandma marched beside the man, hand looped around his arm, like a queen inspecting her new castle. One by one, our fat red-violet suitcases wrapped with white cords disappeared inside, as I fought off the impulse to protect them from strangers. Mom and Lina were swept inside by the crowd, Dad was pointing around while jabbering to the camera, and I almost didn't want to enter. It required several long, deep breaths to convince my legs to step forward.

For once I was thankful for being small. I ran, half-crouched, around the photographers, Mom, Dad, Lina, and Americans swarming in every carpeted room. *Carpets! No cold, blue lino-leum floors, no stupid rugs covering up grime, just soft, warm car-peting. A couch and a short glass table with metal legs I can play with my soldiers on. The kitchen and a huge refrigerator in the corner, full of* everything . . . *Why is that American woman star-ing at me? A tiny porcelain house with a removable roof, cook-ies,* chocolate *cookies, and forks, knives, and tools in a drawer (examine tools later). Grandma's gaping at a weird device, looks like an oven but it's not an oven, it must be something else, like a super-oven. Back into the living room, and another room, a bedroom with a bed, then another room, two beds, and then one more small room with a bed and a door—an open door that's a closet, and it has toys, toys, toys, toys, toys!!!*

My thoughts spun too fast for talking or thinking, rooms, kitchen, yard, toys all pulsed through my body, and I drank them in until I thought I couldn't fit any more, and then I lapped up some more. *How could this happen?* rang in my ears until it came to me that the strangers did it. This was all because of the strangers.

One of the photographers caught Lina and a middle-aged woman in a floral print blouse standing next to the weird super-oven appliance, which turned out to be the dishwasher. Our host gestures as she explains the contraption, while a googly-eyed Lina clasps her cheeks in classic *Home Alone* fashion. The picture wound up on the front page of the next day's paper (West Lafayette is a small college town, and with Purdue off for the summer, our arrival was lead story material). Lina Golinkin is "overwhelmed as Linda Forman describes the furnishings in Golinkin's new home in West Lafayette," was how the caption summarized it. I'd argue that "Lina Golinkin is rocked out of her fucking world like a Neanderthal transported to Times Square" would've been a more accurate description.

Lina was horrified when she saw the photo, and to this day she insists it was staged.

She's lying.

REFUGEE SPONSORSHIP
FOR DUMMIES

West Lafayette, Ind., Summer 1990

The first few months were a blur. Everything was new, old things were useless, and lessons numerous. You didn't walk to a bazaar; you drove to a supermarket. Prices were prices and there was no haggling, doctors made no house calls and required office visits, insurance cards, and copays. You were expected to ask everyone, even strangers, how they were doing, but the answer always had to be "Good!" I'll never forget going to our first Fourth of July cookout and watching the Americans throw away knives, forks, plates, and tablecloths, disposable versions of items that weren't supposed to be disposable. It was like traveling to a land where people toss out their cars after they run out of gas.

And then there were words. Words words words words words. I absorbed them rapidly. When fourth grade began, my teachers realized that if they left me alone, I would take in lessons to the best of my ability and show progress at the end of the day. It was a game, and I would make up little mnemonics to help me with the rules. When do you use "a" versus "an"? Well, "a" doesn't like other vowels, so you have to stick an "n" in between: *an* alligator but *a* crocodile. What's the difference between "embarrassed" and "humiliated"? If you fart in public, you're embarrassed; if you shit your pants in public, you're humiliated. But kids are already wired to soak up languages, plus they're not expected to have jobs or full conversations. Lina and Grandma fared best of the adults: Lina's language was very good, and Grandma announced that she was old and didn't have to learn anything, and America gave her a pass. Dad found out he didn't know as much as he thought he knew, and Mom had to start at the beginning. Thousands and thousands of words: it was like being born, except you didn't have years to build a vocabulary—you had months.

People flocked from all over town to introduce themselves or to assist with particular issues, but Linda Forman (the *other* woman in Lina's unforgettable *Home Alone* photo) was our American mother. There's no other way to describe the woman who arranged discount school lunches, obtained Social Security numbers, taught Dad and Lina to drive, managed doctor visits, filled out food stamp applications, balanced checkbooks, introduced customs, took us to our first Fourth of July, Halloween, Thanksgiving, Passover, and Rosh Hashanah celebrations, all while coordinating the other volunteers in our support network. Before we arrived, she met with my teachers to make sure my classmates knew they were getting a new student who might be scared and wouldn't speak English; shortly afterward, she was already visiting local businesses to inquire about jobs for my parents. For a good part of a year she spent more time with my family than with her own.

The culture shock ran both ways. One evening Linda stopped by to find everyone frozen with fear because the police had just called our house. Linda investigated with the local police chief, who had no idea what Dad was talking about, and after a while she discovered that the "policeman" was actually a Police Benefit Fund telemarketer. "You have nothing to worry about," she assured the family, but her assurances meant nothing. *What do the police want? Why are they calling? What do the police want?* "You have nothing to worry about," Linda repeated a hundred times over, but it required a three-hour explanation of telemarketing, and law enforcement, and civil rights, to make her feel comfortable enough to leave us for the night. She wouldn't forget walking home astounded at how grossly she had underestimated our deep-rooted fear of the police. It was a fear that wouldn't abate for years.

And then there were challenges of a thornier nature. Linda quickly learned that while Lina would readily acknowledge not comprehending something, Dad was reluctant to admit his ignorance. Linda would convey information, *important* information, on upcoming events, U.S. culture, laws, and protocols, Dad would respond with a blank "Okay," and later on she'd find out he had not understood at all. This drove Linda insane, since Dad's misconceptions were multiplied fivefold the moment he relayed the incorrect information to us. But every time Linda confronted him, Dad would assert his understanding. Finally Linda began making Dad recite what she had told him, but using different words, and this tell-and-repeat method became a problem in its own right. Our sponsor believed it was the only way to ensure the message was transmitted. Mom and Dad felt they were being treated with condescension, a callous and arrogant disregard for decades of holding down demanding professional careers while raising a family in harrowing circumstances Linda couldn't fathom.

Linda had hit on a sore spot: the helplessness that smothers many newcomers, especially those who don't settle down in an ethnic enclave (like Brighton Beach in Brooklyn for Soviet Jews or Westwood in Los Angeles for Iranians) and are instead plunged into mainstream America. Tensions between our host and my parents escalated when it was time to nail down jobs. Dad began work as a filing clerk for a medical supply company, a private environment with a small number of employees, but Mom became a barista. Binder's hotel in Austria taught us that not everyone in the West appreciated migrants, and the same was true of Lafayette. Several obnoxious individuals (who weren't known for being coffee connoisseurs prior to our arrival) began to frequent Mom's café, blurting out detailed orders, refusing to speak slower, and ridiculing her whenever she got something wrong. For thirty years Mom had shepherded patients during some of the worst periods of their lives, and now she couldn't brew an espresso. She felt worthless.

Dad channeled his frustration into a more positive direction, spending nights and weekends researching the U.S. engineering sector and shooting out résumés to firms across the country. The rejections returned at an astonishing rate, but that didn't deter my father. "Step by step" was an expression he picked up early on in America, and that's what he'd grunt on the way from the mailbox, before heading to Kinko's to crank out more résumés. Linda, whose prerogative was for Mom and Dad to secure an income and amass equity, viewed Dad's job search as a waste of precious resources, like blowing money on scratch-off tickets. She was the voice of reality and had the statistics to back her up. Mom and Dad were thrashing about, grasping to regain their dignity. Their situation made them feel powerless and humiliated, and Linda's insistence on their *remaining there* fostered their bitterness. Both my parents and Linda were trying to do the best for our family, but they often resented each other.

Linda was neither a social worker, nor a Jewish Federation employee, nor a professional do-gooder. (Her education in sponsorship was limited to receiving a thick binder containing HIAS's version of *Refugee Sponsorship for Dummies*.) She was an architect, with a husband and two kids in college, and up to a few months before my family's arrival, she didn't know or think much about Soviet Jews. To be sure, she belonged to the local synagogue, heard stories, signed a petition or two, but overall she was aware that Soviet Jews were being persecuted in the same vague sense most people know that somewhere in Africa, someone is hungry. But in February 1990, the West Lafayette rabbi put out a call for all community members to attend an urgent meeting with a young HIAS ambassador, and Linda showed up.

The young man from HIAS spoke of Soviet Jews stuck in refugee camps, and the community decided to act. People took out checkbooks, drafted lists of furniture items, volunteered to be English tutors and driving instructors. Linda sat in the back, half paying attention. She was thinking of another young man, a young man swimming across a river, a long time ago. Linda knew little about her grandfather. She knew he was born in Romania, and an army was closing in, and he jumped in and swam for his life under gunfire. She couldn't shake that image. The young man from HIAS kept organizing, and Linda kept thinking of her grandfather swimming across some river in some part of Romania, praying the bullets would miss, praying there was help on the other side. And then the young man from HIAS asked for a community member to take responsibility for the entire project, and Linda Forman stood up. She didn't even remember deciding to say yes.

On weekday mornings during our first two months in the States, Linda would scoop Dad up and start ticking off the countless items on her agenda. It was summer, I didn't have school, and so I tagged along, bound to Dad by old habit. Linda was middle-aged, with olive skin and jet-black hair perpetually coiled in a bun with one or two pencils poking out. She preferred jeans and earth-toned shawls, tan, brown, and gray, which made me think of Indians from old Russian engravings of *The Last of the Mohicans*. If we finished the day's errands early, our host would treat

Dad and me to something enjoyable, swinging by a park, a local landmark, or a funky part of Purdue's campus. Before kicking off the fun part of the day, Linda would fasten her seat belt and turn to Dad: *"English English English. English English."*

Even Linda's slow-paced speech was incomprehensible, and I learned to rely on body language to interpret her mood, just as I did with my teachers and the other Americans in Lafayette. With Linda it was easy: one just had to follow the wrinkles. The corners of her mouth creased up when she was pleased, foreshadowing a smile. When angry, she squinted, emitting little spokes of wrinkles; when she was deliberating, a ripple snaked across her forehead.

"Een-glish, Een-glish . . . Een-glish," Dad would respond in his choppier, hesitant baritone as Linda looked at me in the rearview mirror.

"English English English, what would Lev like to do?"

I knew those words. They were some of the first ones I learned to recognize. Linda was serious: I could track the wrinkles gathering, thinking, asking.

"Let's go," Dad would reply, but the wrinkles remained.

"Ask him. Please."

Dad would tilt back and translate, and I'd say yes. I always said yes. I didn't care what we did—it was the question that mattered. The wrinkles would migrate down and rearrange into a smile, and Linda would shift into gear.

WHERE ELSE DOES SHE BELONG?

West Lafayette, Ind., August 1990

After taking a few weeks to brush up on her English and adapt to our new surroundings, Lina applied to grad school. Both Mom and Dad made it clear that Lina and I were the main reason they had decided to risk it all and flee the USSR. Their children were *going* to have a better future, and there was only one sure way to make it happen. Twin doctorates—an MD for me and a PhD for Lina—would propel the first generation into financial security and allow *our* children to enjoy a normal American life. "Your mom and I will work and get money: that is our task, and you and Lina will study and get A's: that is your task," commanded Dad time and again, adding his voice to the old immigrant battle cry that's been uttered in every corner of America. "You *will* get a top education and you *will* succeed; it's the most important thing in the world."

Conveniently facilitating Lina's achievement of the most important thing in the world was a top-notch engineering program located ten minutes from our doorstep. But when Lina walked down to Purdue's graduate school admissions department, she hit a dead end. My sister had no proof of college education, since her transcript had been confiscated and burned at the Soviet border. The best Lina could hope for, admissions said, was to apply to college and work for her bachelor's all over again.

Lina was devastated; engineering wasn't even her career choice (her dream, after all, had been to become a doctor), and she had struggled for a decade against a biased anti-Semitic school system, then wasted two years taking the medical academy exam only to learn that merit played no part in her future. The burning barrel at the *tamozhnya,* our little parting gift from the Soviet Union, had achieved its intended purpose. The impotence she first tasted in Russia had trailed her to America, and as much as Mom and Dad attempted to console her, they, too, had been plunged into a strange life with no friends and no money, and were as powerless as she was.

What neither my sister nor my parents realized was that a plan to get Lina into Purdue was already in place; in fact, it had been incubating even prior to our little puddle jumper's touching down on the tarmac. As soon as West Lafayette signed HIAS's sponsorship agreement, the organization faxed Linda a list of our names, ages, and occupations. Linda's husband, Michael, was a Purdue biology professor who had recently been appointed as dean. And in July 1990, Michael Forman decided that he was going to get a girl with no college transcript and no standardized test scores admitted into an elite graduate engineering program ranked in the top ten in the nation. And he was going to get it done in the span of two months.

The novelty of Lina's case required Michael to convene a special university hearing. He began with influential professors in the Materials Engineering Department, pulling them aside in the labs, seeking them out between vacations, persuading, cajoling, and strong-arming. "It's only a panel," Michael reassured the hesitant ones, "the First Panel for the Status of Ex-Soviet Graduate

School Applicants. That's all." (The ludicrous title was Linda's suggestion; she didn't want the meeting to smack of any global policy initiatives that would spook the more timid professors.) By that point my family had already landed in West Lafayette and local papers and TV stations were aflutter with stories about us and our sponsors. The faculty understood that this wasn't some distant, ideological cause for Michael; it was personal. By denying him the hearing they would be stepping on the toes of a rising star in the university.

After he had collected a sufficient number of professors to meet quorum, Michael moved on to the administration, and here his pitch changed. Fortunately, it was the early nineties, and ivory towers around the country—including Purdue's nearly all-male graduate engineering program—were buzzing about the concept of diversity. "We *must* get our act together," urged the new dean. "Diversity's becoming a damn prerequisite. And here's this refugee poster girl who landed right on our doorstep—we couldn't *ask* for a better opportunity!" Rabbi Gedalyah Engel, another one of Lina's champions, enjoyed a good rapport with the town and county press, and while Michael was plying the diversity angle, several well-timed phone calls informed Purdue's public relations office that the local media was very interested in running a spotlight on Lina. By late August Michael got his hearing.

Linda and Michael lived a five-minute walk from the gray ranch at 213 East Sunset Lane, and since Linda spent more of her time with us than at home, Michael would often drop by to say hello and bring his wife a sandwich. He was a relaxed, good-natured man, with a sizable belly and a bushy beard that had turned gray long before his hair. When not in the lab or the classroom, he putzed around in his garden and played clarinet for the Lafayette Klezmorim, a traditional Eastern European Jewish band. The first time he strolled down to our house, clad in his

Hawaiian shirt and sandals, he made me think of Santa (I should say "Grandfather Frost") in the off-season, long after all the toys had been delivered and with the upcoming holiday bustle far, far away.

The night before Lina's hearing, however, the man's avuncular attitude had evaporated, because by that point Michael had tacked on another, even tougher, goal to his agenda. Lina couldn't afford the out-of-state tuition. Michael quietly checked with the local banks and was told she wouldn't qualify for a loan: ten suitcases were not enough for collateral. The community's resources were tapped (they had already shelled out eighty thousand dollars to sponsor Soviet Jews), and federal aid was out of the question. In other words, the panel would have to not only accept Lina, but accept her, a non-citizen and non-resident, as an *in-state* student.

When Michael first met Lina, he decided to help her with a *Wouldn't it be neat if I could pull this off* sentiment. But after witnessing Dad toil as a clerk and Mom as a barista, Michael realized that unless Lina was enrolled in a graduate program by September, she would be forced to take a low-wage job, and the odds of her returning to school would taper with each passing year. Dignity, family, social status, or blood, one way or another, every immigrant pays the admission price to America, and the older they are, the steeper the fare. In order to complete her education, Lina would have to be admitted as in-state, and now. Michael knew it, Linda knew it, and so they prepped, Michael debating, Linda playing devil's advocate, revising and tweaking long into the night.

Waiving the prerequisite proof of college education ate up an hour. Michael's star witness was Victor Raskin, a Purdue linguistics professor who had himself escaped from the Soviet Union during the seventies. In truth, Raskin's testimony was conjectural at best. The man was a linguist, not an engineer. All he did was confirm the existence of Kharkov Polytechnic Institute and that, based on his conversations with Lina, she had indeed attended it. But his voice supplied Michael with the gravitas of a faculty member, as well as giving those in attendance a clear example of what an immigrant can become. As expected, the sticklers demanded stipulations, and Michael conceded to having Lina demonstrate her proficiency by spending the fall semester maintaining a B-plus average in upper-level undergraduate engineering courses. Overall, things were progressing smoothly when Michael dropped the bomb. "Just so everyone's on the same page, I want to clarify that Ms. Golinkin is going to be joining us as an *in-state* candidate for a master's in Materials Engineering," he casually summed up, as if ready to bang down the gavel and get back to enjoying the last few days of summer.

Rumbles of a slippery slope erupted right on cue. Purdue University, like all universities, was a business, tuition money was its bloodline, and the difference between in-state and out-of-state tuition was considerable. Even Michael's friends looked perturbed. "Where is this going to stop? What about the kids from Illinois and Ohio—are we going to take all of them as in-state?" one chemist objected. "Absolutely not!"

Michael stuck to the script, jotting down notes and nodding with the utmost empathy. "I understand your concerns; I hear you." He spread his hands. "I, too, have grants, and facilities, and a salary to worry about. Believe me, I've got two kids in college—I know. But I just want to ask one question of this committee. Ms. Golinkin, as you are well aware, is a refugee from the Soviet Union. She fled a tyrannical dictatorship with nothing but two suitcases and the clothes she was wearing. She *cannot* go back. She was granted asylum by the United States government and taken into West Lafayette under the auspices of this community. So I ask you, *if* Ms. Golinkin does not belong here, *if* she is not in-state, then what is she? Where else does she belong? What state are you going to send her back to?"

Michael crossed his hands atop his belly and gazed out the window. It was long past twelve on a muggy August afternoon. Off in the distance, the football team jogged out to the practice field, the season opener against Washington just days away. Prefrosh orientation groups dallied by the quad, a pair of groundskeepers rooted around the chrysanthemum beds by the sidewalk, somewhere across the world the Cold War was petering out, and for a few brief moments the air of a small Indiana classroom hung heavy with the seventy-year struggle of totalitarianism and democracy. Michael leaned back, enjoying the silence, and glanced over at the opposing chemist. *Rebut that, you bastard.*

Five minutes later, Purdue's First [and only] Panel for the Status of Ex-Soviet Graduate School Applicants had adjourned. Lina was in and in-state—they even waived her first-year tuition on their own initiative.

It was the American thing to do.

*   *   *

In March 1991, after hundreds of rejections and eight months of ramming his résumé down the throat of the U.S. military-industrial complex, Dad got a bite from a company called Delaval in New Jersey. His persistence was aided by a bit of luck, because the woman who reviewed his application spoke German and took the time to research the Austrian firm that had supplied Dad with recommendation letters. Dad flew out to Trenton and immediately accepted an entry-level position typically reserved for graduates fresh out of college (Delaval was willing to take a chance on an old immigrant, but they had their limits). Dad was fine with it: the only thing he asked was to have company business cards printed before he flew back to Indiana. His first task upon returning to Lafayette was to distribute the cards across the community. The few believers who had encouraged the job search were given a card; the skeptics got two, lest they misplace one. Linda received a small stack.

Dad started work on April 1 and, a month later, after scouting out the area, he returned to Indiana to pick up me, Mom, and Grandma. Our departure, like our arrival ten months earlier, was a community-wide event replete with media coverage and touching gestures. Happy Hollow Elementary School rushed to have the yearbooks printed ahead of schedule so I could leave with a signed copy from my classmates. Dad gave an oration during a farewell dinner at the local temple, where the community had gathered a year earlier to hear the young man from HIAS speak of the refugee crisis in Europe. After Dad's address, Rabbi Engel, the temple's advisor, came up to us.

"Don't worry, we'll look out for Lina," he promised, protectively draping his arm around my sister, who was staying behind to complete her education. "And listen," the rabbi reminded Dad, "all of you haven't had much time to explore Judaism during the past ten months. There was too much secular work, of course, of course. But now you're on your way, you got your feet wet, as they say, and it'll be up to you to connect with the faith and culture robbed from you by the Soviets." Engel smiled, and his light blue eyes, so full of pain when talking of the Communists, twinkled with joy. The rabbi had spent decades fighting to free the Soviet Jews, even forging an alliance with a Pentecostal pastor to pressure Congress to confront the Kremlin. Our crossing the Soviet border was a victory for him as well. "Don't forget, this is

America, and you have freedom of religion on your side, here, in New Jersey, wherever you go. The choice is yours."

"Thank you." Dad smiled as everyone received a hug from the old rabbi. "This freedom is what makes this country wonderful, and we will be sure to take advantage of it." And take advantage of it we would, but not in the way Rabbi Engel had intended.

UNFINISHED BUSINESS, PART I:
GETTING TO AMERICA

East Windsor, N.J., 2006

Part of my father's collection of mementos from our journey is a copy of the June 21, 1990, *Journal and Courier,* a local
Indiana newspaper that covered our arrival to the States. On the
front page is a photo of me shaking hands with Neil Zimmerman, the mustached man in the checkered beige sports jacket
who greeted us when we stepped off the plane. The accompany-
ing story informs the reader that "the Golinkins opted to settle
in West Lafayette because their son, Leo [*sic*], does not like hot
weather." "Opted" is a curious choice of word in that sentence.
While it's true that I function best in environments below sixty
degrees, neither I nor anyone else in my family had opted for anything—we had little control over the process. And all else aside,
as sentimental as it would be to think that of all the places in
America we would've elected to live at 213 East Sunset Lane, the
disappointing reality is that we weren't even aware of the existence of West Lafayette . . . or Lafayette proper . . . or the midwestern region of the continental United States, for that matter.

Although every refugee story has its unique quirks, certain patterns can be teased out of any given refugee movement. There are
two such commonalities relevant to the massive Jewish exodus
during the waning years of the Soviet Union. First, Austria was

nothing more than a triage center for incoming refugees: migrants came to Vienna, were processed over a period of one to two weeks (a month at peak overflow times, such as the end of 1989, when my family and others were stationed at Binder's), then transferred to Italy. Joint's refugee infrastructure—the camps, teaching centers, food kitchens, clinics—was in Naples and Rome. The only migrants retained in Austria were the gravely ill, people so infirm that relocation to the crammed, filthy apartments of Rome was deemed a medical risk. Everyone else was shipped to Italy.

Second, migrants with no relatives in America were likely to be placed by HIAS into an urban Jewish community, such as Brighton Beach in Brooklyn or its counterparts in Baltimore, Philadelphia, Chicago, and Los Angeles. Cities have dense concentrations of low-level, immigrant-ready jobs coupled with public transportation, Laundromats, pharmacies, grocery stores, and other conveniences of Western life squeezed into a few blocks. What's most crucial is that all those jobs and institutions are staffed by and cater to Russian speakers, which eliminated the crippling effect of the language barrier. The whole idea was to ease the lonely transition to America by plugging isolated refugees into long-established linguistic, ethnic, and immigrant networks.

Problem is, the story of my family flies in the face of both. Every one of the fifty families stationed in Binder's hotel had been transferred to Rome, save us. We were moved to Vienna, to a private upstairs room in a house so packed with invalids that Joint was forced to create space by dicing up the first floor into minuscule curtained-off sectors we generously referred to as rooms. And then there's West Lafayette—even with the entire student body of Purdue University thrown in, the town still comes up a few million short of a metropolis. The Russian enclave of Tippecanoe County had consisted of us and one other family adopted by the community.

Why were we kept in Austria for six months? How did we wind up in Indiana? Time rolled by, my family met other refugees, heard other stories, and the more we shared, the more our story stood out, and still the answers lay hidden, obscured by years and by a transformed world. For many years, I didn't think about any of this—in fact, I did everything I could to ignore, omit, and otherwise bury memories of our journey and of the Soviet Union—but in 2006, as an adult seeking to understand my past, I set out to discover what had happened.

I headed for New York to interview directors of HIAS and Joint, as well as to Vienna, where I tracked down Oswald Prager, who had been responsible for stationing refugees in Austria. I asked all three men if they could think of a reason why five healthy individuals would've been retained in an Austrian purgatory house instead of being forwarded to Rome. Their responses were: "I don't know," "Hmm, that's strange," and "I have no idea." On my way out of HIAS headquarters I picked up a copy of my family's refugee file, and after scouring the blurry, typewritten bundle I discovered that any pertinent information was either omitted or simply not there. One page, dated February 6, 1990, tersely states, "Originally family was supposed to be processed in Rome—now Vienna case." The file continues with numerous correspondences between HIAS and potential sponsor communities in Chicago and Baltimore, when suddenly there appears a sticky note, scribbled on which is "Accepted. Lafayette, Ind. Free case." That's it.

I tried flinging the whole thing on the shoulders of fate, but the longer the story percolated in my mind the more I was certain of a missing factor swirling around me. I'd logged in enough hours with community service organizations to recognize that these groups, especially ones that operate in chaotic environments, are very good at adhering to protocol. There are reasons for established patterns, and explanations for deviations. It didn't require the imagination of a conspiracy theorist to discern a conscious will at work during critical junctures of my family's story, a higher power bending our path to its purpose.

*   *   *

Oberösterreich (Upper Austria), June 2007

Peter still loved his weapons: on the way to the priory he had pulled off at a small village to pick up some rifles he was getting repaired. "The gunsmith was late in repair, so I have convinced him to contribute free bullets!" he happily announced upon returning to the jeep. Peter still loved his haggling. I sat wedged between my friends Steve and Kyle in the back of the Mercedes, listening to the baron and Jeff (the fourth member of Team Lev) discuss Austrian politics as we rolled along the E55 Autobahn on a warm June day. Seventeen years ago Peter had taken my family on the very road we were now on and offered us a choice between the Sankt Florian priory and the Mauthausen concentration camp. Back then we went to the latter; now we were headed for the former.

The maypoles were everywhere, taller than telephone poles, tall like strange ship masts marooned in landlocked Austria, red-and-white pennants fluttering in the breeze. The poles weren't always so tall, according to Peter. They started out as little decorated saplings in town greens, until local children took to stealing the trees from neighboring villages in an Old World precursor to capture-the-flag. Townsfolk responded by affixing the saplings to poles, which made them harder to reach, which only encouraged the thieves to get good at climbing. Over the centuries, the maypoles got taller and taller until they evolved into giant wooden pillars with rings of protective prickly evergreens, inaccessible to anyone, with the possible exception of the Navy SEALs.

Rows of vineyards streaked by the banks of the Danube as I reviewed the interviews I had with my parents concerning the baron. In 1990, when we were still refugees, Peter conversed with Mom, Dad, and Lina about the future during our numerous excursions to the Austrian countryside. The baron never made his own opinion a focus of the discussion, but rather veiled it in hypothetical conjectures full of "if"s and "nice"s.

"It would be very nice if your family did not have to go to Italy," he'd muse. "The living conditions there are much worse. Besides, if you stay in Austria, then Samuel [Dad] can continue working for the engineering company, and get good recommendation letters for employers in America, that is so." My parents replied that they would rather take their chances in Rome, because they didn't want to be separated from our refugee-friends the Zhislins. Their wishes did not pan out.

Once we were inexplicably secured in Vienna, Peter's speculations shifted to the United States. "If you had a choice, where would you like to go in America?" he inquired.

Mom and Lina wanted to move only to Brighton Beach, the Russian enclave in Brooklyn. "It'll be so much easier to be in a neighborhood with Russian speakers all around us," they reasoned.

"Ah, so, that is true, but Brooklyn is *so* impersonal," lamented the baron. "They place you in an apartment in a big building full of little apartments, with a little money, and they leave you alone to get a job and many people get stuck living in there. Mobility is low, so low. It would be nice if your family would go to a small town so you would get attention, somewhere toward the middle of the country, with no Russians so you would *have* to learn English, and yes with a large public university because we require a strong engineering program for Lina . . ."

West Lafayette fits Peter's criteria to a T. In fact, I'm hard pressed to find a town that would've made a better match.

Peter never gave a definitive answer on how big a role, if any, he played in our little refugee inconsistencies. Dad asked him once during a phone conversation in the mid-nineties, but got neither a "yes" nor a "no." Peter muttered something about the past being the past, and shifted the conversation to another topic (in that casually insistent manner of his), and not even Dad had the stubbornness to press on for more. And here I was, almost two decades later, sitting in Peter's car and debating how to tease the truth out of him.

It was easy to see why Sankt Florian was Peter's favorite monastery. The complex devoted to the patron saint of firefighters was a proud Baroque shrine that emanated power and beauty. Aside from a few errant monks, the grounds were empty, and we took our time exploring the courtyard, relics, and a library brimming with enough yellowing scrolls and leather-bound manuscripts to rival Hogwarts. But all those things were appetizers; the best, Peter promised, was the main basilica. The giant front doors were shut, as was a side entrance, but our undeterred guide marshaled us back into the monastery and soon discovered a tucked-away clergy passage. We crossed through the sacristy, spilled out into the front, and immediately discovered why all the doors were locked: inside the basilica was a group of people about to celebrate a private wedding. The guests were already in the pews and the wedding party was assembled at the main aisle in the back. The only thing missing was the bride, and the initial gasps of excitement prompted by our arrival quickly faded as the guests realized that not one out of the five noisy strangers who burst into the basilica was the woman in white. A perplexed murmur rose from the pews. Children began asking questions.

My friends scattered. Kyle and Jeff hid behind a giant column, where Kyle used all his willpower to stave off Jeff's hysterical giggling. Steve just vanished; I have no idea where he went or how he got out, but the next time we saw him, he was outside by the jeep. I trailed Peter, who strolled down the nave, encouraging my friends and me to take in the intricate architecture. Judging by him, one would think we were the only ones in the monastery, if not the entire town. "Look at these carvings—what magnificent stonework!" he exclaimed to the pillar concealing Jeff and Kyle. "Note the pink marble out of Salzburg, that is so, and the frescos on the ceiling. These were crafted by . . ." On and on our little tour went, pausing by an arch, swinging by a chapel, until we stopped at the main entrance, where Peter admired with delight the panes of stained glass shimmering overhead.

Waiting for the bride, neatly aligned across the nave, were the groom, the best man, the photographer, the ushers, and Peter and me. Peter at least had on a suit, while I was decked out in my finest Red Sox regalia. The lanky photographer stomped over, a furious look on his face. He was about to open his mouth when Peter turned his pale blue eyes on him and shot him a nod, the kind used to inform an unruly child that loss of TV privileges is imminent. I don't know how, but with that one little gesture the photographer instantly realized that Peter had come to Sankt Florian with four American visitors and several loaded semiautomatic rifles, that he had come there to showcase Austrian culture to his guests, and that if that meant having to share the basilica with the wedding party, well, Peter was gracious enough to allow them to remain and proceed with the ceremony . . . as long as they behaved.

The photographer froze, then slunk back to his post without

saying a word. Kyle and Jeff joined Peter and me. By this point Kyle had lost the battle against Jeff's laughter, and the two of them were convulsing with mirth like a pair of schoolboys after a juicy fart joke. A hush fell over the crowd as the big doors creaked open: the bride stood at the threshold. I have to hand it to her, she was a trouper, recoiling in horror for only the briefest of moments before commencing her walk down the aisle. The photographer crouched and started snapping away. The groom perked up. The bride floated past us. Peter sent her a smile. I turned my head and threw the groom a nod (a pale imitation of Peter's) to assure him that he had made a good choice and that the blessings of Red Sox Nation went with him on this most special day.

"It pleases me that you finally saw this beautiful place," said Peter as we threw open the main doors and made our triumphant exit from the monastery.

I left Austria without asking Peter about the true extent of his influence on my family's fate. I thought about it, but in the end I decided to let it be. First of all, I accepted that there was no way I'd get him to disclose anything he didn't want to, and frankly, after the Sankt Florian experience, I felt the question had been sufficiently addressed. "God does not play dice with the universe," Einstein famously said, and clearly Peter espoused a similar philosophy.

WHERE THE WEAK ARE
KILLED AND EATEN

East Windsor, N.J., May 1991

Dad's job was in central New Jersey, a land where, according to a popular local T-shirt, "the weak are killed and eaten." We settled down in East Windsor, a quiet middle-class township where two-story houses mingled with cornfields and strip malls. During summers, echoes of engines from the local racetrack drifted across the woods behind our house; on crisp fall evenings, you could hear the drums from the high school marching band. Upon our arrival Dad proudly showed off his almost-new Ford Taurus painted an interesting violet-red that resembled the ten suitcases we had brought with us from Russia. Grandma spent most of her time looking out her bedroom window at kids racing bikes and adults walking dogs. Mom attempted studying for the medical boards: a year later she tried getting licensed as a nurse, then as an EKG tech, then she became a security guard. She didn't have the English to do much else.

Unless an American has been thrown into an utterly foreign environment—not an easy place like Cancún or Madrid, where an English speaker is never far away—they have no idea what it's like.

It begins simply. You have to return a sweater at the mall.

You've studied some phrases from your little ESL worksheets with large print and helpful cartoons of Enrique, the exchange student from Santiago, meeting Sally, the coed from Delaware. You step up to the register and open with the introductory sentences you have prepared, but the clerk says something you don't understand, or fires off something different from Sally's response to Enrique. "Sorry, excuse me," you say, "excuse me" and "sorry" being the two most important phrases in your lexicon, because you're going to have a lot of apologizing to do in the future. And while you're *excuse me*-ing and trying to process what the clerk has said, he says something else, and now you're three sentences behind. Ever speak to someone on the phone and get the repeat echo, where you hear yourself back on a two-second delay? Scrambles your thoughts. Drives you insane. Multiply that by twenty. And now you're completely out of the conversation, and the clerk is waiting. By this point, Enrique and Sally have had a fulfilling exchange and are making plans to hang out. You need another apology.

Maybe the clerk understands what you're going through, but chances are, he doesn't. And now's no time for empathy: there are three customers behind you. Ever feel the stares when you're at the register and your credit card doesn't work or you realize you forgot your wallet in the car? The moment when your whole existence shrinks to you being the asshole holding up the line? Multiply that by twenty. Now you're the asshole holding up the line and you don't even belong there to begin with.

Most people get impatient. Some get angry. Some begin speaking louder—as if that's the problem—or attempt to mitigate the awkwardness with kindly smiles, and you want to tell them that you're neither deaf nor a child, but by this point you're too anxious, angry, hurt, embarrassed, and the mumbling gets worse. And then you panic. You don't understand why they can't understand—you're repeating what the ESL book told you to say, but it's not working. Enrique and Sally already went to the movies, Enrique's got his hand up Sally's skirt, and life is good. You no longer care if you have to keep the damn sweater, or if you're getting ripped off, or if you'll have to come back later and you've just wasted your afternoon. You just want the embarrassment to end and you slink out of the store.

And that was a normal exchange, as far as exchanges go. The bad ones are where someone screams at you, or kicks you out, or tells you to leave their country, or calls you a fucking idiot. Or calls the cops. Those are the worst. You're already terrified of the police. You were terrified of them back when you could speak their language.

It makes you look forward to the next errand. Makes you look forward to going to the doctor, or a job interview. Makes you so nervous you're forgetting Enrique's ESL phrases before you even begin to make an ass of yourself. Except "excuse me" and "sorry"; you'll never forget those.

Then you realize this is it. This is not a vacation; this is forever. This is what it will be like. You're expected to learn the language, except you're also working a menial job, maybe two menial jobs, because you just got to this country and you have no money. And you're raising a family. Forget English: by the time you get home and put the kids to bed, your brain barely functions in your native tongue. Most Americans don't learn a foreign language in high school, when they're young and have nothing to do but learn. You're already old. You will never work in your field again. Find something you can do with your hands, something that doesn't require anything beyond a few words' comprehension. You will never be seen as anything more than an immigrant, or a moron, or a child. For the rest of your life it's you, your family, and a world of impotence at your doorstep. You no longer have opinions. You don't have jokes, or consolations, or conversations, or amusements, or experiences, or perspectives built over a lifetime. They're useless, like you. How are you going to share them? With whom? You are an animal, mooing and mumbling and *excuse me*–ing your way through the smallest chore, the most inconsequential grocery store errand.

And that's how the language barrier works.

I'm in awe of my parents' strength, throughout my childhood, both in Austria and in Russia. Dad was a machine, plowing through obstacles. Failure was the signal to double his efforts; success was another brick upon which to build more success. Mom wasn't as relentless. She'd get discouraged, she'd nurse doubts, but simmering underneath was this *daring* that flared up when we needed it most. *She* was the one who forced the final decision to flee the Soviet Union. *She* was the one who guided us through the exit visa gauntlet in the fall of 1989, when we were racing the deadline to be in Austria. Now, in the States, I watched the hope of being a doctor leech out of Mom, along with her confidence and optimism. I didn't blame America, and I still don't—I believe that immigrants must learn English or pay the price. Instead I blamed Mom, I blamed her security company, her blue shirt and black pants with blue stripes, her little tin security officer badge that looked like the Junior Detective badges cops hand out to ten-year-olds during D.A.R.E. workshops. I lashed out when she'd return home and catch us up on her work shift, and of all things I've done to be ashamed of, ridiculing my mother for trying to contribute to her new society is one that hurts the most.

Dad worked nonstop, just as he had back in Russia, turbines and rotors dominating his brain. His starting salary did not truly permit us to live in a house or in nice, middle-class East Windsor. Dad was constantly juggling old debts and acquiring new ones, but my troubles in Kharkov led both of us to associate apartments with violence, and he didn't want to jeopardize what was left of my childhood. "Let me worry about the money," he'd say during twilight walks we took around our safe neighborhood. "You worry about the A's: that is your job." I felt guilty because I knew we should move, but I shuddered at the thought of leaving the suburbs, so I said nothing and concentrated on the A's.

Dad maintained a detailed record of my job performance in a green folder with a yellow dragon on the cover, which he got at a parent-teacher conference at my East Windsor elementary school. Crammed inside the folder, which Dad keeps to this day, are eleven years of my life, from fifth grade through my junior year of college. Everything is there: report cards, semester transcripts, yearly volunteering statements from Princeton Hospital, student of the month awards, SAT scores, SAT II scores, college acceptance letters, college rejection letters, and college wait-list letters. There are class pictures from high school and middle school, 8 × 10s, and 4 × 6s, and lots of wallet-sized ones. There are multiple copies of them. Dad wanted them taken—I refused to look at any of it—so Dad stored them in the green folder. There are multiple copies of everything; Dad always made copies. I kept presenting, and Dad kept filing, and the folder expanded until the cover ripped off, and still I offered, and still Dad archived, and still the folder grew.

*　*　*

And within three years of coming to New Jersey, the four of us had abandoned all pretenses of being religiously and culturally

Jewish. I did get my Bar Mitzvah, at Dad's insistence: my grandfather Lev had one, Dad's opportunity had been stolen by the Soviet Union, and Dad viewed my ceremony as a symbolic reversal of our cultural castration. I endured the process for Dad, but the day after the ceremony I brought him my tallis, yarmulke, and prayer book. "I don't know if you know this, but becoming Bar Mitzvah means you're a man and can make your own decisions. Here you go." I handed him the Jew paraphernalia. "I'm never going back to the synagogue."

Dad stored the items somewhere near the green folder. He had no room to argue, since he did not attend services himself: the temple had a membership fee we couldn't afford, and even though the rabbi continually assured us the fee would be waived, the offer remained unaccepted. "I've had enough of being a charity case. I'll come back when I can afford it," Dad promised the rabbi, although I suspect charity wasn't the sole issue. I'd seen Dad flounder through my Bar Mitzvah practice, mimicking prayers, moving his lips to blend in with the worshippers, like a D-student lost in an honors class. Jewish observances remained alien to us, and shortly after being divested of their illegal allure, Yom Kippur, Hanukkah, and all the rest became convenient days off, that's all. The only vestigial remnant surfaced during Passover, when Dad bought *matzah* (from a supermarket, not an underground dealer) and munched on the crackers with as much ceremony and meaning as he did back in Kharkov.

The closest we came to exploring Jewish rituals and holidays was during our nine months in Lafayette. In December 1990, Dad wanted to get a New Year's tree, but we were told that was a Christian thing, handed a menorah, and instructed to celebrate Hanukkah instead (apparently all those New Year's family gatherings we had in Russia were meaningless, sacrilegious affronts to our culture—who knew?). So we used the menorah, but once we moved to Jersey, the New Year's tree came back. For a couple of years we lit the menorah alongside the tree, but soon enough it found a home on a bookshelf ledge among Dad's renewed knick-knack collection. And there it remained, next to two moldy boxes of CVS Hanukkah candles.

Truth is, I can't imagine it happening any other way. I can't imagine a reality in which Dad races home in time for sunset and Mom lights the Shabbat candles. But what did shock me is that shortly after beginning to research the last wave of Jewish emigration out of the Soviet Union, I learned that my family's experience was far from unique. Our rejection of the opportunity to embrace (or at least sample) Jewish religion and culture was reflected over and over again as part of a massive national pattern manifested across an entire generation. The ultimate irony of the experience of Soviet Jews in America is that the people who fled to the States in search of cultural freedom adopted irreligious, secular lives, eschewing community and synagogue alike. The vast majority of ex–Soviet Jews did not, to put it bluntly, want to be Jewish.

This phenomenon culminated in widespread frustration and disenchantment for the American Jews who had fought so hard for their oppressed brethren. "They came to us for help," one Jewish Federation leader confided in me, "for food stipends, rent money, all of that. They took what they could, and after they no longer needed us or there was nothing more to be had, they left and we never saw them again. And *these* were the people we spent four decades trying to liberate: organized rallies, marched on Washington . . . As you can imagine, it didn't leave the community with a warm feeling." After all the lobbying, the welcoming, and the funding, the ex-refugees rose to their feet and found themselves facing their liberators across a deep cultural chasm.

One side saw a Jew, the other a *zhid*. In that, the Communists had succeeded.[*]

The four-decade campaign to free the Soviet Jewry was an inspiring victory for HIAS, for Joint, for everyone who marched, pledged, and donated; a victory that reversed the fortunes of hundreds of thousands of people. Forty years is a long time, especially in an age when causes pop up and fade away as quickly as next week's headlines. The fact that American Jews, individuals dwelling in safety, grappled with the Soviet colossus in the name of complete strangers and *persisted* in that fight for forty damn years is a testament to both human rights and the Jewish people. But many Soviet Jews could not be grateful in the way their American benefactors desired, could not bring themselves to celebrate what had for so long been nothing but a dangerous liability. Overcoming our ethnicity was a matter of preservation; it had been branded onto our souls, become instinctual, and instincts, as American Jews had discovered, run deeper than inalienable rights.

The Joint administrator Amir Shaviv once told me a story about attending a conference with Joint officials, American Jewish leaders, and the handful of Soviet immigrants who could be persuaded to appear. "The community leaders were understandably disillusioned, and one exasperated man finally asked: 'Why don't you want to be Jews?'" said Shaviv. "This one fellow stood up and said, 'Listen, back in the Soviet Union I was a roach, I was a *zhid*, and I couldn't stop being a *zhid* for the life of me. I don't want to be a *zhid* anymore, and I am in America now, and I can

[*] The younger generation, those born in America or brought over at a very young age, is different. Brooklyn has plenty of young Russian Jews who converse with shopkeepers in English, their parents in Russian, and one another in Runglish. They keep kosher, chain smoke their cigarettes before sundown on Shabbat, go to pray at the temple, go party on Saturday nights, and go to college during the week. They're Jewish; most are also too young to remember the Soviet Union.

be Mr. No One. I'm sick of being a *zhid,* and if you don't like it that's too bad—it's a free country.'

"I thought that was a good answer."

* * *

Every immigrant expects something from America. People don't scale fences, trudge through deserts, abandon careers, friends, loved ones, the graves of their parents, risk their lives without hope of *something* waiting for them on U.S. shores. Here's what waited for me: America wiped away concerns for clothing, food, shelter, warmth, and I loved it from the start. I loved the freedom, choice, personal space, I blessed the land where I didn't have to cringe at the idea of going to school or walking outside. The red-violet suitcases had been packed away in the attic; the lumpy brown turtle statuette I had rescued at the last moment from the Kharkov apartment was resettled on one of Dad's bookshelves. I no longer needed the wax soldiers I had meticulously crafted from cheese wrappings in Nondorf, but I couldn't bring myself to throw them away, so I rolled them into a softball-sized ball and put it in my closet. And since I started eating more, I also started growing, and soon enough the black bomber jacket from Eva's was donated to a coat drive, replaced with a warm New York Rangers coat. We had made it.

There was no bully I'd brought with me from Russia, no drunk anti-Semite or sadistic teacher. But after five thousand miles and permanent asylum in the most protected and protective country in the world, the sick caricature of the Jew still dwelt in me. A careless glance into a shiny car or a freshly washed window was enough to show me the *zhid,* ugly, diseased, and ultimately worthless. Mirrors aren't complicated: whether in Cleveland or in Kabul, a mirror reflects what the mind sees, no more, no less.

For Mom and Dad, the hardest part of leaving Russia was me. Abandoning your life and possessions and putting yourself at the mercy of strangers is hard; it is terrifying to do so with a child. For years, my parents marveled at how well I had handled it. *No, I'm not scared. No, I'm not tired. I'm a little chilly, but I'm fine.* Partly, I viewed it as my job. From the night we snuck out of Kharkov, it seemed that everyone in the family had assumed a certain role. Dad was the decision maker, Lina the translator, Mom and Grandma the base camp crew, tending to cooking, sewing, and other necessities. I dragged suitcases and ran errands, but my most valuable contribution was simply not to panic. Through cold, hunger, instability, or terror, I was the first thing Mom and Dad checked on, and as soon as they saw I was fine, it had a calming effect on the whole family. I took my job seriously, but to be honest I didn't need to pretend much, because I loved emigration. I *thrived* in emigration.

The best part of emigration was hope. Everything was temporary, nothing was certain, and there was always that blessed chance that tomorrow something would happen and I would come across a place, a situation, a fairy godmother, a genie, something capable of generating a *poof!* that would cure me. But a couple of years after we moved to East Windsor, sometime around middle school, I realized that emigration was over and the *poof!* never came. I woke up and was still a *zhid*, and this time there was no new place to disappear to. We were no longer trapped in Russia; we were no longer refugees in Austria. For the first time in a long time we didn't have to run, and all I wanted to do was keep running.

I lay awake in my safe New Jersey house. The Soviet Union had collapsed, its carcass lay sprawled across Eurasia, and still it shook me at nights. *I'm never going back.* That promise soothed me, for years I chewed on it, it was the last thing I thought before falling asleep. But it wasn't enough. I started purging my life of everything Russian, hollowing myself out until I was no longer a Jew, religiously or ethnically. If America couldn't cure me, I'd do it myself. The religious part was simple—I never prayed or thought of customs and holidays. Here, seven decades of Soviet persecution played to my advantage. I wasn't brought up with Jewish traditions and it wasn't hard to root out what was never there in the first place. The ethnic part required some effort.

I became no one. I was from the Ukraine, once, I'd lived in the Alps, in Vienna, in Indiana, but none of those places had any meaning; I didn't speak of them, and I carried no photographs. It wouldn't do to have friends and neighbors poking into my past, so I carefully isolated myself. Russian was spoken strictly at home and out of earshot. Dad was too proud of being a refugee and Mom had her awful broken English, so my friends couldn't come over or carpool. On the few occasions Mom and Dad showed up at a concert or a swim meet I would feel naked and exposed and panic until they left. A part of me ached for them to be there but the relief of their absence was greater than the ache of their absence, and it won every time. My parents had to go. I was no longer a Jew or a Russian, so I became 32 Winchester Drive, East Windsor, New Jersey, secure in the knowledge that I was ready to ditch that life at a moment's notice and get a new address, and then be from that place. I chased numbers, piled up achievements, became 1510 on the SATs, volunteer #763 at Princeton Hospital, cadet captain with sixty calls a year on East Windsor Rescue Squad 142. My numbers would suffice for my identity.

The world is full of shiny surfaces, but avoiding my reflection wasn't impossible. I knew my surroundings, trained my mind to go blank when glancing over a mirror, learned to shave with my eyes closed. I wasn't about to take a vow of silence, but I found a solution for my accent as well. "New Jersey," I'd tell curious folks who'd hear me speak and ask where I was from. *"East Windsor,* New Jersey," I'd clarify, and most got the point. "Originally," some would persist; "I meant where are you from *originally?"* as if I didn't understand the fucking question. Silence worked wonders at that point. I'd hurl the full force of my ice-blue stare at the nosy prick, and they'd back off.

And that's how it went, through middle school and high school, shedding and running, running and shedding, flitting and darting and hissing *New Jersey,* dreaming of those wonderful days of emigration when I was nothing and no one, didn't need to worry about people and mirrors, just drifted and drifted with no attachment, nothing to remind me of what I was.

THERE ARE NO CATS IN AMERICA

Kharkov, Ukraine, USSR, 1988

"Look at the quality—that's cotton. Nothing else, just cotton."

The clock chimed ten as Uncle Fedya's face swam into the cone of light cast by the anemic lightbulb hanging above the living room table. His thick, meaty fingers gingerly grasped the sleeves of a T-shirt, and the low drone of his voice, which usually bothered me, seemed somehow apt for this occasion. It was the winter of 1988, and Uncle Fedya had recently received a package from a distant someone who had immigrated to the States in the seventies. Earlier in the evening, my family took the tram to his apartment across Kharkov to be entertained with tea, and jam, and news from America. But now it was late and the time had come to unveil the parcel. Uncle Fedya's granddaughter Yulya, whom I was expected to play with, had been mercifully sent to bed, and I nudged my way over to the main table, where I belonged (I was already eight!). Our host shoved aside the cups, stacked the saucers, and displayed the box's contents one by one, his face assuming the same somber expression I would later see on Boston priests presiding over the transfiguration of bread and wine into Body and Blood.

"A real American shirt from Brooklyn," he rasped. "Look at the tag, you can see the English letters. Here, feel it, feel it."

It was a very nice shirt, pale blue, soft and colorful, much better than the ones we had in Russia. But truth be told, it could've been an average shirt or a greasy rag. It had come in a box covered with small square stamps, much different from our gaudy ones smattered with red stars and Lenins. Beneath the circular cancellation marks with queer letters were little engravings of mountains, temples, statues, and mansions, and flowing over each image was that unmistakable striped flag that evokes reverence and hatred all over the globe. The box gave the shirt power.

A potent rumor mill churned through the Soviet-Jewish community of Kharkov, feeding our imagination with tales of America. The stories came from Russian-Jewish expats who had squeaked through the border during détente in the seventies, before the USSR had invaded Afghanistan and emigration ceased. The information filtering in wasn't plentiful: not many had left in the first place, and not all who had left had kept up correspondence. But the rumor mill made up for the scarcity, for any whisper of life in America was repeated endlessly, tirelessly, by friends, by relatives, by friends of relatives and relatives of friends.

The stories were always ones of success: unprecedented, unparalleled, and unimaginable. News from America would not, *could not* be from America unless it centered on a raise, a promotion, a wedding, or a house. After all, Communists and Capitalists alike agreed that America and the USSR were polar opposites. Soviet propaganda averred this with pride, but to those disenchanted and persecuted by the Soviet Union, the notion carried an entirely different connotation. *Not the USSR* meant a place where good things transpired and one succeeded not in spite of the odds but simply because success was in the air. The warm glow of the

Promised Land entrenched itself in our minds, molded our communal viewpoint until it reached the point at which it no longer transcended reality—it *was* reality.

This vision placed incredible pressure on both the expats who penned the letters from the United States and their relatives who read them to others in Russia. An unspoken censorship held sway over the letters: if little Misha had moved to Brooklyn, become a lawyer, gone through a nasty divorce, and was currently drinking himself into oblivion, the only item mentioned in the dispatch back to the Motherland would be "Little Misha graduated from law school," period. The end. The suppression was even more pervasive than its Communist propaganda counterpart, because unlike the blackouts and radio jammers of the Kremlin, *this* censorship was self-imposed. People didn't fail in America; how could they? Even if someone had failed, how could he muster the courage to tell others? Honestly, what can you say: if your cousin fucked up in America, well, your cousin must be an incurable grade-A schmuck, because only an incurable grade-A schmuck could ever find a way to elude the pursuit of happiness.

And so, when my family gazed out of the windows of the Boeing 747 that carried us across the Atlantic in the summer of 1990, what we—like those before us who sailed on steamships and barges—were searching for wasn't the physical landmarks of the United States but the lambent glow of the land of opportunity, the shining city on the hill, the beacon of liberty, the solace of refugees.

*　*　*

Fifteen years after my family landed at JFK, I shared this rosy vision of the States with my friend Kyle, who immediately asked if I'd seen *An American Tail*. He bolted upstairs and fished out a dusty videotape from his attic.

Eighty minutes later I rose from Kyle's couch a broken man. *An American Tail* turned out to be a cartoon saga about the Mousekewitzes, a family of five raggedy mice [read: Russian Jews], including Fievel, the plucky young protagonist, who are persecuted by ferocious cats [anti-Semitic Cossacks]. The mice brave the perilous transatlantic journey and just can't wait to get to America, where there are no cats and more cheese than an honest rodent could nibble. Upon their arrival, they discover that, much to their dismay, cats are plentiful and the cheese supply limited. Several misadventures, musical numbers, and one wacky ploy to scare the crap out of New York's cats later, the Mousekewitzes learn that with a little teamwork and a can-do attitude, they can enjoy a better life in the New World. The movie ends with a close-up of the Statue of Liberty winking at the camera as the credits roll on.

"H—h—how?" I croaked out.

"Oh there are no cats in Ame-ree-ca, and the streets are paved with cheese"—Kyle launched into the refrain—"there are no cats in Ame-ree-ca, so set your mind at—"

"Stop it! Please! Yes, you like it—that's absolutely wonderful. Unfortunately, I can't join in on your nostalgic childhood memories because I just learned that *my* childhood perfectly parallels a movie about mice . . . wide-eyed, idiotically optimistic, musical mice. I am Fievel Mousekewitz. I am a fucking cartoon mouse! I'm having a crisis here. How could this happen? Even a ten-year-old kid doesn't expect to go on safari and see singing warthogs and 'Hakuna Matata' bullshit! But me, Mom, most of us, it was just like that mouse movie. Mom's a smart woman, not some naïve idealist, but she didn't study English or prepare a résumé: she acted like those mice! How?"

"I don't know," said Kyle. "Have you tried asking her?"

"I've interviewed her dozens of times."

"Don't interview her. Ask her."

The opportunity presented itself several days later, when I went out to eat with Mom and Dad. I sat across from Mom. Over the past six months she had grown used to fielding random emigration questions and spontaneous requests for clarification, so I brought up America smack in the middle of the entrées. "Didn't you consider, before you got here, that people may have been exaggerating, that the stories weren't real? Didn't you plan ahead for getting a job, learning the language, banking, paying rent? Didn't you foresee any of these challenges?"

"No, we didn't discuss too much of those details," Mom shook her head. "It was just a feeling, America, not specific details, and—"

I cut her off. "And that is why doctors become security guards here." Mom winced. It was a shitty thing to say, but that moronic mouse had me furious. "You wanted to live here, right? So shouldn't you have prepared more realistically? I hate to say it, but the refugee vision of this country was naïve and ridiculous!" I jabbed my fingers in the air to accentuate the point. "America's not heaven: there's bills, and rents, and fine print, and a language barrier, and people get fired, get mistreated, humiliated . . . I mean, Mom, what is it you wanted from America?"

Mom rested her elbows on the table and for a while I watched her gaze off at the wooden divider next to us, and I could tell she was far away. When she spoke again, her voice was both calm and quiet. "I didn't want to be afraid of the government anymore, to live in fear of them going to my home. I didn't want to watch my daughter suffer and be denied from school because she was Jewish. I didn't want to stand on the schoolhouse steps and worry to death about explaining to my nine-year-old son why being a Jew was bad, and why he should prepare for a long and painful life."

I remembered the last day of second grade, standing on the steps of Kharkov's School Number Three, the cold rag damping the bruise spreading over my left eye and cheekbone. Mom dashed in from work and I asked her if it was possible to stop being a Jew. I had been so ashamed of that moment, not because of the beating, but because I was weak enough to ask Mom for help. I hadn't meant to upset her; I just figured she was a doctor, she knew how to cure all sorts of illnesses, and it was worth a shot. It was the only time I ever brought up Jews to my parents. I didn't realize Mom even remembered that moment, and now, as an adult, I shuddered at seeing it from her perspective.

She didn't need a job, I realized as the waitress refilled our drinks, snapping me back to the present. *She had a job. She had a career. She didn't need English to read books, and have friends, and watch the news, and carry on meaningful conversations. She'd done that for decades before I was even born. She sacrificed it all for peace and dignity, not a paycheck.*

The laughable thing, it hit me, was not that intelligent, sane people bought into an unrealistic vision, but the fact that I was fussing over logistics when deeper factors were at play. We *needed* America. Shit, I needed America. When I was a kid huddling inside the apartment, scared of the world beyond our black-leather-upholstered door, scared of my neighbors, my teachers, of drunken men by the bakery, when I lost my best friend to the grotesque thing in the mirror, when I had no dreams other than to escape the Ukraine, I *needed* America, Fievel Mousekewitz's America, shiny and golden, without the warts and fine print. How could any immigrant write home anything but good news? People are suffering: tread softly, comrade, you're walking on their salvation. The stereotype of America had anchored itself to dreams and fears, drew its power from hope, operated on a level beyond logic. It didn't bother to contend with rational thinking for the simplest of reasons—it didn't have to.

The waitress cleared away the plates and left us the check, and for a few quiet minutes my mother nibbled at her cake while I sipped my coffee, a little subdued and immensely grateful.

*   *   *

America *is* the land of opportunity—that's a true stereotype, and thank God for that. The seeds for meaningful change were there, in the States. They were there through middle school and high school, as I gnawed on disappointment and hate, but they would require a commitment beyond landing on safe shores and passively waiting to be healed. Fievel and the mice did it with musical numbers and half-baked schemes that were just crazy enough to work. In my case, it would necessitate another journey, one that began at an unlikely place.

Senior year of high school came, and with it, the ritual choosing of colleges. I had only two requirements: the school had to be highly selective (a top education being the most important thing in the world), and could not have a Jewish studies program. I gravitated toward nice Catholic schools, figuring they'd provide me with a good diploma while minimizing my contact with the sick race. Boston College grabbed my attention: it was ranked in the top forty national universities by *U.S. News & World Report* and boasted of being not just Catholic, but "Catholic Jesuit." I had no idea what that meant, but it sounded delightfully not-Jewish, and that's what I went with. Little did I suspect that from Boston College I, who had enrolled as an anti-Semite, would emerge a Jew.

WHERE AM I AND WHY DO I
SMELL LIKE BANANAS?

Chestnut Hill, Mass., March 2001

The campus is desolate; spring break has begun. I'm in my dorm waiting for tomorrow, when I will join my Appalachia Volunteers group to begin the long trek down to Georgia, where we will spend a week building houses with Habitat for Humanity. Tonight is my birthday, and in a few hours I will turn twenty-one. I do not plan on going out: I want to be fresh for the trip, all of my friends have already left the campus, plus I hate birthdays to begin with and I thank the BC administration for being prudent enough to schedule the first day of spring break right on my birthday.

Enter Pete, the only friend who's staying in town for the week. Earlier this year I made the mistake of telling Pete the date of my birthday, and now he's calling to make plans. When I tell him there are no plans, Pete grows incensed. He fumes that there are disadvantaged children who would give anything for a chance to binge drink once in their grimy little lives. He reminds me that getting blitzed the night you turn twenty-one is an American tradition, and the Founding Fathers didn't shed their blood for my right to party just so I could "pussy out" on them. But what hurts Pete the most, as an American, is that I have just gotten my citizenship, made a commitment to this country, and the moment I have to do something that "inconveniences" me I go ahead and trample the proud American spirit without any regard for my actions.

By the time Pete's finished with me I feel like Benedict Arnold, Simon Legree, and Richard Nixon all rolled into one. Without delay I lug my bags to his apartment, and we take the fateful walk to Mary Ann's, the mother of all Boston dive bars. The place squats next to a tram station. It's small, brick, and brown, with a green-and-yellow sign and a side yard littered with abandoned keg carcasses. It looks like it was originally a cheap build-it-yourself fallout shelter and now, with the nuclear race over, someone slapped a sign on it and opened for business. We arrive five minutes before midnight and loiter outside while I have a cigarette and listen to Pete regale me with stories of the joint. It turns out Mary Ann's is a perpetual contender for the coveted Worst Bar in Boston award. Pint glasses are neither washed nor rinsed, but dipped into a sink with soapy water, then into another sink with tepid water, and then deemed ready for refills. Practices like that have caused some misguided BC students to select more reputable establishments for their birthdays, but the stalwarts, Pete assures me, true maroon-and-gold, retch at Mary Ann's on their twenty-first. I am pumped up. I feel honored to partake in this venerated, albeit blurry rite of passage and tread on an entire generation of alumni puke stains. Off in the distance, a church clock strikes twelve and Pete smiles and holds open the padded black door as the last few strains of "Tiny Dancer" escape into the night.

Saturday Evening

I wake up around 6:00 p.m. I am miserable and achy. I reek of vomit. I'm supposed to meet my Habitat group in two hours, which means that I should probably take a shower, but I'm also extremely nervous about getting into a van with twelve strangers and trudging down to spend a week in Georgia, so I do nothing. And the worst part is, my stupid birthday locked me into going on this trip: all Appalachia drivers have to be covered by Boston College's insurance policy, which only applies to those ages twenty-one and up. If I back out I'll be screwing the group. I lie on Pete's couch in my grimy blue sweatshirt and search for some magical way to elude this trip. I bargain with the universe. I promise the universe that if I get a pass on this, I'll devote my spring break to building something here, in wonderful, safe Boston. Of course I can't manage a house by myself, but I can probably recruit Pete to assist me with something smaller, like a doghouse for a homeless dog. That has to count for something.

The universe doesn't budge. Homeless dogs in the greater Boston area aren't high on the universe's agenda. I've really fucked myself on this one. Throughout my three semesters at BC I've exerted great care to keep my shit nice and delineated. I'm no longer 32 Winchester Drive, East Windsor, New Jersey. I'm 140 Commonwealth Avenue, Chestnut Hill, Massachusetts. I've already severed contact with people from high school, and I barely leave Boston, returning to Jersey only for winter break, when the campus shuts down. Mom and Dad require daily schoolwork updates, and I talk to them (in Russian and out of earshot of my roommates), but as long as the A's keep coming they're satisfied. I don't have a girlfriend, and if a girl likes me, I make sure to get out of the situation. Girlfriends come with questions, and besides, I don't want to be with anyone who'd want to date a *zhid*. I study, but don't live with my classmates; I live, but don't hang out with my roommates, and the people I hang out with, like Pete, are potheads whose activities are centered around a black light, a joint, and Phish on the stereo. Potheads are safe—chip in for your share, lie back on the couch, and don't worry about dealing with inquiries about what you are and where you're from. I do what I can; I delineate and run.

Initially, I signed up for Appalachia Volunteers because I liked the idea of showing up to an empty work site and leaving a framed house a week later: I've been investing myself in purely figurative things like GPAs and test scores, and it'd be nice to get something tangible done for a change. But as the trip drew closer, it dawned on me that building a house involved spending a week with twelve do-gooder strangers who give big, sweaty hugs and want to get to know you, and it scares me out of my freaking mind, and I'm reduced to cursing the urge to play construction worker that made me sign up for Appalachia in the first place.

"What's your problem?" Pete interrupts my pouting. "You're about to have a great time and meet lots of interesting people!"

I gape in disbelief. *You'll have a great time, You'll meet lots of interesting people,* and *You'll get more out of it than you put in* are the three clichés of Appalachia Volunteers, which ring through the campus during orientation and after spring break. People sign up for fun, community service, résumé building, but everyone, from the altruistic to the career-minded, is drawn in by the three magnetic slogans that have transformed Appalachia into the biggest club on campus and the largest volunteer spring break program in the nation. Pete's never gone on a service trip—none of my friends have—but that doesn't matter, because with 540 people participating every year, the sayings worm themselves into the brain of every BC student. Forever.

"Are you gonna tell me I'm going to get more out of it than I put in? That is pathetic."

Pete's attempts at encouragement have failed, but the blond, ruddy-faced man doesn't give up. He gets his first-aid kit and rolls a very fat joint, crushing up a codeine pill and sprinkling the powder over the weed. "We're going to smoke this; it'll help you relax, and you'll be all set for the trip."

I vaguely recall signing a No drugs or alcohol pledge for Appalachia, but as Pete points out, the trip hasn't started yet. Plus, Appalachia Volunteers operates under the aegis of BC's Campus Ministry and Pete's a theology major, which somehow makes it okay. We smoke the whole thing.

Pete's plan has worked in the sense that while still terrified, I no longer possess the ability to articulate my emotions. Pete packs me a Gatorade and walks me to the T, the tram that returns me to campus. As the tram pulls away he gives me an encouraging wave, like a proud mother on the first day of school. I never wind up showering.[*]

A lonely van waits under a lonely lamppost by the main church at the edge of the campus. With each step the ground feels like it's situated a few inches above or below where it's supposed to be. I try to adjust my walking, but whoever's in charge of the ground elevation continues to mess with it as well, and progress is slow. The van's loaded and there are people milling about in the yellow haze. Some are hugging. We've accomplished nothing, we haven't built so much as a Popsicle house, and they're already hugging.

I climb into the very back. My limbs are contorted into unnatural positions. A fifteen-passenger van is designed for fifteen people to sit in uncomfortably; we have just crammed in thirteen people along with a week's luggage and sleeping bags. Trapped in the back bench with me are some guy with a hammy face and a girl who thinks she's better than everyone else.

[*] Later on I learned that Pete was something called an "enabler," that I should surround myself with "constructive" individuals, and that smoking crushed-up codeine to alleviate anxiety was not a "healthy" decision, but that was all way down the road.

Five minutes into the ride I discover that I've been sitting on an overripe banana Stuck-Up Girl brought along with her. The banana mush has already colonized the seat of my jeans and is rapidly soaking through the boxers. I hate Stuck-Up Girl. My only consolation is the nauseating smell emanating from my sweatshirt; I've already caught her suppressing a gag. We merge onto the Massachusetts Turnpike and someone cranks up the radio, just in time for the chorus to "You Give Love a Bad Name."

The van's only speaker is mounted in the rear of the cabin. I know that because my head has been resting on it. My brain explodes. *"Shhmaaa . . . eeeeehhhhhh,"* I attempt to plead for a lower volume but the codeine is inhibiting the formation of complete sentences, leaving me in some cheap, sticky hell with a Bon Jovi soundtrack.

Location: Uncertain
Date: Uncertain

Where am I and why do I smell like bananas? is the first clear thought to congeal in my mind. All I know is that I'm standing, it is day, it is overcast, and there's a gray granite wall inches away from my face. I tilt my head to follow the wall as it soars up and up and up, leaving me dizzy and losing itself at an apex somewhere in the clouds. I stagger backward from the monstrosity; around me I hear cloth flapping on wind, and the wall morphs into a giant stone obelisk encircled by American flags. There's nothing else around—no people, no cars, not even a bird—it's like a crappy post-apocalyptic movie. I manage an awkward U-turn and spy the van parked along a faraway curb, the group lined up in front. They must've survived the apocalypse. Part of me is a little relieved. Part of me is very disappointed.

It is 6:00 a.m. on Sunday, I'm in front of the Washington Monument, and my entire ass and the backs of my legs are plastered with a thick crust of dried banana mush. The wind changes and I get a good whiff of myself. I reek of weed, and puke, and bananas. For some reason it's the last smell that concerns me; I don't want to smell like bananas. I am sad. I look around for a hose.

There is no hose. I am indignant. I don't understand why the government can't maintain basic amenities near a beloved national landmark. One of the trip leaders, Seth, approaches me. He's wearing a shit-eating grin, has a bottle of water in one hand and a coffee in the other, and he can't stop smiling. "You, sir, look like you've had a fantastic birthday."

"Thenk yehhh," I croak as Seth hands me the water and briefs me on the past eight hours. It turns out I had remained staunchly motionless during the night's ride to D.C. When the group pulled into town to grab breakfast, they voted to let me sleep off the coma. Upon their return they discovered the van empty and me trying to stare down the Washington Monument.

Seth orients me toward the van and hands me the keys, since the only other driver has already logged in nine hours and the rest is up to me. I hate it when people touch me. "Wonderful birthday . . . what a fantastic, wonderful birthday," Seth wistfully sighs. I jump the curb, the van erupts in a hurried clicking of seat belts, and nine hours later we arrive in Eastman, Georgia.

*   *   *

Eastman, Georgia, is a town where southern stereotypes come to life. It boasts a Main Street with a small diner that serves coffee, grits, and corn bread (I'm still not sure what grits are, save that they have the taste and texture of soggy paper). It has a Walmart. People in the Walmart, employees and shoppers alike, immediately notice that we're from out of town and refuse to release us until they're convinced we've been fed and have a place to stay. On the way back to the van I see a pickup truck with a ratty Confederate flag tied to the antenna and a revolver strapped to the back of the driver's seat headrest. Up north this would've been alarming, but here it's authentic. In fact, I would've been disappointed if the truck *wasn't* equipped with a Confederate flag and a revolver.

A rickety railroad track slices through Eastman. On one side of the tracks is an enclave of large mansions, descendants of the old plantations, inhabited by wealthy white people, some of them descendants of the old plantation owners. Immediately on the other side of the tracks is an overgrown field strewn with rusty propane tanks. Black children play hide-and-seek among the tanks. Beyond the field is a collection of dilapidated shacks. There are lots of moldy beams and crumbling cinder blocks. Some appear to serve a purpose but others simply jut out of the ground, as if they had supported something at some point but now that something isn't there. Everything leans everywhere, and the walls are riddled with holes big enough to see through one shack to the shack behind it. Except for the beams and cinder blocks, the whole neighborhood has no infrastructure. It feels like a strong gust of wind is all it would take to send the whole thing back to the trash heap from which it came.

We don't see many inhabitants during our tour of the shacks. The ones we do see are black. We look at them. They do not look at us.

Monday afternoon, and I'm hammering together a house frame in a lot across the tracks from the field with the propane tanks. The first problem is that I'm awful at hammering. Compounding this is the fact that Habitat for Humanity of Dodge County, Georgia, must've gotten a hell of a bargain on three-million-year-old petrified wood. The fucking wood is rock solid. It belongs in a natural history museum, not a work site. The nails refuse to go in. I'm inching along at a half-hour-a-nail pace and find myself thinking of Sisyphus and the starting roster of the 0–14 1976 Tampa Bay Buccaneers. The sweat's dripping from my face, my wrists throb, I alternate arms because both hurt, and I'm getting infuriated.

The nail bends. Apparently, giant four-inch metal nails can do that—I had no idea. It *folds* and I pull it out, painstakingly tap it back into shape, focus my anger, slam down the hammer, and again it bends. I've curved this nail into fifty unique and grotesque positions, but it won't go in. I am angry beyond belief, and *I hate my life, I hate how I look, how I am, how my body looks, how my body hurts, and I hate how everyone around me hates me, and I hate them right back for it. I am validated by achievement, and right now my entire self-worth is hanging on a fucking nail that refuses to go into a piece of petrified wood, and I can't do anything about it and I can't stop and I can't fail and I'm nothing and my arms are so drained that I can't even grasp the hammer, and I hate how weak I am and I try to rest as little as possible until I can—*

"Hey."

The girl is Katie, she's the other trip leader, and she is looking me over because I'm clearly not going fast enough for her.

"You want some water?"

I hit her with the *I'm from New Jersey* stare, through her burning red hair and green Scranton University sweatshirt, rumpled from hugging and hammering. That's the best way to do it: you focus on a spot a little bit behind the person. It makes them feel transparent, brings them to your level, where you're comfortable.

"You want some water?"

I push out with my eyes, through her invisible body, willing her to back off, but the insult doesn't come. What's more concerning is that the stare doesn't do shit. Usually people back down; sometimes they start a confrontation. This girl doesn't react. I pry out the nail. This time it's bent into a cursive Z. The head's squished into itself and the rest is a wicked curve. I don't know what to do so I hand it to her.

"Z."

"What's that?"

"Z. It looks like a cursive Z."

"It kinda does." She smiles, cocks her arm, and chucks my nemesis into the weeds. "I think it's time for that nail to retire."

"Can you do that?" The option never crossed my mind. My plan was to hammer, and hammer, and hammer. Until kingdom comes.

"Yeah, you can," Katie says, and I drink her water, and it feels good, and two little streams dribble out the corners of my mouth, making me realize that I am smiling.

As I walk over to the equipment truck for more nails, I spy a yellow drill. I covertly drill small holes all along the length of my section, where the nails are supposed to go, and sneak the drill back. The nails glide in—it's like I'm hammering them into butter—and when a nail does bend, I toss it away. My body's working and I leave it alone. The site echoes with the disjointed *clank clank clank* of fourteen hammers each going at its own pace, and I love that clanking. I think about nothing. I hammer and I'm at peace.

It's time for a coffee break and Wendell and I are perched on the rafters our group nailed up earlier this morning. Every day Wendell gets dropped off at the work site by an unmarked white van, and picked up by an unmarked white van. The van comes from a halfway house where Wendell is undergoing rehab. He's a court-mandated volunteer. It's Wednesday morning, it's sunny and the sky is really blue, and we chain-smoke cigarettes and sip southern sweet tea and look out over the field with the black kids and the propane tanks across the tracks from the site. Most of the group avoids Wendell, but I'm okay with him. We get along.

Wendell starts talking about how he got to the halfway house. He got involved with the Ku Klux Klan, got hooked on meth, became a dealer, got arrested, went to prison, and lost custody of his son. His goal now is to clean himself up so he can hang out with his son and go to NASCAR races and play ball with him.

Wendell is here because he has to be here. I don't know why I am here. I'm not an ex-Klansman, but I know what it's like to blindly hate. I've never been to prison but I'm always on guard and don't trust people, and from Wendell's description, that sounds like a key element of prison life. I don't have an overarching goal, but I desperately want to want something. It'd be nice to have a real goal.

He tells me that he was recently transferred to the halfway house and is still orienting himself within the program. "What's that like?" I ask.

"You know what?" he drawls. "In prison, in rhehab, everyone tells you you gotta git God, or prayer, or whillpower . . . you can change the way you been raised, the way you thought all yer life—git yourself some whillpower and you'll be rhight as a fucking June bug."

Wendell's a big fan of his *h*s. It's a bit charming, but I don't think Wendell would appreciate being linked with the word, even in my inner monologue, so I once again resort to "*authentic.*"

"But you eva drink a bottle of castor oil?"

I shake my head. "I'm more of a Busch Light guy myself."

He spits and squints at the black kids racing around the propane tanks. "Whell, you want to find out about *whillpower,* try drinking a bottle of castor oil and *whill* yourself not to shit yer brains out. Whill all you want, pray all you want, it ain't gonna do you a damn thing.

"People talk about 'whill this' and 'whill that,' but what you need is hard work to change the way you think, the way you look at the shit around you, and *that's* the part people don't want to hear and don't want to tell you. I may be an ex-junkie, and an ex-Klansman, and an ex-con, but I've learned that much."

Below us the group starts to stir. Wendell spits again and clambers down the rafters. I watch him yank leftover splinters from his palms (Wendell eschews work gloves) and return to work. I don't know him, but I still want to say thank you for the sincerity, but I'm not sure how to do it, so I spit and follow him down the ladder.

*   *   *

The outgoing senior leader for Appalachia Volunteers was either not very good at leaving messages or had an interesting sense of humor, because the voicemail he left me began with "We've had many strong applicants this year, which made it a very difficult decision," and continued in that vein for a good thirty seconds before congratulating me on getting the position.

Immediately upon returning to Boston College from Georgia, I had applied to be an Appalachia coordinator, one of six students who assume the burden of organizing 32 trips, recruiting 540 participants, training 58 trip leaders, and raising $200,000 for the mammoth spring break program. Before the outgoing coordinators started the interview, they made sure to inform me of the immense workload involved. They mentioned it to everyone, but they stressed it to me, since I was entering junior year, which is when pre-meds sequester themselves from the world to prepare for the MCAT med school admission tests. I thanked them for the warning and immediately accepted the position.

The graduating coordinators weren't exaggerating about the workload. At the beginning of fall semester, Boston College's legal department had informed us that due to safety issues, we could no longer use fifteen-passenger vans. Their decision placed the Appalachia program in jeopardy: the number of drivers had to be doubled, logistics had to be reworked, and an already-packed budget had soared by an extra $20,000. None of us wanted to see the twenty-five-year-old program die on our watch.

At the end of spring break I was on a Greyhound bus returning to BC from Appalachia after spending the past six months helping to keep the program afloat. Buses lined the main campus drag, dropping off students returning from Mississippi, Alabama, Georgia, Kentucky, West Virginia, and the Carolinas. Elsa, another Appalachia coordinator, was sharing my bus. Without saying anything the two of us stood up and met in the center aisle. She was crying. Everyone else on our bus was beaming at us. They realized it had been a tough year, but Elsa and I were the only ones who really knew how close Appalachia had come to folding.

Outside, volunteers were chatting, hugging, unloading, laughing, sharing stories. It hit me that I had been a part of 32 communities and 540 students, and the notion left me both honored and humbled. That's when reality inverted a bit. In the time it took us to wend down St. Thomas More Drive and find a parking spot, I saw smiles and knew they were genuine, and I wanted to be myself and no one else. For nearly two solid minutes, I could've looked straight in a mirror.

I sat down on the steps across from the cafeteria, toying with the straps of my sleeping bag, watching the world settle back to normalcy. Clusters of students broke off from the group, carting duffel bags and memories back to their dorms. A line of freshmen snaked up the giant staircase leading to underclass housing at the top of the hill. My mind began compiling to-do lists to keep busy and keep moving; the long row of large, shiny windows on the campus theater radiated with familiar danger once more.

I tucked those two minutes away. It was the second time in my life I was absolutely, utterly happy. By coincidence, the first time also took place on a bus. It was December 21, 1989, the night I climbed onto a bus at 4:00 in the morning, the bus that would take my family off the grid and out of Russia.

It's when I first began to run.

UNFINISHED BUSINESS, PART II:
STAYING IN AMERICA

Chestnut Hill, Mass., October 1999

"Do you have your citizenship?" asked Dan.

It was around eleven at night, and the three of us—Dan, the dog, and I—were in the middle of our nightly walk. Dan lived two doors down from me. We were both pre-med bio majors, and every night we took a twenty-minute break to loop around the quiet neighborhood behind the freshman dorms, and smoke Camel Lights, and talk about getting laid, which, of course, is the real goal of becoming a doctor. The dog, a silver lab, lived in one of the houses. It wasn't kept on a leash, and one September evening it tagged along with Dan and me, and ever since then it always joined our walks, trotting around the block a few times, then going off to wherever it lived.

Dan was a Russian Jew, like me. He came to the States when he was young, like me. How he escaped Russia, where he was stationed in Europe, whether he got beaten up in school, or how he wound up in the States, I did not know. I wasn't even sure which city or republic he was from. I'd overhear him mutter Russian on the phone to his parents, and I know he'd caught me doing the same, but we never exchanged a Russian word between us. This mutual reticence is what bonded us in the Catholic Jesuit milieu of Boston College. It's like we were the only two on campus who

263

knew where the body was buried, and as long as I didn't squeal and he didn't squeal it would remain our little secret. Dan and I never spoke about the past beyond America, which is why his citizenship question surprised me.

"No, I don't," I answered. "I applied, but they lost my paperwork. Twice. I've been meaning to reapply but I haven't done it yet."

Dan looked concerned. "You should do it soon. I just read online about this immigrant who got caught doing something stupid, like public urination, and got deported, even though he had a green card."

"How can they deport me? I don't even have a country to get deported to—the *Soyuz* is gone. Where the fuck are they gonna put me?"

There was an uncomfortable pause as both Dan and I registered the use of Russian. *Soyuz* means union, as in the Soviet Union, which had fallen apart into its fifteen constituent republics in 1991.

"I don't know," Dan said. "The guy I read about, they shipped him to Somalia. It doesn't matter, man: you *gotta* get your citizenship."

"Public urination?" I glanced down at the dog, who looked positively horrified.

"Public urination."

"Somalia?"

"Somalia."

I applied for my citizenship the next day; I did *not* want to go to Somalia.

*   *   *

On a crisp autumn afternoon one year later, I stepped into the gray Immigration and Naturalization Service Center in Cherry

Hill, New Jersey. Inside was a stark vestibule monitored by a bored security guard as well as a six-foot-tall Statue of Liberty made out of green plastic. I signed in, took a seat next to the rest of the tired, the poor, the huddled masses yearning to breathe free, and listened for my name. After about an hour, a middle-aged lady ushered me into her cubicle.

"Mr. Golinkin, we have your fingerprints, documents, and application fee. You will now take the citizenship test to demonstrate your knowledge of U.S. history."

I was in college. I was in mid-term mode. *Bring it.*

The woman produced a sheet of paper with ten questions. A cursory survey revealed that the test had been designed by an avuncular middle-school teacher who wanted everyone to get an A. "What do the thirteen stripes on the American flag represent?" the first question asked. A few rows down was "How many original colonies were there in America?" *Brilliant.* I breezed through the questions, nursing my disappointment. I wanted to discuss the Boston Tea Party and the Hayes-Tilden affair, the Truman Doctrine and the Marshall Plan; I wanted to show America that I cared about the little things, that I had forgotten neither the *Maine* nor the Alamo. Instead I had to reaffirm that yes, our union was still comprised of fifty, nifty United States . . . just as it has been since 1959.[*]

The case officer didn't share my indignation.

"It's time for the writing part. You will find some blank space on the bottom of your test sheet. In it, I would like you to write down why is the sky blue."

Oooh, I perked up. *Here we go! Finally, a real question. A*

---

[*] In the interest of full disclosure, I'm not 100 percent sure of the exact questions on my test, but I can assure you, a remedial sixth-grader would've aced it.

little strange, a little unexpected, but still, an opportunity to make my country proud. Last year, in chemistry class, we covered optics and how Earth's atmosphere diffuses white light into its components. These, in turn, get absorbed by the atmosphere, save the blue wavelength, which gives the sky its characteristic hue. But that's only the scientific explanation. The ancient Egyptians believed the sky was a heavenly ocean upon which the celestial spheres journeyed in boats. I need to integrate these various perspectives into a coherent yet terse—

"Mr. Golinkin?"

"I'm sorry, ma'am, I'm just thinking it over."

"Mr. Golinkin, this is a dictation exercise. Would you like me to repeat the prompt?"

"Did you say dictation?"

"Yes. Would you like me to repeat the prompt?"

"I know stuff about the presidents," I mumbled. *Benjamin Harrison was the Lucky Pierre of the Cleveland administrations. Harry Truman played the piano.*

"Mr. Golinkin"—she anxiously glanced at the clock—"all you have to do is write down the sentence 'Why is the sky blue?' and we're *both* done."

Why is the sky blue? I methodically printed in big letters. It was a bit girlie (the *y*s looped a lot), but overall a decent sentence. Definitely citizenship material.

"Very good. We will contact you within two months to make arrangements for the naturalization ceremony." The woman squeezed out her most reassuring special-ed smile. "Goodbye, Mr. Golinkin."

On the ride back to Boston I contemplated the fact that I had already become a young, jaded American and I wasn't even an American yet. I didn't know whether to feel concerned or ahead of schedule.

INS must've been impressed by the handwriting; the natural- ization ceremony invitation came within a month, and back to Cherry Hill I went. Dad wanted to come for the ceremony, but I told him to stay home: I was tired of standing around govern- ment offices with members of my family. The vestibule was full of people from all over the world, all of whom had come to take the final step to naturalization. I plopped down in the back for about forty-five minutes of waiting and listening to the jumble of languages mixing together in the room.

"Ladies and gentlemen, please stand and raise your right hand."

Our swear-in officer, a graying man in a standard-issue navy suit, strode into the room. He took a few moments to scan the ranks, as if to make up his mind whether he was going to go through with it. An elderly Indian woman next to me had brought her granddaughter, who was constantly taking pictures, trying to capture the perfect before-and-after citizenship shot. The Oath of Allegiance commenced, the officer prompting, the crowd repeat- ing the various stipulations: fight for the government, reject other citizenships, "renounce and abjure all allegiance and fidelity to any foreign prince, potentate, state, or sovereignty," and so forth.

By the time the oath was over, everyone was eyeing the offi- cer's assistant, who cradled a stack of citizenship certificates in her arm. But before we got a chance to move in, the officer segued into the welcome speech.

"Congratulations, everyone. America is based on immmgrants, we're all very proud to have such hard-working men and women . . ."

The speech droned on. He didn't even need a cue card: judg- ing by the monotone voice and perfunctory delivery, he'd done this hundreds of times. After the first few sentences everything decomposed into an interminable trickle of nouns: America, work, opportunity, you, long history of, melting pot.

He finally ran out of nouns and nodded to the assistant. The Indian granddaughter snapped away furiously. I took my certificate and gave the room one parting look. The vestibule was awash with exhausted, jubilant faces. People of all colors, cultures, backgrounds, chattering, beaming, hugging their documents. Even I was a bit touched. *I'm an American. I'm safe. I'm free. I can go outside and publicly urinate from sea to shining sea, and they can handcuff me, they can fine me, they can throw me in jail, but they can never, ever drag me out of this country. Not to Russia. Not to Somalia. No sir, all you motherfuckers are stuck with me. Let freedom flow.* The Indian grandmother caught my gaze. She smiled. I smiled. I bet she was thinking the exact same thing.

ALICIA

Chestnut Hill, Mass., November 2002

The cold November wind rushed through the brick avenues formed between the BC dorms and it was already late and it was going to be a lot later by the time I first told someone my story.

I met Alicia at the very end of junior year, and I spent a lot of the fall semester of senior year with her. She was kind, compassionate, very beautiful, and a little sad. She was smart, and she was an idealist, and she wanted to change the world. I felt safe with her. Every time I felt rattled, felt that I had made myself too accessible, she'd say or do something funny, or silly, or endearingly vulnerable, and my jaw would unclench and I wouldn't run.

I had just returned from one of the numerous retreats offered by BC. The retreat, like most retreats, was supposed to instill the participants with a feeling of identity, a sense of belonging, and hope for the future. It was a good retreat, powerful and thought-out, but none of that happened. I sat in the group circles and shared the minimum, and when others smiled I said that I was also happy and when others cried I said that I, too, was sad, but being there and watching the emotions flow over other people left me aching to talk to Alicia and tell her *something* real.

I wasn't happy about doing it so I just vomited it out in a

continuous stream. I told her that I hated myself. I told her that I hated others and that I had never believed a single good thing anyone had said about me, because whoever gave me a compliment must've been a liar, or delusional, or worthless to say they saw worth in me. I told her that I had been afraid for as long as I could remember, and I told her that I had a good memory.

I took Alicia back to the USSR, walked her over to Austria, brought her to the States, and drew her into the paralyzing, hopeless existence that comes with not having a shred of self-esteem.

We sat on her blue couch. I spoke and stared unwaveringly into the darkness outside her window, but I could feel Alicia trying to sit closer, peek into me. She was always trying to hug me and I finally explained why I hated hugs, why I hated having someone touch my body, how it evoked memories of the beatings, and why I froze and cringed whenever she tried to hug me, just as I had done with everyone since I left Russia. I told her that I hadn't looked in a mirror in years, and I explained to her why. I choked up when I explained that whenever I finally did open up to people during the last two years, whenever I found something that I cared about like the Appalachia program, that feeling of love, friendship, communion would vanish.

Build all you want, pretend all you want, you're still a zhid, *you can't stay away from mirrors forever,* said the sickly little thing in the mirror. And it was right.

I kept talking, not because I wanted to, but because I was afraid of what would happen when I stopped—Alicia thought so well of me and she was so damn kind. She'd silently mouth "bless you" when someone sneezed in class . . . not because the person would hear her or it was dictated by the situation, but because she meant it. Upstairs in her bedroom lived a group of ugly stuffed animals she'd bought over the years because she was afraid nobody else would buy them (I'd done the same thing and for the same reason, except that my purchases involved the timing and execution of a special forces raid as I raced to make sure no one I knew was in the immediate vicinity of the store). When I finally stopped talking it was past three in the morning and I could look outside her glass door and see that the campus, which was usually teeming with people, was completely dormant, and I listened to the silence and stared at the blackness of Alicia's window, afraid to turn and see the inevitable disgust and horror in her reaction.

She remained quiet, waiting until I forced myself to look at her, and when I did I saw that her dark eyes, jet-black, darker than even the windowpane, were full of tears, and more tears were already on her face, and she would sometimes wipe them away with an absentminded gesture, but more tears kept coming. I looked at her eyes and at that moment I knew that I could have gone on for hours, I could have completely emptied all the hate, and guilt, and vileness in my heart and she would have absorbed it all, and she would have never been repulsed.

I don't know how to cry, and I don't mean that in the *I'm all cried out* emo way. I literally can't do it. I'd burned it out of me by the second grade. I couldn't avoid the beatings or the fear, I couldn't get my friend Oleg back, but I could decide not to cry, no matter what. I tried it one day and soon it became a reflex. It's a trick, a matter of concentrating, clenching your jaw, and grinding out the knot in your throat until it travels up your neck and dissipates into a dull headache. Headaches were fine, I'd reasoned to myself back in Kharkov: sad people cried, weak people cried, but everyone got headaches.

A scratching from under the kitchen cabinets broke the silence. "Is that a mouse?" I went to investigate. I didn't hear Alicia move, but when I turned back I saw that she'd teleported onto the far-thest piece of furniture from the kitchen. (Love for ugly animals had its limits.) "It's probably just the stove," I lied, and walked over to the chair she was standing on. She was looking down at me from the chair, an embarrassed smile showing through the tears. It seemed like an hour had passed as I stood there aching to help her down, but reflexes kept my arms pinned to my sides. After a few awkward moments, she stepped down herself.

"Can you do something for me?" she finally said. "Can you promise me that if I tell you something, you'll believe me, if just for a moment?"

I didn't say yes, or maybe I did and I just don't remember.

"Can you promise me that you'll believe me when I tell you that everything that you just told me—the hating, the beating, the kids in Russia, your friend Oleg, the mirror—can you believe me when I tell you that it's not your fault?

"It's not your fault. I just want you to believe that."

I wanted to tell her *I'll try*. I wanted to tell her *I will*. I wanted to kiss her. There were times when I was with her that I felt I could, or I should, and it would just feel right. I wanted to take whatever it was that whispered that a beautiful girl would never be interested in a *zhid*, and tell it to go fuck itself.

I slid open the glass door and stepped out into the empty campus.

* * *

The matches refused to ignite. They jerked across the matchbook and did nothing, or caught fire and instantly puttered out. I kept tearing them off and striking them and cursing them and cursing the wind, and at some point after I'd gone through seven or eight,

I realized that there was no wind, and I couldn't light a match for the life of me because my hands were trembling.

Something was different. As I fumbled with the matches under the still black sky of Alicia's backyard, suspended between the momentary sparks in front of me and the dim glow of her window, where I knew she was still standing, I knew beyond a doubt—something had changed. The cold sky, the frozen grass littered with burnt matches, my dorm on the hill somewhere ahead, all of it was eerily distant, and I found myself shrunk inward, my senses focused and acutely self-aware.

I felt wrung out and exhausted, weary and victorious. I was scared, terrified, more than I had ever been. I commanded my hands to be still, and with a single deliberate motion I lit my cigarette, walked toward the hill to my dorm, and didn't look back.

There's a complacency that comes with hopelessness, a strange relief in giving up. You don't have to try anymore; you can just lie, and that's it. I can't explain it except to say that it feels safe, or rather that it used to feel safe, because by the time I had finished my cigarette, swiped my entry card, and heard my feet clanging on the brown stairway of my dorm, I knew that I could no longer be safe in my misery.

Years of yearning had finally broken out, and a rhythm, long ignored, beat through me. *To be happy, to no longer feel empty and unwanted; to work with the world, to become a full person. To have a real identity, not one based on numbers. Alicia. Appalachia. Service. Hugs. Walking through campus. People saying hi. Saying hi back. Not feeling shitty.* Louder it grew, steadier, and surer. *To be desired. To desire. To have someone need me, to let someone in. To look in a mirror . . .*

I could feel the fear and the hatred welling up within me, surging, stretching, registering danger, rallying, scrambling, scratching at my heart, and reminding me of how weak I truly was.

The cadence did not stop. The cadence grew stronger.

To be able to sit down with another human being and let them hold my soul for a moment, to hold it and return it, and to do so without judging, or controlling, or hating, and to do the same to them—that was the gift of Appalachia. That was the gift Alicia gave me.

ONE MAN, ONE JACKET

Tijuana, Mexico, January 2003

"Is it always this awkward?" the guy next to me whispered. "Depends on the group," I muttered. *With this group it's awkward. Tonight will be especially awkward. Tonight will suck.*

"Don't take it personally," I said aloud. The room was silent. The doors were shut, the shutters were shut, nothing was lit but a tiny stub of a candle, and I could barely make out the people next to me, and still I felt fifteen pairs of eyes hone in on my sweatshirt. "Trust me, don't take it personally," I added, but they couldn't trust me and I couldn't blame them. These people were sad and confused, and throwing empty platitudes at them wasn't helping.

An outburst of growls and yipping drifted up through the shutters of the migrant house. In the mornings, the city buzzed with trucks and day laborers, evenings brought drunk tourists from California, but this late at night, Tijuana belonged to the dogs.

Shut your mouth, let it go, they're not going to jump off the roof, they'll be fine, pleaded years of training, but as much as I wanted to listen, I couldn't. Problem was, there really is no such thing as a free lunch. Oh, I've had free lunches, too many to count, free suppers, free clothes, free rides, but some things aren't paid for with money. I could feel the debt pricking me like a splinter in my mind, telling me to speak. It was the most frustrating obligation, a quiet little IOU in your head, the easiest thing to brush off, and also the most impossible.

A cheap convenience store matchbook slid around its cover inside my right hand. *In, out, in, out,* my fingers fumbled with the cardboard. Across in the other sleeve, my left index finger kept digging at the soft flesh below the thumbnail. I had a hood on, a hat on, I had my sleeves pulled out over my hands and the ends bundled up so you couldn't see a single fingertip, I had both bundles shoved far into the sweatshirt pouch, and still I felt naked. I prayed for the darkness to obscure me, wrap me in the safety of its gloom. I prayed for the shutters to pull themselves a little tighter, I begged the candle to burn a little less, just a tiny bit, for just five minutes. Suddenly I felt the wind knifing through the sweater and the thin layer of shirts, and I was two feet shorter and twelve years younger, and shaking from the cold.

* * *

"One man, give one jacket," instructed Hilberto earlier that evening. "Be careful. No time to try on. One man, one jacket, next man, next jacket. Understand?"

We filed out of the van and into the church parking lot. The sun was setting as the hills of Tijuana receded into the night sky. Tijuana was an earth-toned city, a massive sprawl of squat, box-shaped buildings intermingled with squat, box-shaped shacks. As the day faded, the earth got browner and the shacks became grayer and the whole area seemed to sink, as if the hills themselves were burrowing into the ground, seeking shelter for the night.

I was in Tijuana with a Boston College student group working at La Casa del Migrante, a large homeless shelter that resembled a cheap motel. This afternoon, Hilberto, La Casa's director, asked the male volunteers to assist him with a clothing donation at a local church, where a long line of men had already assembled. Inside the church storage room waited boxes stuffed with sweaters and jackets collected by San Diego parishes. Judging by the desperation of the men in the hallway, these types of events did not happen often.

Hilberto repeated his warning and unlatched the door, and the men rushed in. They moved quickly, so quickly that we had to devote half of our group to crowd control alone, trying to prevent an all-out stampede. I barely had time to reach for another jacket before the next man was already there.

I straddled two worlds. The volunteers behind me were caught in a hurricane, a whirling frenzy of cardboard shuffling, opening, emptying, collapsing, vanishing. Every time I turned back for more jackets, I was struck by how quickly the boxes were disappearing. It was like looking at time-lapse photography that compacted several hours into a few frames.

In front of me, nothing changed. The line wound around a corner, making it impossible to see its end. I was so busy shoving jackets that I was barely able to see anything but the men's hands, which instantly replaced one another, making it seem as if there was just one hand in front of me, an empty, weathered hand that kept coming at me from some inexhaustible source of empty, weathered hands.

The volunteer next to me handed out the last jacket, and we froze. The men in front didn't move but the line behind them kept undulating, shoving, pushing, until those around the corner rushed forward, spilled into the room, and realized all of the jackets were gone. Some were angry; all were disappointed. Our group stood still, unsure of what to do, when Hilberto shouted something in Spanish, then pointed to the limp heap of cardboard: "Put in van, then get in. Thank you for help." He ushered the men outside, locked the room, unlocked the van, and climbed in. I joined him.

I could see the church parking lot in the van's side mirror. The church was functional at best; it looked like a shabby middle school, and only the lonely cross reaching up to the sky imparted it with any sense of sanctity. Outside, small groups of men were dissipating, returning to their homes or going in search of one. Our volunteers remained in the lot, standing alone or squatting on the pavement. Hilberto and I sat in the van. Hilberto stared ahead, an impassive look on his face. "You can*not* let it get you," he said. "You do your job, and you go home. You need to make yourself a heart of stone, because if not, your heart will break."

I said nothing. Hilberto lived, as I had once lived, in an imbalanced world, where the number of jackets was markedly fewer than the number of jacketless men. It was an unforgiving ratio, as true in Vienna as it was in Tijuana. It was a world where cynicism and despair waited around the corner, ready to pounce on any act of kindness, a world where you smile at a refugee kid and give him a black bomber jacket with golden zippers and he snaps at you for no reason. *You can't let the situation consume you.* I understood. It was probably why I was the only volunteer ready to go home.

Back in the shelter, we held reflection, a nightly exercise to debrief the group. Reflection was tough that evening. People were saddened, utterly. Many felt guilty, as if they were responsible for the lack of jackets in Tijuana. Others felt that the angry, desperate stares of the men had been directed at them. I was fighting the urge to walk out of the room. Thinking about my past was uncomfortable; speaking about it made my hands shake, made me want to run, be someplace else, but the guilt was too strong. I owed a debt to the Joint and HIAS workers in Austria, to the blond girl who gave me a jacket at Madame Eva's house, to Oswald Prager, who pulled us off the train station in Vienna, pudgy Mr. Prager in his crumpled blue blazer who almost drowned in a sea of migrants and still kept his shit together. I owed them, and tonight, twelve years later, the bill came, pried open my mouth, squeezed out the memories, compelled me to say something encouraging.

So I hid in the darkness and spoke of Eva's house, the house with the red door, and the girl who made me feel warm, gave me a chance to be a child for a few moments. I stressed that even though we helped only a small number of people, we made an enormous difference in their lives, warming their nights, enabling them, I hoped, to get jobs, get money, help their families.

After reflection ended, I padded out to the shelter's top-floor walkway. Three stories of silence stretched below. The migrants went to sleep early: they worked odd jobs and long hours and would be out hunting for more work at dawn. It was cold, and I was tired and tempted to go to bed, but I couldn't: five minutes earlier, I had assured the group they shouldn't take it personally, but it was different for me. I crouched against the wall and lit a cigarette, my eyes drifting up with the smoke. It was hard to see the stars. The sun had long since set, but it never got dark in Tijuana. A sickly glare hung over the city: the glow of carnival lights and strip clubs on Avenida Revolución, of sprawling highways and factories, and, overshadowing it all, the massive floodlights that lit up the U.S.–Mexico border.

I made my body as still as possible and then I left; I floated up through the courtyard, out of Tijuana, out of Mexico. I bent my entire will, and I sent myself across the ocean, to Vienna, to Eva's, to the girl who once handed me a jacket, who smiled at me, whom I sneered at, who probably went home wondering what on Earth she did to make me hate her. For years I thought of her quiet smile, her demeanor, her warmth. For years I still felt ashamed for lashing out at her. I hoped she understood I was just a stubborn kid, that it was instinct, and sitting in that courtyard in Tijuana, after all that time, I was finally able to smile back at her.

KILCOYNE

Chestnut Hill, Mass., March 2003

Everything came to a head in March of my senior year, as I sat in an empty Boston College cafeteria, sipping a coffee, sipping away the end of college. I had just informed my parents that I was not going to med school. Mom and Dad reaffirmed, in no uncertain terms, that I was a failure who had wasted the past twenty-three years of their lives and thousands of dollars of their hard-earned money, not to mention the enormous sacrifice of emigration. I had braced myself to hear all that. Mom and Dad had gotten their citizenships, voted, paid taxes, but America would never be their country. I knew it every time I heard them refer to Americans as *them*, and Russia and Russians as *us* and *ours*. I was reminded of it when Mom would come home in her security guard uniform, or talk on the phone to her friends five thousand miles away. "The day you graduate from med school is the day I can go and find a noose, because everything I needed to accomplish here will be done," Dad told me, again and again, in high school and in college. *Now Dad won't be able to hang himself and it's all my fault.* It would've been hilarious if it didn't hurt so much.

Across the cafeteria table from me towered Dr. Kilcoyne, my freshman-year philosophy/theology professor and advisor, who had unofficially retained the latter role throughout my time at BC. The man had always instilled me with awe, in the true sense of the word: admiration mixed in with a healthy bit of fear. Standing in at six feet five, 250-plus pounds, the undisputed holder of several advanced degrees, Francis P. Kilcoyne was the type of professor one expects to find in movies like *Dead Poets Society,* not on an actual brick-and-mortar campus. He had traveled the world, supervised archaeological digs in the Middle East, and worked a couple of stints for the government in Washington. Prior to December finals, he had the class at his house for Christmas dinner; several times he nearly bankrupted an all-you-can-eat buffet by taking his advisees out to lunch. He'd bonded our class into a unit, not just faces stocking a lecture hall, and even three years later I always stopped and chatted with my old classmates. Kilcoyne's only weakness was ties: he wore these comically short, dinky ties that rested atop his belly, the tips poking out in front of him, and as childish as it was, on the few occasions I'd been forced to wear ties, I made certain mine were nice and long, the opposite of those donned by the man who surpassed me in everything else.

We sat in a forgotten corner of the cafeteria and talked about the twin options I saw before me. Both had begun with hope, and both had ended in disappointment. For Mom and Dad, who'd roamed a strange land depending on the mercy of others, who learned firsthand that there *are* cats in America, med school embodied safety: financial, social, lasting, and complete. It was the quintessential American Dream: to transplant oneself to a foreign country, endure the myriad sacrifices of being the first generation, and retire in peace knowing your children will thrive. But for me, who'd racked up achievement after achievement only to remain No One, med school loomed like a gargantuan trophy for an endless mantel that stretched beyond the horizon, an insatiable trophy case that would never be full. *So what if No One has an MD after his name? What's the point of the American Dream if it isn't your dream?* I couldn't explain it to Mom and Dad at the time, and even afterward it would take them a couple of years to understand, but then again, it would take me a few years to see their side as well.

My second option was equally, if not more, frustrating. After Boston College, chasing accomplishments and scurrying from one address to the next was no longer possible, because I finally recognized that behind each achievement, emptiness still lurked. I loved my freshman mentoring and community service trips, I'd walk across campus and say "hi" to people and feel connected, and be at peace, but as much as I had tasted that feeling of belonging, true engagement remained beyond me. Every time I got close to someone, every time I edged out a little too far, the overwhelming urge to protect myself would kick in like a stubborn governor function set inside me and I couldn't do a damn thing to fight it. As cliché as it sounded, I told Kilcoyne, I felt like I was standing before two paths, both dead ends. I felt like I had no future.

"You don't, of course," Kilcoyne coughed. "You do not have a future. But it's much more serious than that."

I wasn't looking for a "there, there" (Kilcoyne wasn't the type), but the immediate confirmation of my fears skewered me to the chair. Not having a future seemed pretty damn serious on its own. I almost didn't want to know what could be more serious than that.

"It's important to realize you're heading down a potentially dangerous path. You've got a bit of knight in shining armor in you—you're an idealist, and you want to make a difference—which in itself is not a bad thing. But be careful to always stay in touch with reality: there's the dream, the desire, and then there's the real world, where not everyone wants to be helped or can be helped, and it is crucial, *crucial,* to be able to negotiate between the two worlds."

The professor was hunched over the table. His normally placid face tightened as if an electric current had shot across it, and his voice pierced me. It was quiet, barely above a whisper, and what came across more than words was the rhythm, with its sharp yet quiet pauses, like the muffled cadence of a drum. I'd heard that voice before, but only a handful of times, in the classroom, when Kilcoyne spoke of something important and dangerous, very important and very dangerous, like the bloodshed and hope intrinsic to and triggered by Jesus suffering on the cross, or of the false allure of Fascism, of Jews rising up in the Warsaw Ghetto, and Buddhist monks immolating themselves in defiance of the Vietnam War.

"Career, Appalachia, parents, all of that doesn't matter right now. Your parents will get over it. Or they won't get over it," he waved. "But it's not about them; it's about you. I've watched you closely over the past four years, I've seen you grow and you have grown, but not nearly enough. I've sat with you in my office and you talked about medieval history, and Appalachia, and girls, and parties, but today was the first time you have ever divulged anything about your past. Do you realize that I can quote your views on Plato and Kierkegaard, I can recite your attempts at getting a girlfriend, but aside from the little scraps you mentioned just now, I know nothing about you beyond New Jersey? You act as if your life began at Boston College, and it—did—not. You have no foundation, Lev; you must go back."

A legion of "if"s and "what about"s was itching to jump out of my mouth, but the words wouldn't form. The jumble of conflicting thoughts in my head had been unceremoniously thrust aside, leaving me and the voice, rhythmic, deep, hushed, hypnotic, sinking itself into my mind and forcing me to listen.

"If you keep running up to life, and tasting it, and scurrying away, if you only go by the ideal world, the real world will consume you, and instead of an idealist you will become a *cynic*"—he spat out the word like it was venomous—"a person so fed up with futility that you will come to despise the very dreams you once espoused. The line between the idealist and the cynic is a thin one, and too often people—especially people of your age and situation—cross over that line.

"You are not ready. *If* you want a meaningful future, *if* you want to become part of something larger than yourself, then you must root yourself, reach out, and understand. *You have to go back.*"

The cafeteria was so dead that the distant chiming of the campus bell tower startled me. Kilcoyne rose. There was no small talk, no goodbyes; he simply shook my hand and headed for the main exit, toward the heart of the campus. He had a class in five minutes. I, too, had class, but I took a different exit, through the door leading away from the college. I walked across the street and past the little pathway meandering up to the freshman dorms. I went by the ring of houses owned by the BC administration, and the old mansion on a hill where every year a few imprudent freshmen might get busted for smoking pot, and huddled by an oak at the edge of campus, Kilcoyne's warning pounding in my head.

Kilcoyne was . . . well, he wasn't a friend, he wasn't family, but friends and family didn't mean much at that point. Talking to my parents was out of the question. Lina and I had been growing apart for years. She wanted nothing to do with Russia, and neither did I, which left us with meaningless progress reports on her PhD and my studies, and in every conversation there was less to say. The last time we talked was when I called her, excited that I had been chosen for the Tijuana service trip, and she asked why I was wasting time on Mexicans instead of concentrating on med schools. I knew exactly where she was coming from, but I didn't know what to say to make her understand, so I just hung up the phone. Kilcoyne was what I had. When he talked, I listened.

I passed houses with unshoveled sidewalks, wandered past a shopping mall, and into the tiny hamlet of Newton, where I bought a coffee and kept going. I had no destination; as long as I had coffee and cigarettes, I continued to walk. I smoked the cigarettes, and my hand would freeze, then held the coffee, and my hand would warm up again. I slunk past Boston College, past the dull years of high school, past New Jersey, Indiana, the cobblestone boulevards of Vienna and the hoary valleys of the Alps, back through the endless steppe and the gloomy, industrial streets of Kharkov. I walked past Linda and the swearing cabbie from New York, Madame Eva and the blond girl with the jacket, the manic grins of the *tamozhniki* at the Soviet border, the frozen shape of Kolya the coin dealer as the *druzhinniki* walked through our apartment yard. Even thinking of their names was painful. Ten years of rigorously excising the shreds of my childhood had left me raw and exposed: Russia, Vienna, Indiana, the Alps, any of it was enough to transport me back to a dark brown hallway, a dirty mirror, and the specter that dwelled inside. It was an image I'd never challenged. It was an image that triggered the most visceral reaction I knew.

"Hate" is a strong word. I heard that over and over from well-meaning adults in America, but it's not true. Hate's neither strong nor weak. Given the proper environment, hate can settle down into an annoyance, or a baseline, or a norm. I knew strong things, things beyond hate, things that made hate seem pretty fucking trivial. I didn't have clever aphorisms for them, but I knew them well. I knew blinding and paralyzing anger. I knew isolation, so crushing that my tiny shreds of self-esteem would wither to noth-

ing, and I knew sadness and I knew that I was helpless against them, and compared with those, hate wasn't so bad.

Hate is what came through after I chanced to glance at a mirror and felt so alone, so scared, unwanted and unwanting, naked and trembling. Hate's what drew me out when my whole existence shrunk to an insignificant pinpoint of ugliness; hate is what took over, shook me, ground my teeth, utterly exhausted me until I reached the point where I could collapse and not feel sad and unwanted anymore. Hate's what protected me, and as I walked it awoke, rejoiced, swelled until I was so flooded with it that by the time I limped back to my dorm room I no longer wanted to be well, or have a girlfriend, or be able to hug people, or have a good evening—I just wanted to be numb.

I walked again the next day, and again the day after that. Every day I walked, several times a day. Where I went didn't matter—graveyards, apartments, country clubs—as long as it had a path it suited me. About two weeks after my conversation with Kilcoyne, I asked Dad to mail me his scrapbook of our journey to America. We had no camera when we left the USSR, of course, but Dad had grabbed what he could, and despite the chaos of emigration he managed to hoard a surprising number of items. He saved a napkin from Binder's, from when we waited in line to receive those precious rolls with butter when Joint moved us to the mountains after that terrible night at the Soviet border. He spent a bit of our meager refugee stipends on postcards of the palaces and gardens we strolled past when we were stationed in Vienna. He grabbed an extra copy of the customs form we filled out at JFK and the Indiana newspaper from our arrival to Lafayette. He stored away our coveted exit visas (except Lina's, because my sister insisted on shredding hers the day she got her citizenship), and traced our route on maps he photocopied from the library. All that he stashed and more, and when he made enough money he bought an enormous magnetic-page scrapbook and arranged everything inside.

For years, Dad's album had terrified me. I could feel its filthy presence whenever I walked by his closet, mocking all the costly efforts I'd put into concealing my identity. I begged him to never show it to anyone, raved about how unfair it was that Lina was allowed to shred her exit visa and I couldn't shred mine ("Lina is an adult, and she has the right to be an idiot," was Dad's unyielding answer). God, I hated that scrapbook, and suddenly it became the only item that mattered. I sat with the album and watched the past unfold before me, I walked as words and stories cautiously tiptoed into my mind. Here, my experience as an Appalachia coordinator proved invaluable: I knew how much work went into organizing even the dinkiest fund-raiser, and what I was staring at went way beyond a bake sale. In flickers and glimpses I saw them, thousands of individuals across the globe, praying, debating, marching, lighting candles, and holding vigils. People I've never met and will never meet, people who didn't know me, people who died before I was born, grappling with the most powerful dictatorship in history because they believed in my cause. Because they believed I was worth it.

Spring came and thawed out the sidewalks, and I ventured out farther. I circled around the Chestnut Hill Reservoir, among runners training for the upcoming Boston Marathon on Patriots' Day weekend. I took the tram into the city and followed the banks of the Charles, past couples cuddling on benches and students reviewing for final exams. Amid the weirdness that descends on campus in the last month of college, I called up a few students and some trusted professors who had asked me about Russia. People always inquired, in retreats, trips, classes, and I'd silence them, snapping, "I'm from Jersey." Now I sought them out, showed them Dad's album, recounted the little I could verbalize. As I talked, I paid attention, listened to their responses, heard them be amazed, or tearful, or grateful, and I bottled that, too.

Facts became faces, details rushed in, fleshing out events, hints of emotions played in the periphery, and I clung to them, the stubborn shards of my past. Instinct flared up every time I touched on something new, and I fought to inure myself so that I could probe further. Back and forth I went, as two sets of images wrestled for control of a crazed kaleidoscope. *Otto Binder, converting his hotel into a refugee camp, risking his business for migrants. Anna Konstantinovna, placidly staring at the cuts on my face. The drunk man by the bakery, hissing* We're sick of you, *grabbing me, reeking of vodka, and an Austrian baron getting a stranger an illegal job.* Panic set in when I'd poke out too far, and the images would quiver and scatter, and leave me again in front of the mirror, reminding me of what I was and why I ran. *You did this to yourself,* I'd think as a feeling would dissipate, *so get up and undo it,* and I'd launch into another walk, have another conversation, conjure another memory, grasp it for a bit longer. And as maddening as the process was, I really had no choice: chasing achievements didn't work, and hissing "I'm from Jersey" and intimidating people into silence didn't work either. I was trapped, and Kilcoyne gave me an exit. When you're stuck at a dead end, any way out is a good way out.

* * *

Mount Laurel, N.J., August 2006

One August morning three years later, I sequestered myself in the back room of my job, picked up the phone, and dialed the offices of the *Journal and Courier* in Indiana. In my hand was a copy of the paper from my family's arrival to the States, which showed me shaking hands with our Jewish community greeters after we landed on the tarmac. But newspapers always have more photos than they print; the photographer goes on assignment, the editor picks one or two shots, and the rest are consigned to an eternity in the archives. I was calling the *Journal and Courier* because I wanted the other photos from that roll, the ones that didn't make the cut. For the past three years, since Boston College, I'd been residing in my cozy zone of reading about Soviet Jews, speaking with my parents, and ruminating over coffee. It was time to step outside the cocoon, and obtaining a handful of photographs from a small-town newspaper seemed like a safe and easy objective.

It wasn't. In fact, by the time I hung up the phone I was seriously considering trying something more realistic, like breaking into Fort Knox. I was informed that the *Journal and Courier* had long-ago switched to digital media. The film processors had been shoved into an out-of-the way closet, everything past the mid-nineties had been relegated to the archives, and the archives were closed. The policy of the *Journal and Courier* was to release only those photos that had been originally printed in the paper. No exceptions.

My initial August phone call turned out to be the opening kickoff of what would essentially become a six-week harassment campaign. For the first three weeks, I badgered the photographer, who finally crumbled and passed me off to the photo editor. Then came the photo editor's turn, and then the general editor's, until I convinced the editor in chief to grant me a minute of his time. "Can't you just get some expendable intern to run the photos?" I suggested. All the expendable interns were already occupied with other duties, he replied. "I'll make it worth their time," I said, trying to sound like a man who regularly leaves financially satisfied people in his wake. It's not a question of money, he assured me;

it's a matter of policy: if they do this for me, then little Timmy is going to want his Little League photos, and then little Susie is going to ask for her birthday party photos, and where would that leave the *Journal and Courier* then?

"Why do you want these photographs, Mr. Golinkin?" the exhausted editor finally asked.

Everything stopped. No more than a few seconds had elapsed, but those few seconds were like the moment right before an accident, or opening a college admissions letter, or asking a girl on a date. I had the world on pause. I could simultaneously track a thousand branching thoughts, follow each one to its logical conclusion, and still have time to spare. This was it. If I gave the editor anything but the truth, the conversation would be over and it's goodbye, photos. And if I told him the real reason, I'd probably get the pics, but then I'd be committed. Yes, I could have them mail them to me, I could stash them on my hard drive and forget about it, but I wouldn't. If I took this step, I would drive to Indiana and get them myself. And then I would track down Linda, and Michael, and the various families who had sponsored us. I would talk to them. I would talk to the refugee groups in New York and Vienna. I would accept myself, as an ex-refugee, and a Jew, and a Russian, and an immigrant, and while I was at it I'd try to do something for my future as well. I'd write it all down into a book. There'd be no more tiptoeing around. This was the plunge.

"Listen, I understand what you're worried about, sir. You have to deal with the public and you can't set precedents you can't follow; I get it. The reason I'm asking you to make an exception is because *unlike* little Timmy, I don't *have* Little League photos. I don't have any childhood photos. I don't even have a birth certificate, because it was taken from my family when we crossed the Soviet border. The closest thing I have to a birth certificate is a copy of your newspaper from the day we stepped off the plane in West Lafayette and began our new life. I need those photos because I need to understand who I am and where I come from. They aren't going to accomplish that all by themselves, but I think they'll help. I hope they'll help, in any case."

The next pause was not on my end.

"Mr. Golinkin, would you be interested in cooperating with us on a follow-up story?" he finally said, in a tone that made it clear that the fate of the negatives trapped in the dark room hinged on my answer. *Quid pro quo, Clarice.*

"I'll see you tomorrow," I said.

"Wait, they tell me you currently reside in New Jersey: Is that correct?"

"Yes it is, but I'll see you tomorrow anyway . . . before you change your mind," I blurted out.

Five hours later, after calling Linda and Michael Forman and the other people in Indiana who had adopted my family, I bought a notebook and a voice recorder and was filling my car at a truck stop on the Pennsylvania Turnpike. It was a beautiful afternoon for a road trip. The summer vacation traffic was gone, fall had come early to Pennsylvania, and I took a moment to sip cheap roadhouse coffee while watching the sunlight play with the trees in the Poconos. I jumped in the car, tuned to the college football chatter for the upcoming weekend, and pulled out onto the highway, off to claim my future, off to reclaim my past.

It helps, now and then, to step back and take a long view.

The kingdom is not only beyond our efforts, it is even beyond our vision.

We accomplish in our lifetime only a tiny fraction of the magnificent enterprise that is the Lord's work.

Nothing we do is complete, which is another way of saying that the kingdom always lies beyond us.

No statement says all that could be said. No prayer fully expresses our faith.

No confession brings perfection, no pastoral visit brings wholeness.

No program accomplishes the Church's mission. No set of goals and objectives includes everything.

This is what we are about. We plant the seeds that one day will grow.

We water seeds already planted, knowing that they hold future promise.

We lay foundations that will need further development.

We provide yeast that produces effects far beyond our capabilities.

We cannot do everything, and there is a sense of liberation in realizing that.

This enables us to do something and to do it very well.

It may be incomplete, but it is a beginning, a step along the way, an opportunity for the Lord's grace to enter and do the rest.

We may never see the end results,

But that is the difference between the master builder and the worker.

We are workers, not master builders; ministers, not messiahs.

We are prophets of a future not our own.

—Prayer of Oscar Romero

EPILOGUE

East Windsor, N.J., 2011

In the spring of 2007, after interviewing my parents, researching the struggle to free Soviet Jews, speaking with various individuals who'd been involved in the fight, and returning to Indiana to reconnect with the families who had adopted us, I assembled the trio of hooligans known as Team Lev and set my sights across the Atlantic. I wanted to return to Austria, journey along the shoulderless roads of Niederösterreich, tear down the autobahns past ruins and vineyards, and walk once again under the shadow of Vienna's cathedrals. Most of all, I was ready to thank all the people who'd provided my family with love, sustenance, and support.

This trip went beyond arranging an interview or shooting over to a quiet midwestern town. Seventeen years is a long time: things change, as I would discover after three hours of trudging around Vienna in pouring rain only to learn that the neighborhood around the old ex-villa where my family was stationed had been bulldozed and rebuilt as condos. Dad's scrapbook proved invaluable once again: shortly after starting preparations, I was able to track down Otto Binder, Peter, and the Joint worker Oswald Prager, as well as map out all the places we had stayed. The one glaring omission was Madame Eva, the philanthropist who owned the house full of free clothes, where the blond girl had handed me a jacket a long time ago. Online searches as well as inquiries to my Austrian contacts yielded nothing, which wasn't surprising. By the late 1990s, the refugee flow into Austria had largely subsided, thanks to the collapse of the Soviet Union and the end of the Yugoslav Wars, and while this was good news in general, it also negated the reason for Eva's charity. HIAS and Joint, at least, were established international entities with all the concomitant headquarters and websites. Madame Eva, on the other hand . . . I didn't even know her last name.

There *was* one piece of information at my disposal: my father remembered the old refugee who first told us of Eva mentioning that the mysterious "crazy woman who gives away perfectly good clothes" was originally from northern Europe. Dad had no idea why the old timer knew that or whether it was even accurate, but it was all I had. I *really* wanted to find Madame Eva—her charity had affected me deeply, laying the foundation for my own volunteerism and inspiring (during my service trip to Tijuana) the first hesitant steps toward acknowledging my past. *Originally from northern Europe*—as the trip loomed closer, the wispy little rumor came to dominate my thoughts. For weeks, I poked at it in my mind until one night, after feeling particularly saucy, I pulled out an atlas and e-mailed the Vienna embassies of every Western country north of Austria:

Dear Embassy Staff:
    I am looking for a woman whose first name is Eva (I do not know her last name), who may or may not be from your country, and who distributed free clothes in Vienna seventeen years ago. If you happen to know her, please contact me.

"You can be sure they'll have their top staffers working on it," quipped Jeff, the team's blunt voice of reality, and I had to agree; immediately after hitting "send" I could almost hear the echo of eleven embassy clerks clicking "delete" at the other end of the line.

The morning Team Lev was shipping out for Austria, I was dashing around between last-minute errands when I got a call from Kyle, who'd been assigned to monitor my e-mail account for any straggling messages from Europe. "You're not gonna believe this," my friend exclaimed. "You should probably send them a thank-you card, or a *danke* card, or whatever they call it."

"Send *who* a *danke* card?"

"Finland, man!" said Kyle. "Good ol' Finland came through for you."

"Dear Mr. Golinkin: it is not a usual policy to disclose contact details, but we are familiar with the individual you are talking about, we have established communication with her, and obtained permission to share her information. She is most interested in speaking with you," went the e-mail, ending with a line I will never forget: "We thank you for allowing the Finnish embassy of Vienna to be of service to you in this matter."

I made the call as soon as we hit the tarmac.

Madame Eva's backstory was both simple and moving. She, like many I had encountered on my journey, was not a professional humanitarian; in fact, she hadn't engaged in full-scale philanthropy prior to 1986. The seeds for her actions, however, had been planted much earlier, in the aftermath of World War II, when the world first opened its eyes to the horrors of Hitler's empire. Rumors of the Holocaust had been spreading through Europe for years, but for years they'd been dismissed as dramatic exaggeration or outright propaganda. Humanity had never been confronted with such diligent, mechanized slaughter, and many couldn't conceive the extent of the carnage until after the war, when the camps were liberated and the photographers walked through the ashes.

At the time, Madame Eva was just Eva, the young daughter of a Helsinki pastor, but she remembered the night she sat in her parents' safe Nordic living room and learned of the Final Solution. A suffocating helplessness washed over the little girl. She felt the *unfairness,* the acute, absolute, and overwhelming unfairness that can only be experienced by a child, the notion that millions of people had perished and millions more were suffering, and there was nothing she could do to help. On that night in a remote Finnish apartment, little Eva made a silent promise to herself and to the Jews: if the Jewish people ever needed her in the future, she would not idly stand by.

The skinny girl from Helsinki grew up, became a journalist, traveled widely. Hers was a familiar face in the social circles of Austria, Italy, Switzerland, and her native Finland. Decades flowed by, life happened, career happened, one marriage and two children happened, until one autumn evening in the mid-1980s, as "We Are the World" was topping international charts and acid-washed denim hijacked fashion sense, Madame Eva Huber-Huber first noticed the shivering individuals ghosting by on the streets of Vienna. This time, she wasn't helpless.

Eva began simply, soliciting donations, which allowed her to open a distribution center at the house on Schüttelstrasse. Advertising was unnecessary—Gorbachev's reforms were rapidly taking effect, and more and more Jews braved the emigration process. Old refugees told new arrivals, and shortly after the first wary migrant ambled away from the house with the red door, clutching his new duds and shaking his head in disbelief, word spread, and soon Eva needed help. Friends across Europe provided clothing and served as regional collection hubs. The Schüttelstrasse center expanded into a headquarters and a dormitory. Helsinki churches and youth groups allowed Eva to tap into a network of Finnish teenagers, such as the ones who had assisted my family, girls with an eye for fashion and a mind for community service. Donations, as well as funds from Madame Eva herself, supplied money needed to transport and house the volunteers, who were recruited to serve in Vienna for two to four weeks. The Cold War was hurtling to a close, the Soviet Union kept shaking and groaning and spewing out more refugees, the Schüttelstrasse house started operating day and night, and an organization named Hilfe und Hoffnung (Help and Hope) emerged into being.

While doing my research I had erroneously assumed that Madame Eva had wrapped up her charity work with the collapse of the Soviet Bloc; in truth, the house with the red door was only the beginning. Since the refugees no longer came to Austria, Eva had realigned the group and went mobile. In 1990, a transit camp sprang up in Budapest. Aid caravans embarked for the town of Oradea in the wake of the Romanian Revolution. Shortly afterward, the Balkan conflicts devolved into outright ethnic cleansing; by the time the Yugoslav Wars were over, twenty-six separate Hilfe und Hoffnung aid missions had snaked out across war zones in Belgrade and Sarajevo. The convoys were serenaded by gunfire and mortar explosions, and at one point Eva was forced to do some quick talking as a militiaman threatened her life at gunpoint. But with the increased danger came increased opportunity to help those in peril: back when migrants still flocked to Vienna, Hilfe und Hoffnung had assisted 60,000 people; in the first two years of the Eastern European convoys, that number ballooned to 212,000, and it has only risen since.

Madame Eva couldn't stop the Holocaust. She wasn't able to

reverse the past, erase the terror, give the survivors back their lives and their lost. She couldn't undo the damage of diligent Soviet persecution or tackle the Communist colossus. But she could do *some*thing—she could give out clothes on the streets of Eastern Europe, bestowing a quarter million people with a basic human need—and she did it very well. This staggering success had not gone unnoticed, and in 2006 the Austrian secretary of state awarded Madame Eva the Gold Medal of the Republic, one of the highest civilian honors of the Austrian government.

Eva was on a fund-raising trip in Italy during my visit to Vienna, but after we spoke she connected me with Hannu Ylilato, the Finn responsible for organizing Hilfe und Hoffnung's latest service trip, which was set to begin in a week. Hannu scooped me up from my hotel and drove us over to the Schüttelstrasse house, which now serves exclusively as a supply post. Pallets laden with furniture, baby carriages, and crates of supplies waited to be loaded, and boxes bulging with clothes, books, toys, and Torahs were already packed. While gaping around the main room I almost tripped over a pile of menorahs near the doorway. "These just arrived out of Belgium," Hannu apologized; "the trip is very shortly, so I left them out to save time with storage."

"You didn't show me the whole house," I said as Hannu began to lock up. "There's another room, over there somewhere . . . it's a small room, but it has a large window that faces the canal."

Hannu gave me a strange look, then silently took out his keys, walked across the hall, and wheeled aside a pair of clothing racks and a large black screen leaning against a corner. Inside the little room hidden by the screen, we edged past plastic crates plastered with medical symbols. "I hold the medical supplies here—they are the most expensive and most hard to replace. No one has broken in, but I want to be careful," my guide explained as he flung aside a thick wool blanket to unveil the window behind it.

"Yeah, that's it," I said. "That's the room. The window's not as big as I remembered it, but that's probably because I grew up since then."

Hannu was staring at me.

"You were here when?"

"Seventeen years ago."

"And of what age were you?"

"Ten."

"And how is it you remember this one room?"

"It's a very important room, Hannu." I smiled. "It's where they kept the children's jackets."

Hannu unzipped his backpack and fished out a camera. "I think we'd better take a picture of you for Eva," he said.

"How'd the date go?" Jeff glanced up from his bed when I returned to our hotel room. "Was he cute? Did he drive a nice car?" I'd grown used to overcoming my fears, but the anticipation of meeting people and groups that had succored my family still left me "giddy as a shy lass on prom night," according to Jeff's unsolicited description.

"It was good," I replied. "I got good info, plus I got to come back as an adult and say thank you, which doesn't happen too often with these groups.

"And yes, douchebag, he has a very nice Audi."

*   *   *

"How is it you remember this one room?" Hannu had asked, and I smiled because the first thing that went through my head was

How could I not? I understood Hannu's incredulous question, and it was a valid reaction from his point of view. The Finn was a volunteer—a veteran volunteer, but a volunteer nonetheless. "How could you expect a man who is warm to understand one who is cold?" said Aleksandr Solzhenitsyn, and as much as I wish it were otherwise, perhaps Solzhenitsyn is right. I wouldn't expect Hannu to recall a minor detail from a specific service trip many years back, no more than I can remember the structural layout of every house I built with Habitat for Humanity. I'd be shocked if the original owner of the black bomber jacket was able to recollect stopping by a clothing drive with his parents when he was ten years old. All those experiences come from one side of an invisible divide, where a coat is just a coat, and a house a house, and when one's world is full of coats and houses, they recede into memory. But how could I forget scrambling out of that pile of clothing, the thrill of golden zippers flashing down *my* jacket, warmth and dignity snuggling up to me, the shiny black window pane standing witness to a wish granted and a need fulfilled? How could I forget listening to the brutal Vienna wind as it howled down the Danube, rendered impotent by Eva's kindness? Everything's magnified on the other side of the divide.

I've been fortunate enough to reach a point where a new piece of clothing no longer elicits such a fierce response, but whenever I think of Eva's jacket, a different kind of joy surges through me. I look back and see my childhood, the result not just of the dark streets of Kharkov, but of the combined efforts of thousands of protestors, dozens of human rights workers, politicians, philanthropists, activists, and everyday people. I've been lucky to meet a few of them; most I will never know. Some devoted their careers to the struggle; many had done nothing more than sign a petition, or mail a check, or process paperwork, or drop off a jacket. Small deeds that wound their way through the world to become a part of me and shape me in ways unexpected and unknown. And now that I'm on the other side, I look out and rejoice in my ability to transform a can of soup into dinner or a ten-dollar bill into hope. Crackling around me I can feel the invisible strings connecting me to people I will never meet, and I *know* I can help another human being feel appreciated, important, *worthy*. As much as I'm still a work in progress, I have no doubt about the power of the seeds I can plant.

I pray that I plant my seeds well.

ACKNOWLEDGMENTS

New York: Michele Rubin and Brianne Johnson of Writers House, who believed in this book. Robert Bloom of Doubleday is an incredible editor who pushed, prodded, challenged, and encouraged me to bring the manuscript to a new level. Amir Shaviv of Joint started out as an interviewee, became a character, then an advisor and a friend. Many thanks to Valery Bazarov of HIAS; Carolyn Starman Hessel of the Jewish Book Council; Sandra Cahn, Kaylie Jones, and David and Alice Caputo.

New Jersey: Mike, Anastasia, and Dar Vanderbeck; Tricia Elliott; Sabrina Spector at Cherry Hill Katz Center (the best damn marketing and publicity guru you can imagine); Rabbi Eric Wisnia; Rev. Barbara Heck and Rabbi Esther Reed, who shared this project with their students at Rutgers; Cynthia Cherrey, Rabbi Julie Roth, John Kolligian, Stan Katz, and Nino Zchomelidse at Princeton; Elizabeth Cappelluti Sheehy; Sauté Dean; Congressman Chris Smith; Drew Wintringham; Steve Lafferty; Ryan Kotarski; Zack Kiensicki; Chris Stibol and Laura Burns; John Walsh; Dan Swango; Brian Patterson; Kati McMahon; Jamie Baglivi; Kevin Higgins; the Bond family; Delia Hegarty; Stephanie McArthur; and the lovely Tony and Judy Covington. A special note goes to Kara Kiensicki and Allison Gilchrist, who made absolutely no discernible contribution to this project yet loudly insisted on being included; their years of whining have paid off.

Boston: I am extraordinarily fortunate to have the friendship and guidance of Boston College Jesuits: William Leahy, SJ; William Neenan, SJ; John Paris, SJ; and Donald MacMillan, SJ. Additional BC advice and support came from David Quigley, Paul Christensen, Joy Haywood Moore, David Hadly, Ben Birnbaum, and Cathryn Woodruff. Hugh Truslow assisted with research into early Soviet culture. Many thanks to Rich Masotta, Doug Most, and Dante Ramos at *The Boston Globe.*

Indiana: Michael and Linda Forman, Rabbi Gedalyah and Marilyn Engel, the Zimmerman family, the Lillianfeld family, John Norberg, Pastor Charles Hackett, and David Smith of the *Journal & Courier.*

Austria: the beautiful Eva Huber-Huber, Hannu and Anna Ylilato, Peter and Gabi, Otto and Agnes Binder, Ottilie and Amadea Gabmann, Oswald Prager, Traude Litzka, and the Finland Embassy of Vienna.

Here, there, and everywhere: the wonderful Nancy DeJoy; Rita and Ben Grace; Roberta Spivak and Bill Gotthelf; Karen Petrone; William Husband (who knows pretty much everything about the USSR); Barbara Engel; Sister Barbara Reid, OP; Judy Holmes; Jennifer Keup, Tim Delaney; Kim Frankwick; Katinka Bellomo; Petra Seibert; Rachel Schnold at Beit Hatfutsot; and Nick McIlwain, producer for *The Preston & Steve Show* at 93.3 WMMR.

One of the biggest encouragements for a first-time writer is the support of an established writer. I was lucky to have Roya Hakakian, Chuck Hogan, Mike Christian, Steven Hart, Nicholas Lemann, Lee Kravitz, Bruce Feiler, Nathan Bransford, Noah Charney, Bob Woodruff, Brian Sloan, and Joel Chasnoff.

Readers: Bridgett Ross (who provided invaluable detailed

feedback and question ideas), Lynne Hamilton, Claire LaZebnik, Liz and Alex Castro, Katie Abrahamsen Borer, Ed Baruch, Keri Badach, Keith Bush, and Diane Fowler.

Team Lev: the red phones, the true believers, the ones who spent years enduring my whining, plotting, and endless problem solving. Mom and Dad, Chris Edenfield, Kyle Bond, Peddie School headmaster emeritus John Green, Helene Stapinski, Michael Casey, Peter Lovenheim, and AJ Jacobs—I hope you enjoyed being a part of this as much as I enjoyed siphoning off your time, energy, emotions, connections, and, in my parents' case, money. Special thanks go to the four people this book is dedicated to: Jeff Vernon for harassing me into becoming a writer; Bettie Witherspoon for her compassion; Amanda Porter for her wisdom; and Dr. Vernon for teaching me how to get shit done.

ABOUT THE AUTHOR

Lev Golinkin came to the United States as a child refugee from the former Soviet Union. He is a graduate of Boston College and lives in New Jersey.